◆**ALTERNATIVES** *is a series under the general editorship of Eric S. Rabkin, Martin H. Greenberg, and Joseph D. Olander that has been established to serve the growing critical audience of science fiction, fantastic fiction, and speculative fiction.*

Other titles in this series are:

SCIENCE FICTION IN THE REAL WORLD

Norman Spinrad

Southern Illinois University Press
Carbondale and Edwardsville

93 92 91 90   4 3 2 1

Library of Congress Cataloging-in-Publication Data

Spinrad, Norman.
    Science fiction in the real world / Norman Spinrad.
        p.   cm. — (Alternatives)
    1. Science fiction—History and criticism.   I. Title.
II. Series.
PN3433.5.S65   1990
809.3'8762—dc20   89-19705
ISBN 0-8093-1538-6   CIP
ISBN 0-8093-1671-4 (pbk.)

The following essays first appeared in *Isaac Asimov's Science Fiction Magazine: Inside, Outside, Books into Movies, Must There Be War?*, copyright © 1985 by Norman Spinrad; *The Neuromantics* (retitled, *The Neuromantic Cyberpunks*), *Critical Standards, Science Fiction Versus Sci-Fi*, copyright © 1986 by Norman Spinrad; *Sturgeon, Vonnegut, and Trout, Dreams of Space, Emperor of Everything*, copyright © 1987 by Norman Spinrad; *The Hard Stuff, The Strange Case of J.G. Ballard, The Graphic Novel*, copyright © 1988 by Norman Spinrad.

For
Shawna McCarthy
Sheila Williams
Gardner Dozois
Eric Rabkin
The editors who made this book possible

Contents

Introduction

For a period in the early 1970s, I was a film critic for the *Los Angeles Free Press*. Among the films I reviewed was Stanley Kubrick's *A Clockwork Orange*, and I said in a rather long and detailed piece that the film struck me, as had just about everything of Kubrick's since *Dr. Strangelove*, as a technically brilliant but essentially soulless and mechanical exercise—that is, that *A Clockwork Orange* was a clockwork orange.

A week or two after the review was published, I got a late-night long-distance phone call from Warren Beatty, who was in New York at the time. He had read the review and had gone to the not inconsiderable trouble of ferreting out my Los Angeles phone number because he had to tell me that, in his opinion, my review of *A Clockwork Orange* had gotten to the essence of Stanley Kubrick's strengths and weaknesses as a film maker as had nothing else he had previously read.

Well, there aren't many better conversational ice-breakers than that, and we had a rather long and interesting talk about the film, Kubrick, and film in general, during which it became clear that Beatty knew only my film criticism, indeed perhaps only this one review, and had no idea that I had published half a dozen novels.

But toward the end of the conversation, Beatty paused, then said to me in a strange, guarded voice, "You don't write criticism for a living, do you? I mean, you're a creative artist of some kind yourself, aren't you?"

"Well yeah, I write novels. How did you know that?"

"Because," Beatty said with no little vehemence, "someone who is not a creative artist himself couldn't have written the kind of criticism you did. All these guys who write criticism without ever having practiced an art themselves are just a bunch of jerk-offs."

Well, Warren Beatty has had his problems with the critics, and maybe he was moved to overstate the case, but that part of the conversation stuck with me.

How could it not? Beatty had made his point by guessing the truth about me blind. I had never been a film maker, but Beatty, an artist in that form, had read from my criticism alone that I must be a creative artist of some kind, even though he had no idea what art I practiced.

Which is not to say I necessarily agree with him that critics who have never been anything else are jerking themselves off, for the evidence is quite persuasive that a good deal of excellent criticism has been written by people who have never been primary creative artists. And a great deal of crap has been written by fiction writers convinced that anyone who could write fiction successfully must certainly be able to successfully write mere criticism of same.

But I think that Warren Beatty's central point was quite correct, and it has stuck with me for a long time, and it may have been in a way the genesis of this very book, for—while not everyone who can write good fiction can write cogent criticism and while much good criticism has been written by people who were never working artists—there is a kind of criticism that can be written *only* by a critic who is.

What sort of criticism is that? What was it that Beatty had seen in my criticism that told him I was a working artist?

In one sense, I am hardly the one to attempt that level of convoluted self-criticism, though on the other hand, I have the feeling that no one reading *Science Fiction in the Real World* would need to know the name of the author or see a list of his credits to know that it was written by someone who practiced the art he was analyzing.

On an obvious level, I know personally many of the authors I'm writing about, and when personal knowledge is relevant, I make no bones about including it. I even, upon occasion, bring my own fiction into the discussion. I have been a part of some of the literary phenomena I am writing about, and if that may limit my objectivity, it certainly has also enhanced my intimate knowledge of some of the topics in question.

No one who didn't know Ted Sturgeon personally could have had a prayer of explaining why the text of *Godbody* is what it is, no matter how brilliant a critic they were. Anyone could see *how* I screwed up the closure of *The Solarians*, but only I can explain *why*.

Ah, but the Norman Spinrad whom Beatty recognized as a working artist from the reading of a single film review certainly had never been a film maker and had never even met Stanley Kubrick!

So on a not-so-obvious level, it would seem there is something that a working artist brings to criticism that he may generalize to an art form that is not necessarily his own, something that another working artist may recognize immediately from what he is reading even though *he* is not primarily a writer.

How do we working artists recognize each other's spoor? Why did Beatty consider critics who weren't working artists jerk-offs? What's the dead giveaway?

For one thing, all working artists know damn well that all working artists have to pay the rent. And that there are likely to be times when the landlord is pounding angrily at the door or worse. And the film is way over budget. And you have to stretch your own canvas. And your publisher has just been taken over by I.G. Farben. And the only offer you get is a bit part in a toilet-paper commercial. And you're only halfway through the tank-town tour of the universe.

All working artists who write criticism are constrained to be marxists of a certain kind, for every working artist must admit in his heart of hearts that more artistic decisions are economically determined than are dreamt of in the genteel groves of academe or than he would really care to think about.

Then too, all working artists recognize that almost no work of art is ever perfect, that compromise, or—more bluntly—fudging, is often an artistic as well as a commercial necessity. The painter must sometimes force perspective for design purposes, the song writer must slur a rhyme or squeeze a beat to make a line work, the general fiction writer must at times resort to coincidence to make a story point or stretch a point of logic for characterization's sake, and the science fiction writer is practicing an art form that requires playing fast and loose with the scientific facts in order to exist at all.

In a sense, when you do it yourself, you know it's all done with mirrors, with compromises and fudges and technique, and so you cannot help but be attuned to these things in the work of all other artists, let alone your own partners in crime.

And that's one reason why I've called this book *Science Fiction in the Real World*. That is my critical angle of attack, and that is probably what Warren Beatty recognized in my review of *A Clockwork Orange*.

Because in the real world, someone in probably less than entirely ideal financial circumstances, and with at least as many personal hangups as anyone else, was inspired by the random conjunction of elements in the environment to come up with a story that then had to be pounded out word by word under the influence of a relationship with a spouse, last night's dinner party, this morning's state of health, and maybe booze or dope besides.

A generalist like me will never be able to explore any one critical approach with the depth and fineness of detail of the dedicated specialist. But a dedicated specialist will never convey the real texture of multiplex literary reality either.

I suspect that this inherent schism of perception between the writer of fiction and the writer of criticism is the source of the age-old tension between writer and critic. This is why Robert Heinlein claimed he never read reviews. This is why many science fiction writers regard academic criticism with skepticism. This is why it is often greeted with the desire to "get SF back in the gutter where it belongs."

For after all, to the specialized critic who complains that the full-spectrum approach is unwritable in practice, the novelist may modestly point out that he does it all the time, and no novelist more so than the writer of science fiction.

The novelist knows that it's all smoke and mirrors, that there are techniques for creating the literary illusion of fully rounded reality without filling in all the fine detail, and the writer of science fiction has to invent such detail itself, ofttimes from scratch.

If one is accustomed to writing in this manner in the first place, one will naturally tend to bring the tools and techniques and tricks of the novelist to the work when one turns away from creating fiction and toward telling the story of literature.

And that is my critical approach in *Science Fiction in the Real World*: a novelistic one. What else? I was a storyteller before I was a critic, and so if I'm telling a story about a book I've read, or a film I've seen, or a literary phenomenon, I'm going to feel free to use the tools of the storyteller to do it, even, upon occasion, bits of scene and dialog.

Why not? I have been very fortunate indeed that Shawna McCarthy and Sheila Williams and Gardner Dozois at *Isaac Asimov's Science Fiction Magazine* have given me carte blanche four times a year to publish critical pieces of some length that need not confine themselves to discussion of current books and need not conform to any stylistic critical conventions. And aside from this introduction, the concluding essay, and the essay on Philip K. Dick, all essays in this book were first published in *Isaac Asimov's Science Fiction Magazine.*

In a sense, I've tried to write a kind of science fiction about science fiction, to relate what gets written to the lives of the characters that write it and the world that shapes their consciousness, which is not too different from relating the lives of made-up characters to the made-up world you create for them.

That may sound a tad pretentious, but as often as not it can mean something like the revelation that Philip K. Dick wrote *The Unteleported Man* around a magazine cover because he needed the money, or that Anthony Burgess once churned out eleven novels in one year, including *A Clockwork Orange*, to build up an estate for his family because he had been (erroneously) told his days were numbered, or that Lawrence Durrell batted out *The Alexandria Quartet* at high speed because he sorely needed the bread, or that I did likewise with *Agent of Chaos.*

Even if you live in an ivory tower, as I've said elsewhere, you've gotta pay the rent. And the rent is usually outrageous.

If this is marxism with a very small *m*, it is certainly also Capitalism with a great big fat *C*, you better believe it! Nor, of course, is literature created in pristine laboratory conditions in a socialist system either.

There are those who will say that a good deal of the foregoing is a commercial genre writer's rationalization of the satanic pact he has made with Mammon, that a serious literary writer does not allow his work to be shaped and molded by landlords, the publishing apparatus, his current wife's opinion of his potency, what he sees on television, or the state of his health, financial and otherwise. Indeed, there are those who contend that only those works written with such pristine literary intent are fit subject matter for serious literary criticism. All else is commercial genre writing, to be studied by the Popular Culture department as artifact.

So in a way it is true that *Science Fiction in the Real World* is a rationalization of the plight of the writer of science fiction confronting the critical tradition, in that it is a revisionary examination of where we are and how we got there, and a revisionary redefinition of the concept of "genre" itself.

For in the real world of human life and passion there is no such thing as the writer as unmoved mover, and in the real world of modern

American publishing, *everything* is a genre, you better believe it, even "serious literature," with its own stylized packaging, its own spectrum of distribution expectations, its own stable of bankable writers, and the effects of all these on what writers end up writing. That is another reason why this book is called *Science Fiction in the Real World*.

"Science Fiction" is a term that has always been highly elusive of definition, and this is not merely a matter of clever little word games. Is it school of literature? Is it a genre? Is it a subculture? Is it an industry? Is it a set of image-systems? Is it about space and the future? Is it scientific speculation? Is it bug-eyed monsters?

All and none of the above.

From a certain critical perspective, science fiction has its roots in the tale of wonder as the Ur-story of the species, but from another, equally valid perspective, it was born with the first issue of *Amazing Stories* in 1926 as a genre spun off from the boy's adventure pulps.

From one perspective, it is the fiction that best copes with matters of transcendence and destiny in our present rapidly mutating reality, yet from an equally valid perspective, it is the totemic object of a cult.

It is a severe error indeed not to consider the many ways in which the existence of a subculture called *Science Fiction Fandom* has influenced what is published and what gets written and how science fiction as literature is critically perceived. The exclusion of this matter from the sphere of literary discourse weakens any overall viewpoint on science fiction quite drastically for the same reason that critics are generally unequipped to deal with it.

Namely, that it is a unique phenomenon in the history of the world.

Where and when else has a genre of fiction accreted such a subculture around it?

Science fiction fandom has existed as a subculture since the 1930s. By now it is international; conventions are held every weekend in the year somewhere, and World Science Fiction Conventions (Worldcons) can draw over 10,000. Science fiction fandom started half a century ago with readers publishing their own amateur criticism, but by now it includes costumers and creative anachronists, the roots of the national space community, and the Trekkies who kept the legend of a dead TV show alive for years until they could finally resurrect it as a series of movies.

Science fiction writers regularly attend conventions, where they are literally surrounded for long weekends by thousands of their fans. They perform for them, they party with them, get loaded with them, and sleep with them.

What other writers in the history of the world have ever experienced such an intimate relationship en masse with the most involved segment of their readership?

Writers emerge from this subculture of science fiction fandom, and so do editors and publishers, and much literary business is done among them in the bars and at midnight parties.

How can anyone hope to understand what gets written without factoring in this unique phenomenon?

Science fiction fandom has been a fairly popular object of study as a phenomenon of popular culture, but not too much gets written about its relationship to the actual creation of a literature that is far more than rocket ships and ray guns.

This is a subject that both fans and writers find sensitive, the former because they feel they have long been the object of derisive coverage in the media and in print, the latter because on the one hand, their work tends to get tarred with the same brush and on the other, because many of them also feel a certain fannish solidarity.

General media and print critics tend to use the existence of this extravagantly costumed horde to dismiss science fiction as cult material, and, in fact, a good deal of the commercial product is indeed tailored to be just that.

Over the past decade or two, there has arisen a scholarly community dedicated to the academic study of science fiction. Some of these science fiction academics will admit to being closet fans, while many others are engaged in trying to connect science fiction to the general literary canon. This has produced some valuable work and even valuable changes in the real world, but dedicated fans are not well equipped to analyze the fandom factor, nor are scholars attempting to give the genre literary legitimacy exactly motivated to deal with this untidy subject.

One would think that a science fiction writer would be the last person in the world to want to confront such a subject in print, and from a certain perspective one would be right, but from another perspective, it would hardly be honest or accurate for someone who knows how pervasive the subculture's influence on the literature has been to say it ain't so.

Indeed, science fiction has a powerful feedback relationship with the real world, as witness the Starship *Enterprise* and the Shuttle

Enterprise, the atom bomb and the moon landing, *Star Wars* the movie and Star Wars the Strategic Defense Initiative.

Science fiction fandom is only part of it. The relationship between science fiction writers and generations of scientists by now is part of it too. So is the critical ghettoization of a huge sphere of discourse into a narrow genre and the ghetto-mentality warpage created thereby.

All this is as much a part of the story *Science Fiction in the Real World* is attempting to tell as literary history or formal analysis or class self-interest or semiotics. The novelist, particularly the science fiction novelist, must be a generalist, must have at least some knowledge of a great many diverse areas that are known in greater depth by those who devote their lives to the special study thereof.

A Renaissance man or an intellectual pack rat, and probably both, the science fiction writer interfaces with science while he is writing fiction in a way not so different from his relationship with the critical tradition when he writes criticism.

The science fiction writer ransacks science for the germ of thematic material and learns much from intellectual intercourse with the creators thereof, and scientists in turn gain from science fiction the unexpected connections generated by freewheeling extrapolators who could not care less about degrees of probability.

So too, I would hope, the relationship between *Science Fiction in the Real World* and more traditional criticism. I have borrowed from everywhere here without feeling the need to follow traditional critical forms and conventions, or, admittedly, scholarly rigor; pack-rat style, I have assembled the stuff I have gathered into a montage whose value, if any, resides in the cross-connections, not in the depth of detail.

As a writer of fiction, I have from time to time learned much from critical analysis, just as I have been inspired from time to time by scientific evolution. As a writer of science fiction, I hope that I have from time to time repaid the debt by connecting the evolution of science and technology to the human spirit in the real world.

As a science fiction writer writing criticism, I hope that this book may serve a parallel purpose, that if it may not tell any specialist anything he doesn't know about his own critical territory, it will in some small way connect that territory with the mainland of the whole.

Literature and Genre:
A Critical Overview

When I first started writing a column for *Isaac Asimov's Science Fiction Magazine*, Baird Searles was covering what was being published from month to month: it was never intended that I would ever do such a thing, and so what the editor, Shawna McCarthy, commissioned from me was four critical essays a year on more or less what I chose, as long as current novels were tied into the discourse.

It wasn't long before I realized I had begun to write a book, namely this one, and the columns included as essays in this section of *Science Fiction in the Real World* represent this discovery.

"Critical Standards" was written first, inspired by the general ire evoked by the notorious Luc Sante piece in *Harpers* attacking science fiction and by reading Le Guin's *Always Coming Home* and the reviews thereof more or less at the same time. It was coherent critical standards applicable to science fiction that Sante's piece so sorely lacked, and the wrong critical standards applied to her work which had led Le Guin away from her strengths and into her weaknesses. That was when I realized I had been given the opportunity to meditate on what proper critical standards might be in the process of applying them to current specifics.

Upon re-reading "Critical Standards" in the context of what to me was the bizarre popularity of Orson Scott Card's novel *Ender's Game*, I realized that if I had written an essay bemoaning the lack of coherently applied literary standards from *outside* the genre apparatus, I could not in all conscience fail to deal with the lack of coherent *internal* literary standards, which was exactly when I realized I was in the process of writing a book.

"Science Fiction versus Sci-fi" was written in the light of this

1

realization, and so was the final essay in this section, "Inside, Outside," which is a reworking and combination of the original magazine column of the same title with a subsequent column called "The Edge of the Envelope."

Only when I was preparing this book did I see how those columns complemented each other, with their discussions of science fiction as a literary absolute unbound by genre, with their consideration of SF by hands as diverse as Mark Twain and Margaret Atwood, Russell Hoban and George R.R. Martin, Norman Mailer and Lisa Goldstein, H.G. Wells and Samuel R. Delany.

In truth, while I was reading these books, I was looking for no overarching theory of the relationship between science fiction and the mainland of literature, and only in retrospect did I see that that was what I was groping for when I reviewed them.

As elsewhere in *Science Fiction in the Real World*, I have reworked these columns into book-chapter form, but nowhere else have I revised and combined so extensively. For this opening section of the book is where I not only explicate my critical overview of science fiction in its relationship to the real world, but where, in the hot writing to deadline and publishing flow of the column, I truly discovered it for myself.

Critical Standards

At the outset of this essay on critical standards, I'm afraid I'm going to have to violate one of the most generally accepted principles both within and beyond the SF cannon: don't review a book you haven't read.

I have before me *The Eleven Million Mile High Dancer*, by Carol Hill. It is a science fiction novel. Its heroine, astronaut Amanda Jawarski, dresses in a Wonder Woman suit, rollerskates around the corridors of NASA, and has a magical cat named Schrodinger. After my third try at getting past page 60, I still can't figure out whether Ms. Hill is trying to be funny or not.

True, the book is filled with silly characters, sillier science, cartoon-level feminism, and the use of garbled quantum theory to legitimize vibrating mysticalism one would expect of a writer who appends a two-page explication of quantum mechanics for the unwashed masses, nearly half of which is a quote from Fritjof Capra's *The Tao of Physics*.

On the other hand, little of it is really funny; it is merely ludicrous, not humorous; trying to read this book for laughs is like watching a borscht-belt comic in his own nethermost pit of Hades, bombing out forever with jokes that don't get even a hollow giggle.

But if *Dancer* is failed satire, one must then ask of *what*, and the only possible answer, alas, is of *itself*. That, if the book is meant as satire, is why it is so agonizingly unfunny, for satire just doesn't work when it has no reference reality to play off.

I mean, give me a break, will you? I've saved you from the ghastly experience of trying to plow through 441 pages of this thing, so don't expect me to subject *myself* to such exquisite torture. Mea culpa, mea maxima culpa! I just can't drag myself through *The Eleven Million Mile High Dancer* to the bitter end, but I really must talk about it anyway.

Why?

Because I do not think that this novel is a failed attempt at humor. I think it much more likely that it is a failed attempt at *science fiction* by a writer of some talent who hasn't the foggiest notion of what science fiction really is.

Breathes there an editor who has not seen this sort of first novel over and over again in the slushpile and sent it back with a form rejection slip after reading maybe twenty pages? If for some reason such an editor felt perversely mellow enough to write a personal rejection letter, it would go something like this:

Dear Ms. Hill:

While *The Eleven Million Mile High Dancer* displays ample evidence of your prose skills on a sentence and paragraph level and a firm grasp of the mechanics of scene, dialog, and description, it is equally evident that you have attempted to write a science fiction novel with little or no study of the form itself.

Science fiction may be serious extrapolation, space opera, satire, or metaphysical speculation, but not all at once in the same novel, let alone in the same paragraph. If you intend to use scientific extrapolation as a story element, you must understand it at least well enough to convince a general reader that you know what you are talking about. If you are writing action-adventure, you must keep your tongue from getting stuck in your cheek, and if you are writing humor, try reading some of it out loud to see if anyone laughs.

Don't be too discouraged by this rejection, Ms. Hill. You obviously *do* have some talent for writing narrative fiction on a professional level. But I would strongly advise *reading* a wide sampling of science fiction novels before attempting to write one again.

Harried Editor

I can see you scratching your head out there. Okay, so some lousy first novel managed to escape from the slushpile into marginal publication; why bother to agonize over it in print at such length? It happens all the time; all it means is that some overworked editor needed something quick to fill a hole in the schedule, and this was the least offensive thing available at the time.

Ah, but *The Eleven Million Mile High Dancer* is *not* Carol Hill's first published novel, but her *third*. It comes festooned with laudatory blurbs for previous work by literary high priests like John Leonard and Alfred Kazin. It was reviewed—on the whole, quite favorably—in important critical journals and national newsmagazines. Since it is so manifestly science fiction, albeit of a rather amateurish sort, one is led to the inescapable conclusion that a significant segment of the American critical apparatus considers it *good* science fiction.

What does this have to do with intelligent, informed critical standards?

Alas, one is led to another inescapable conclusion: not very much.

But it has a great deal to do with current American literary politics.

Science fiction, of course, has long been subject to a standard form of scatological abuse by the established American critical apparatus, a textbook example of which is the notorious Luc Sante cover story in *Harpers*. If nothing else, it demonstrates conclusively the extent to which this form has become genrefied itself, since the very same magazine had published very much the same article several years earlier under a different byline.

The genre formula is as follows:

Hire a writer with some critical credentials, though not an established heavyweight, someone who has either read little science fiction or regards it as an addiction of his youth, discarded along with the bubble-gum-card collection.

Have him select (or select for him) about a dozen SF novels, a few acknowledged fannish icons, the rest mediocrites chosen by a random-number program from the tens of thousands of such novels that have been published in the genre since it was incarnated as such in 1926.

He can then proclaim in innocent horror that what is touted by its practitioners and advocates as a visionary literature of ideas and scientific speculation actually consists chiefly of pulp action stories set in outer space, gadget-pornography for adolescent wimps, and militaristic power-fantasies.

SF can then be deported en masse from the sphere of serious literary discourse back into the ghetto for another few years, until it's time for the next pogrom.

Indeed, this form has become so genrefied that the SF apparatus has even developed its own genrefied form of response, a neo-Marxist one, at that.

According to this analysis, the motivation for these periodic hatchet-jobs, as well as the scanting that SF and SF writers get from the American critical establishment between them, is economic. A perusal of sales figures and bestseller lists reveals that the SF ghetto has become the high-rent district, while the ivory towers of what is deemed "serious literature" by the impoverished practitioners and critics thereof are being torched by the landlords for the insurance money.

Science fiction is being read by larger and larger audiences and making more and more money, while these threadbare literateurs, having lost all contact with their readers, can only stand like Canute before the rising tide, impotently and forlornly commanding the wave of the future to roll back.

Certainly, human nature being what it is, this indeed does much to explain why significant science fiction works by significant science fiction writers are not regularly reviewed by significant critics in the literary journals and the newsmagazines. In their literary subculture, the authors of all those SF books they perceive as having usurped *their* rightful rackspace are a class enemy, competing all too successfully for the same bucks.

But higher things than the Darwinian demographics of market share are involved in this conflict, for in a certain sense there *is* an intellectually legitimate disjunction between the world views of these two tribes of humans.

The preamble to the aforementioned *Harpers* piece railed against technology, change, modern times, fancy TVs and cameras, and finally, with admirable unconscious honesty, amazingly enough, *innovation itself:* ". . . innovation itself has become an aesthetic quality, existing for its own sake. . . . Technology has long been science fiction's conceit, now it is a conceit in real life as well."

This is a *complaint*, as far as this world view is concerned, not a compliment; this may need to be pointed out to those who do not share it, for science fiction writers are forever boasting about the technology they conceived before the inventors of same, and more to the point would generally quite enthusiastically endorse the proposition that intellectual, emotional, cultural, technological, literary, even *critical* innovation is indeed its own ding an sich as an esthetic delight for both writer and reader.

This delight in innovation, of course, is what the genre alludes to as "sense of wonder," the heartfelt conviction that the experience of novelty—sensual, geographical, scientific, technological, esthetic, or emotional—is one of the deep intellectual and spiritual pleasures of being human.

Anglophone literary culture, like our civilization, has long had a difficult time with the concept that "science" and "spirit," "reason" and "emotion," "transcendence" and "realism," "esthetics" and "accuracy," the "soul" and the "intellect," "truth" and "multiplexity," "technology" and "the natural world" are not mutually exclusive dichotomies. That reality itself, as Brian Aldiss once so elegantly put it, is a multivalued motorway.

Why this is so and of what crisis in our evolution it speaks would be the subject of endless novels, several of which I have already written, so suffice it to say for present purposes that these matters are central to the great historical nexus our species is presently attempting to negotiate, that they are the thematic material for much seriously intended science fiction, and that, sadly, the fiction generally regarded as "serious," "contemporary," and "engaged" by the arbiters of literary culture has encountered severe conceptual and stylistic problems in coming to terms with the multiplexity of post-Einsteinian reality.

If all you can see in the wave of the future is shock and dislocation and yourself being washed over, then of course you will take a dim and uncomprehending view of the space cadets and cyberpunks trying to ride the crest on jet-propelled surfboards.

So by extension into down-and-dirty *intellectual* social Darwinism, the neo-Marxist explication from within the genre can even account for the rough and iniquitous treatment that seriously intended and literarily successful works of science fiction so often receive at the hands of the critical establishment, when they are attended to at all.

The traditional critical establishment is well equipped intellectually to mercilessly skewer the prevalent literary vices of science fiction—action-adventure plotlines, absence of complex emotion, lack of ambiguity, merely serviceable prose, stereotyped characters—in short, the vices that critics inside the field all too often elevate to virtues as "the pulp tradition."

Come on, let's face it, there are something like 500 new SF novels published each year, and the vast majority of them are going to be exactly what the critical establishment would deem them, commercial action-adventure fiction with SF symbology, mere light entertainment, and intended as such by their authors.

This, while not quite the moral equivalent of child molesting it is sometimes painted as, is undeniably true. So those who are truly interested in the literary evolution of science fiction as an art form should concern themselves not only with the odor of pulp this smears on their own covers, but with the danger that some of it may seep inside.

So when it comes to Sturgeon's famous 90 percent, the critical establishment is quite right. The vices and shortcomings of the great wad of science fiction published to fill all those rack slots are all too apparent to any critic perusing it with a remotely functional shit-detector.

So what goes wrong with said instruments when they are passed over something like *The Eleven Million Mile High Dancer*?

Okay, Carol Hill is a certified member of the tribe, so we can expect she'll be treated more tenderly than auslanders like Dick or Bester or Disch. But there really *is* a degree of integrity in established critical circles, and even if there weren't, few critics would be so self-defeating as to call a turkey like this a good book in public no matter *who* wrote it unless they really believed it themselves.

The thing of it is that most of the traditional critical establishment is entirely unequipped to deal with the other 10 percent , with the twenty or thirty science fiction novels of serious intent that are published each year and that to a greater or lesser degree fulfill both the general literary parameters of excellence and the unique central literary virtues of science fiction.

Rigorous visionary extrapolation of the future evolution of culture and consciousness, based on a wide-ranging understanding of the physical nature of the universe and the individual psyche's feedback relationship with it, is so alien a virtue to most establishment critics that they have big trouble even conceptualizing it, let alone *recognizing* it as a virtue or making a measured judgment as to what extent a work of fiction achieves it.

So while the critical establishment may dismiss science fiction from its sphere of serious discourse as the commercial entertainment genre that grew out of the pulps, it is an ignorant dismissal that has never developed a comprehensive or remotely intelligible overview of what is actually being written by the best of the writers working behind those ghetto walls.

And in the best science fiction, written inside or outside of the ghetto walls, there is something that all natural men and women crave in their heart of hearts, in one form or another, unless they are totally spiritually dead: namely, to transcend—if only for a moment or the length of a book—time, space, and mortality and contemplate some credible vision of one's destiny in the universe entire.

Bad science fiction and not much of it, like bad sex, is at least better than none at all. So the traditional literary critics, having categorically dismissed genre SF and its practitioners, look to their own favored sons and daughters to satisfy that elusive itch.

Which explains why something like *The Eleven Million Mile High Dancer* can be reviewed so favorably.

They read it with open minds because it was written by someone they were predisposed to take seriously. They liked it because it was something they could scratch that itch in public with, something that got them off without violating their belief system—science fiction free of distasteful genre identification.

They couldn't recognize that it was *bad* science fiction because they have no adequate conception of what *good* science fiction is. To a horny virgin, even the performance of another sexual naif is probably going to seem like hot stuff.

Too bad for them, poor babies! I mean, anyone who could actually *enjoy* reading 441 pages of *The Eleven Million Mile High Dancer* would surely enjoy much better even Doc Smith or Kendall Foster Crossen, let alone *The Stars My Destination* or *The Three Stigmata of Palmer Eldritch*.

Too bad for us, poor babies, that we visionary dreamers are confined to a literary purdah from which we must drive, crying in our beer, to the bank.

Too bad for a civilization, poor babies, in which the apparatus of literary evaluation has malfunctioned to the point where the main literature dealing with its central cultural concerns at this evolutionary nexus is removed from the mainstream of intellectual discourse.

But worst of all for any science fiction writer of merit who is adopted as a "token nigger" in the grand high salons of literary power and allows ignorant praise to influence the work itself.

By all means accept the invitation to the party and all that it means—the enhanced advances, the better publication, the wider critical attention, the society of celebrities both of the media and the spirit. Trip the intellectual life fantastic.

But beware the Jabberwock, my son, the jaws that bite, the claws that catch, beware that in the process of reshaping your public identity as a science fiction writer into something more fashionable, you don't start tailoring *the work itself* to the specs of your less-than-expert intellectual admirers.

Alas, read *Always Coming Home*, and weep for what this process has done to Ursula Le Guin.

Le Guin's first three novels, *Rocannon's World, Planet of Exile*, and *City of Illusions*, were Ace SF paperback originals, a loosely connected trilogy set in a rather ordinary galactic future, certainly competent, but not considered noteworthy at the time.

Then her fourth novel, *The Left Hand of Darkness*, an Ace paperback special published and edited by Terry Carr, won both the Nebula and the Hugo, and her career as a seriously regarded major writer within the genre was launched.

The sequence of what was actually written next is a bit unclear, but the next books to be published were the Earthsea books, a fantasy series for young adults that won the prestigious National Book Award as such. More or less meanwhile, *The Lathe of Heaven* was published, a multi-reality novel—strongly influenced by the work of Philip K. Dick—that, though it didn't create the stir that *Left Hand of Darkness* did, showed a sure grasp of the form and a deepening of Le Guin's sense of irony and ambiguity.

Then came the publication of *The Dispossessed*, Le Guin's "ambiguous utopia," which won another Hugo and Nebula, which is generally regarded as her magnum opus to date, and which is the last true science fiction novel she has written.

For by design or happenstance, the National Book Award for a juvenile series became her passport to higher literary realms, and her career began to change direction. Her stories stopped appearing in SF magazines for the most part and began being published in little magazines and literary quarterlies. She cracked *The New Yorker* and became something of a regular.

One must admire her idealism and effort. She set out to use her good fortune as an entre into writing herself out of the ghetto and into literary respectability, and she succeeded, knowingly sacrificing a certain amount of income in the bargain, at least initially.

Who within the ghetto walls but the meanest of spirits could do anything but congratulate her with communal pride?

Alas, only those willing take a hard look at what happened to her work in the process.

As a science fiction writer, Le Guin's strengths have been a good descriptive eye, the ability to pile up details of an imagined world toward thematic ends, better-than-serviceable prose, and the ability to place believable if not memorable characters firmly in the matrix of their specific culture.

Her weaknesses were a tendency to turn her forthrightly political fiction into didactic exercises, and the unfortunate fact that her political insight tended to pivot simplistically about a dualistic misreading of Taoism in which yin is considered the way of virtue and yang the root of all evil, most nakedly stated in *The Lathe of Heaven* but present as well in her portraits of the planets Annares and Uras in *The Dispossessed*.

Sometime after the publication of *The Dispossessed*, Le Guin began to take pains to deny that she had ever *really* been a science fiction writer, and with the publication of *Always Coming Home*, she finally got the critics to agree entirely with her: all those Ace paperbacks were apparently a fluke or nonhistory, and now it has been discovered that she was a "visionary" writer, not a science fiction writer, all along, to hear Peter Prescott tell it in *Newsweek*.

While this public transformation from "science fiction writer" to "visionary" was taking place, Le Guin's major published works were *Orsinian Tales*, a kind of generalized Ruritania story cycle; *Malafrena*, a novel in similar vein; *The Beginning Place*, a fantasy that may or may not have been intended for young adults; and several long novellas.

Far from being visionary, these latter-day works are pretty pallid stuff, lacking the extrapolative rigor and cultural specificity of Le Guin's science fiction, weak on character development, and too often coming off as schematic set-ups for her political message.

Which all too often is a *devolution* of the rather more ambiguous and sophisticated version to be found in *The Left Hand of Darkness* and *The Dispossessed* into a political cartoon of the supposed moral dichotomy between evil yang (militarism, technology, male dominance, capitalism, Faustian philosophical activism) and virtuous yin (passivity, ecotopia, socialism, decentralization, the noble granola-eating natural woman).

And now, with the publication of *Always Coming Home*, we see the awful truth, for precisely in the process of transforming herself from a science fiction writer into a "visionary." Le Guin has strayed far away from her cardinal virtues and into the self-indulgent morass of her worst weaknesses.

For it was precisely her virtues as a *science fiction* writer that gave her work vision, and having abandoned them as the things of childhood and bad literary karma, she has lost the creative center, sense of irony, and intellectual discipline that every would-be visionary writer must retain if she is not to devolve into a hectoring guru.

Always Coming Home is, on several levels, an enormous act of ego-tripping self indulgence, yang to the max in yin clothing. The form of initial publication itself was an arrogant act of commercial seppuku, apparently insisted upon by the author. For $25, you were privileged to purchase a trade paperback that should cost about $9, packaged in a slipcase with a cassette of amateurish technical quality on which you are treated to a pseudo-anthropological collection of song and music from "the Valley" of the novel, an all-too-faithful overture to the tedium of the text.

Imagine that Frank Herbert had written *Dune* as a 20,000-word novella, and then padded it out to 523 pages by doing a cut-up a la William Burroughs with the text of *The Dune Encyclopedia*, and you have the formal structure of *Always Coming Home*.

Conceptually audacious, it could have worked. The "nonfact" article is a well-established SF form, *The Dune Encyclopedia* itself was rather entertaining, and there is certainly esthetic respectability within the SF genre for making the created world the central character and the story and humans secondary. And indeed, if the fictional thread was really well-integrated with the pseudo-documentary matrix, and insightful in and of itself, such a work could become a masterpiece of Nabokovian formal complexity.

But for it to work, the created world must be a sufficiently fascinating character in and of itself to carry a whole long novel, and the embedded novella must contribute in a way that makes the whole greater than the sum of its parts.

Le Guin's retrogressive ecotopia is a valley and its environs in a future central California, in an era when the entire world has apparently been balkanized down to a tribal level; technology, scientific inquiry, and the exploration of the universe consigned as hopelessly yang to a net of artificial intelligences; and the Kesh, the yin white hats of the novel, live the bucolic good life of noble, re-created, and somewhat Disneyized American Indians.

The storyline, such as it is, concerns a woman called Stone Telling, of Kesh mother and Condor father, who ends up living for quite a while in nasty Condorland (a nearby dystopia), and then goes home, where she narrates her story into Le Guin's pseudo-anthropological annals.

So basically *Always Coming Home* is *Coming of Age in the Valley of the Kesh*, with Le Guin (or "Pandora," as she calls herself when she addresses the reader directly from within the text) as Margaret Mead. Customs, poetry, folk-tales, made-up language complete with glossary, religion, agriculture, and even recipes. Audacious! Ambitious! Four years in the writing! Coulda been the champ!

But only as interesting as the Kesh and their world itself. And the Kesh are boring. They lack eccentricity, real passion, ambiguity, complexity; their culture is a kind of generalized Potemkin village designed to exemplify the Le Guinian political and spiritual virtues, yet another recitation of the virtues of the yin half of the great wheel.

The yang half of the equation is represented in political-cartoon style by the Condors—evil, male-chauvinist, paranoid imperialists who conjure up a Reaganoid arms program literally deus ex machina and are defeated by the peace-loving third-world peoples when they conveniently trip over their own dicks.

And what of the center about which the great wheel must turn, the center which, we all know, is Void?

Alas, the void at the center of *Always Coming Home* is called science fiction.

The Le Guin of *The Left Hand of Darkness* and *The Dispossessed* just might have made this work as a novel, whether one could accept the politics or not. Le Guin, the science fiction writer, knew how to build up a real world, characters, story, out of a wealth of inherently interesting detail, how to raise her didactic impulses to thematic material for literary art. This is what it *really* means to be a visionary writer, flavor of the vision aside.

But the Le Guin of *Orsinian Tales* and *Malafrena* and *The Beginning Place*, etc., is no longer a visionary writer in that deeper sense. Here we have almost a laboratory experiment examining what happens to a science fiction writer of merit who heeds the advice of her admiring establishment critics, not on matters of prose style, characterological depth, or formal structure, which they understand well, but on what is the wheat and what is the chaff when it comes to visionary science fiction, about which they know nothing.

Too many establishment critics confuse science fiction with allegory, too many of them see the medium as merely the mouthpiece of the message. Le Guin's political and cultural message happens to sync quite nicely with the current consensus zeitgeist in these circles, so if only she would get rid of the SF paraphernalia, they would be pleased to admit her to the drawing room.

But certainly at least *we* by now know that the medium *is* the message, or it should be, for it is precisely by applying an active innovative imagination to embedding the thematic material in the cunningly designed details of a living, breathing, striving, morally ambiguous world, that the science fiction writer, and arguably in our time the science fiction writer alone, may elevate the politically engaged novel out of the nether realm of didacticism and onto the level of literary art.

Once Ursula Le Guin set out to purge her work of that which made it science fiction, she was inevitably led down the primrose path of less and less cultural specificity, less and less complex world-building, less and less true visionary extrapolation, more and more generalized fabulation, nakeder and nakeder didacticism, a deadening confusion of her weaknesses with her virtues, and an elevation of the former at the expense of the latter.

Until at the end of this road, we have *Always Coming Home*, fave rave of the critical establishment, where the didacticism is quite dominant, and the relative vapidity of its vision is unfortunately revealed by the almost total absence of the extrapolative rigor, saving irony, and visionary imagination of the author of *The Left Hand of Darkness* or *The Dispossessed*.

Yes, we have righteous reason to hiss and boo at the critical establishment for their ignorant hip-shooting, their mean-spirited economic envy, and their intellectual incomprehension of the inner esthetics of science fiction, and certainly someone or something deserves to be pied for steering the likes of Ursula Le Guin down such a creative blind alley.

But perhaps rather than patting each other on the back on the way to the SFWA suite, we should look in on the hucksters' room before we cast the first critical stone.

Not all critics from outside the genre are envious bounders and mountebanks; and some of them, such as Leslie Fielder and Bruce Franklin, have brought their powers to bear on works of science fiction with justice and understanding.

So what of a hypothetical top-flight outside critic who wishes to perform the noble task of explicating science fiction to the American intellectual generality, not in terms of its shortcomings, but of the best work it produces?

What can a poor boy do, one who was not raised on Doc Smith or Heinlein, who wasn't raised on science fiction at all, an eclectic intellectual sincerely seeking to expand his range of literary knowledge?

He can't go into a bookstore and tell the action-adventure stuff from the essays at literary greatness, since it's all packaged the same. And while the famous Big Four of Asimov, Clarke, Heinlein, and Bradbury all have their characteristic virtues, they can hardly be said to fairly represent the literary cutting edge.

So if he's to delve beyond the obvious or the random at all, his only reasonable recourse as a gentleman and a scholar is to peruse the existing critical literature for an overview with which to orient himself.

At which point he and we have met the mutual enemy.

And it is us.

In sheer quantity, the existing critical commentary on science fiction leaves nothing to be desired. For while material on science fiction may be quite sparse in the annals of the established critical tradition, science fiction fans have been piling it up in enormous stacks of fanzines from here to Betelgeuse since the early Pleistoscene, or at least since 1930.

And there are Hugo and Nebula lists going back twenty years and more to contemplate. And enormous literary congresses called "science fiction conventions," where the leading literary lights, editors, and critics engage in learned symposia on the esthetics and thematic philosophies of their art for the delectation of the avid masses.

When it comes to quality, though, the level of literary discourse turns out to be not quite what he's used to, as he's menaced by sword-wielding barbarians, propositioned by Brunhilda in furs, given the hitchhiker's tour of the galaxy, and then sits down with the clap and a hangover to read through the archives of the Ackermansion.

Somehow, Professor Leavis, I don't think we're in Oxford.

It's not his planet, Monkey Boy.

The fanzines are no help. Most of the reviews are plot-summaries, and those that aren't vary randomly between the twin poles of insightfulness and complete babble, often within the same issue of the same publication, since most fanzine editors have no informing literary philosophy or even standards of critical professionalism.

The critical academic journals? There are several of them, and some of the criticism in them is reasoned and intelligent, but all too much of it either assumes the specialized knowledge our sincere intellectual naif is seeking in the first place, or sticks to examining the works of a few icons or exploring some literary theme *within* the SF canon. Very little of it is an attempt at a grand orienting literary overview for the innocent newcomer.

The Hugos and the Nebulas?

Let's face it, the Nebulas and the Hugos have about as much to do with measured critical judgment and as much to do with personal politics and random factors as the Oscars or the Nobels or the Balrogs or any other set of artistic awards dreamed up by the mind of man.

They are by nature determined by an electoral process. All electoral processes have a political component, and the outcome is determined by some form of numerical tabulation. So even in the best of worlds, the Hugos and the Nebulas cannot be other than literal popularity contests, measurements of the numerical popularity of works among the paying members of a science fiction convention on the one hand, and the creators of those works on the other.

Not surprising then that both of them are indiscriminately awarded to masterpieces and trivia, pace-setting works and cult-objects, as popular trends come and go.

Interesting for tracking such trends perhaps, but not much help to our poor would-be friend of the family trying to put together a coherent critical overview.

The science fiction magazines? A little better, at least when it comes to the current stream of SF publishing, but not by much. There are only four of them publishing reviews regularly, and most of *those* are intended as buyers' guides rather than as analysis for practitioners or serious critics.

And of course there is a novelist—who maunders on in essays like this, writing about the likes of *him*—who hasn't been so much help either.

Hey, guys, will you drag yourselves out of the bar long enough to advise me what to tell this righteous professor? Any of you know where to find a rigorous, informed, and comprehensive body of critical literature adequately explicating the sixty-year literary history of science fiction for the nonconverted?

If we can't score him some soon, he's going to think we don't know how to party, throw up his hands in disgust, storm out of the convention, and write another of those ignorant hatchet jobs!

Guys . . . ? Guys . . . ?

Whoops, sorry professor, catch ya later, they just told me it's time to go to the autograph party in the huckster room!

Science Fiction Versus Sci-Fi

Synchronistically enough, at about the time I was writing the preceding piece on critical standards or the lack thereof as applied in a rigorous and consistent manner to the literature of science fiction by critics within and without the SF genre apparatus, Thomas Easton, who reviews regularly for *Analog*, published a column based on the thesis that "what's wrong with SF is sci-fi."

I will leave the full explication of Easton's thesis to Easton (you could look it up, as Casey Stengel used to say), but with a bow in his direction, I will blow my own riff on his pithy aphorism, which certainly admirably served to crystallize some of my own thoughts on the whole question of literary standards *within* the SF genre.

After all, if it is better to light a single candle than to curse the darkness, someone who has just expended considerable wordage bemoaning the nonapplication of consistent, rigorous, absolute literary standards to science fiction would seem to be honor-bound to attempt to explore what such critical standards might actually be. And Easton's theme is an excellent point of departure. Much science fiction and fantasy fails literarily because it is infected with the vices, commercial strictures, and pulp conventions of "sci-fi" (as often as not without the writer being consciously aware of the process), and much criticism of SF, within and without the genre apparatus, ignores the crucial distinction between "science fiction" and "sci-fi."

For the purposes of this discussion, let me first define "SF," "science fiction," and "sci-fi," as I will use the terms in the rest of this book.

"SF" will by my all-inclusive term for the marketing genre, as in "SF is anything published as SF," or "SF is anything that an SF editor buys." Since SF editors certainly buy fantasy these days, and publishers customarily publish it in their "SF lines," "SF" includes fantasy too. It also includes "science fiction" and "sci-fi."

"Science fiction" and "fantasy" will be my labels for the two literary branches of SF, as defined in *literary* terms. I will mercifully spare you and myself the usual futile attempts to define the indefinable. Suffice it to say that what I mean by "science fiction" is any work of fiction containing a speculative element belonging to the sphere of the "could be, but isn't," and what I mean by "fantasy" is any work of fiction containing an element that openly and knowingly contradicts what we presently consider the "possible." Thus, for example, *Ender's Game, 1984, Timescape, A Clockwork Orange*, and *Riddley Walker* are all works of science fiction, and *The Lord of the Rings, Winter's Tale, The Odyssey, Conan*, and *Ancient Evenings* are all works of fantasy.

Defining "sci-fi," however, is a good deal trickier, for it cuts to the heart of the matter.

"Sci-fi," as many of us already know, is a word coined decades ago by Forrest J. Ackerman, one of the first of the Big Name Fans, and it has long since become the media's fave label for the genre, denoting, in the general public's consciousness, those books festooned with rocket ships and BEMs (and, more recently, unicorns and dragons too) in the SF sections of bookstores and libraries, the SF specialty magazines, most modern comic books, and of course "sci-fi movies" ranging from *2001* to *King Kong vs. Godzilla*.

Fittingly enough, the contents of the Ackermansion, Ackerman's definitive collection of sci-fi memorabilia, nicely epitomize the bounds of sci-fi, including as it does books, pulp magazines, fanzines, comics, artwork, toys, movie posters, bits and pieces of film props and models, and a photographic record of science fiction fandom and its conventions.

The Ackermansion is a museum dedicated to the artifacts and history of sci-fi, to what the term will mean herein, to the SF *genre*, or, to put in the other way around, to *genre SF*.

But what does "genre SF," aka "sci-fi," mean in *literary terms*?

Well for one thing, sci-fi, unlike science fiction or fantasy, which have been around as literary modes for centuries in the one case and since time immemorial in the other, has a well-defined and relatively brief history.

It began with the publication of the first science fiction specialty magazine, *Amazing Stories*, in 1926. More specialty magazines followed. Science fiction fandom evolved out of the interaction between readers in the letter columns of these magazines. Fans began to publish fanzines. They began to hold SF conventions, then an annual Worldcon, out of which came the Hugo awards. A subculture accreted itself around the kernel of the SF genre. After World War II, SF novels began to be published in paperback. General publishers established regular "SF lines." A flourishing SF small press evolved. The Science Fiction Writers of America was founded, along with its Nebula awards. During the so-called SF boom of the 1970s, the SF genre became an economically important segment of general publishing.

Thus "sci-fi" as a historical development, a subculture, a marketing concept, and a publishing genre.

A genre that evolved out of the SF pulp magazines, which in turn came into existence as a subset of a whole galaxy of pulp adventure magazines that flourished in the 1920s, 1930s, and 1940s.

This is what Algis Budrys means when he writes about SF's evolution out of the "pulp tradition." American SF, or at least "sci-fi," did not evolve as a subset of the general sphere of serious or "elitist" American literature, but as a subset of *commercial popular literature*, and though by now much SF has long since transcended the literary limits of commercial fiction, its public image is still tarred with the sci-fi brush, to the detriment of the general literary reputations of its more serious and accomplished practitioners.

And to the detriment of much of the work itself.

Even today, the majority of the working writers and editors in the SF field are people who evolved into "pro-dom" through "SF fandom," who attended science fiction conventions, who receive more critical attention in fanzines than in literary journals, who measure their literary success by Hugos and Nebulas, and whose work is therefore influenced to a greater or lesser degree by the literary values of the subculture of which they are perforce a part.

And *those* literary values are what I mean by sci-fi, the sci-fi that is what is wrong with so much of what is published as SF, and that tends to insidiously infect even the best of it.

In his excellent textbook on surviving and flourishing as a commercial writer in the marketplace, forthrightly titled *Writing to Sell*, the literary agent Scott Meredith, himself a one-time SF fan and the literary representative of many of the writers in the genre for decades, sets forth the so-called plot skeleton, the formal template for viable commercial fiction.

A strong, or at least sympathetic, hero, with whom the reader can identify, is confronted with a problem he must solve or an unsympathetic villain he must overcome. As the story progresses, the attainment of this goal becomes more and more difficult through a series of plot complications, rising to a crisis at which point it seems he must fail. But through intelligence, courage, physical prowess, or some combination of the three, he turns the tables and triumphs at the climax of the tale, which should end soon thereafter in a coda or resolution that wraps things up.

This indeed is a reliable formula for successful commercial fiction. Crank it through cowboys and outlaws and you have a western; spies and counterspies, and you have an espionage thriller; cops and criminals, and you have a detective story; rocket ships, alien planets, a galactic overlord, an intrepid spaceman, and you have . . .

Sci-fi.

Notice that the plot skeleton is the formal backbone of virtually *all* commercial fiction. Notice that commercial genres are created by running recognizable image systems through it. Notice that it is the generalized plot skeleton, *not* the particularized image system, that connects a work of sci-fi to the so-called pulp tradition.

Notice too that what we have here is a formula for manipulating the reader's level of arousal in an escalating series of sine waves not unlike the dynamic structure of a proper lay. Some foreplay, segueing into a driving rhythm of tension and release, building and building up to a peak, an orgasmic climax, and then a slide down into a satisfied afterglow.

What does this have to do with what are generally regarded as the higher literary virtues?

Not very much.

For notice what it leaves out, or even precludes.

Brian Aldiss once castigated SF (or, in the current terms, sci-fi) for "lacking a decent sense of despair," perhaps an unfortunate choice of terminology: I suspect that what he meant to say was that SF lacked a decent sense of *tragedy*. In the classic definition, a work of tragedy requires that an otherwise noble figure come to ruin through some flaw in his character. A more modern sense of tragedy allows the possibility that a good person may be destroyed by the indifferent machineries of an unjust or at best amoral universe. (See Tom Godwin's "The Cold Equations" or, for that matter, Aldiss' own *Greybeard*.)

Notice that adherence to the pulp tradition, the plot skeleton, the literary values of sci-fi, precludes the possibility of tragedy in both senses of the term. The sympathetic hero with whom the reader identifies *must* triumph over adversity, lest the reader whom the writer is quite literally mindfucking be left angrily tumescent.

The universe of sci-fi, unlike the universe in which we unfortunately find ourselves, is relentlessly moral; good always triumphs over evil, the white hats always triumph over the black.

And notice that this also precludes the thematic exploration of the spiritual ambiguities confronting imperfect creatures in a less than morally just universe, which is ultimately what almost all fiction that attempts to touch the heart and higher philosophical brain centers of the reader must be about. Which is perilously close to saying that "sci-fi" and "literature" are by definition antithetical.

Sci-fi's exploration of morality is generally confined, as so many book jacket blurbs proudly proclaim, to the "battle of good against evil"; the teams have their names clearly lettered on their uniforms, and the home team must always win.

Yet—as we have all long since learned, to our discomfort—in the real world, it is not so easy to tell good from evil, even *with* a scorecard. No man is a villain unto himself, everyone from Saint Theresa to Adolf Hitler sees themselves as the hero of their own tale, and so the real moral questions almost always arise as the result of conflicting value systems. In true literature, as in the inner life it mirrors, the real moral dialectic is not between good and evil, but between conflicting concepts of virtue.

I was rather perplexed at a certain reaction to my novel *Child of Fortune*. Many people who are not regular SF readers expressed the same kind of surprised pleasure.

"I don't like science fiction, but I like this book; but then *Child of Fortune* isn't science fiction, is it?"

Child of Fortune is set several thousand years in the future and takes place on four planets and three spaceships.

If *that* isn't science fiction, what is?

But when I read Mr. Easton's column it all became perfectly clear.

Child of Fortune is a bildungsroman, a tale of the growth of a young girl to the beginning of her maturity as a woman, and while there are a certain number of perils for her to overcome, they are mostly perils of the spirit, and the focus is kept on the evolution of her character, not on a thrill-a-minute plot. There is no black villain, and no one in the novel would lay claim to being a paragon of moral perfection. It has little to do with a dualistic struggle between good and evil.

Right. You got it.

Child of Fortune is science fiction.

But it is not sci-fi.

Notice that we are not necessarily talking about relative literary quality here, but about *form*. It is certainly possible to set out with the highest intent to explore the moral ambiguities of the human heart and end up writing a bad book. It is also possible to take the sci-fi plot skeleton as your formal structure and turn out literary masterpieces like *The Man in the High Castle* or *The Stars My Destination*.

Ask a commercial writer, aka hack, why he wrote a given book, and he will tell you, for money. Ask him what it is about, and he will, more likely than not, give you a plot summary.

Ask a writer with literary ambitions why he wrote a given book and what it is about, and you will be treated to a philosophical discourse of some passion and varying degrees of coherence.

I do not say that the hack is the moral inferior of the writer with an ambition to create literature. It is when a writer of more than commercial ambition confuses the manipulative requirements of the commercial plot skeleton with the literary parameters of science fiction, the plot-climax with the thematic resolution of the novel, that sci-fi becomes what is wrong with so much SF.

Take Orson Scott Card's *Ender's Game*, for example.

Humanity has beaten back an alien invasion of the solar system and is now preparing itself militarily to confront an expected second attack. Six-year-old Ender Wiggin is drafted into a program designed to produce spaceship officers and ultimately the strategic genius-hero to lead the whole human fleet into battle. Ender, we are given to understand, is destined to become this hero.

Ender and other tykes like him are taken to an asteroid, where, in addition to pursuing their formal education, they play endless rounds of a zero-g personal combat team sport designed to mirror the strategic and tactical exigencies of space warface. Ender later graduates to a more advanced school, where the game is played on computers and TV screens with ships and fleets. The description of the playing of these games and Ender's growing mastery of them dominates the novel. In the climax, Ender is playing the commander of the whole human fleet on his video game machine, and it turns out that the *real fleet* is slaved to his controls as it destroys the home planet of the aliens at the cost of many real human lives while Ender sets the arcade record.

Card has faithfully followed the plot skeleton. He writes a terse, well-paced, transparent line of prose that expertly moves the reader through the story without calling attention to itself, which is the stylistic ideal of the pulp tradition.

It is not surprising, therefore, that *Ender's Game* would be a successful work of commercial sci-fi. But it ended up winning both the Hugo and the Nebula and, indeed, made Card's commercial career. Yet from the plot-summary, it is not so easy to see why such a work should stand out from the pack.

Something must be going on at a deeper level.

Something certainly is.

For one thing, there is a truly bizarre subplot, in which Ender's brother Paul and sister Valentine take over political leadership of the Earth while still in their teens. They do this by creating pseudonymous letterhack personas who debate each other on a worldwide computer-network bulletin board. I kid you not, you could look it up.

For another thing, Ender, Valentine, and Paul simply do not come off as the young children Card tells us they are. Their speech patterns, their level of intellection, the style of their interaction with their peers, what they say, and what they do all mark them as adolescents.

Except for one factor. Superficially, at least, sex never rears its head. What Card gives us in the guise of young children are *desexualized adolescents*.

Well, not exactly, for beneath the surface there certainly is a strong sexual subtext in *Ender's Game*. Paul and Ender compete throughout the novel for the affections of sister Valentine, and in the denouement, Ender, the hero, gets the girl. Valentine goes off with Ender to colonize the home planet of the aliens in a complex, hurried, over-dense final chapter that reads like an outline for a whole other novel, while poor Paul must content himself with being ruler of the solar system.

Why has this novel struck such a strong chord with SF readers? The main plot would seem to be a rather ordinary variation on the standard plot skeleton. Card's realization of his future civilization is narrowly confined to a few self-contained locales and game-realities, the subplot is entirely unbelievable, and the main character relationship is a thinly sublimated incestuous love triangle.

No, the strength of *Ender's Game* as a piece of sci-fi can't rest on the plot, or the uniqueness of the speculation, or the world building, all of which, while certainly craftsmanlike, are no stronger than similar jobs of work in hundreds of novels.

But when we compare the psychic profile of the typical sci-fi fan to the characters Card has created as reader-identification figures, we see at once why *Ender's Game* does such a world-class job of pushing the buttons of the targeted audience.

Talk about sympathetic heroes with whom the reader can identify! How about a sexually arrested adolescent who becomes the savior of the human race through his prowess at war-sports and video games? How about two other sexually arrested adolescents who take over the world as electronic fanzine letterhacks?

This is as close as identification of the audience with the hero can get—the identification figures *are* the audience's fantasy images of themselves.

We are getting onto admittedly shaky critical ground here, in which textual analysis skirts perilously close to attempts by the critic to psychoanalyze the author.

Did Card *know* exactly what he was doing? Did he study a psychological profile of sci-fi fandom and cynically craft his work accordingly?

Or is Card himself a psychic citizen of that subculture, unselfconsciously expressing its wish-fullfillment fantasies?

I *told* you we were on shaky critical ground. There is nothing more invidious than a Freudian critic who assumes he knows more about the real motivations of the characters and the author than the author does himself, unless it is a Marxist critic holding forth on the economic determinism of the author's motivations.

When in doubt, the critic should assume that the author is as aware of what he is doing and why as the critic is and then some, and in the case of *Ender's Game*, Card provides ample evidence in the text itself that what we are dealing with here is not so much an exemplar of successful sci-fi as partially failed science fiction.

For one thing, thin as it may be in terms of flowing logically out of the bulk of the novel, there is a nice little piece of moral judo when Ender, all unknowing, commits his act of genocide via game console.

For while the adults laud him as savior and hero, he views the result of what he has been conned into doing as just that, genocide, and in the confused final chapter, we see him, in skimpy outline form, expiating his guilt.

In other words, *Ender's Game*, in the end, essays irony; a twist on the dynamics of the sci-fi plot skeleton, which, if successfully executed, would bring the reader up short, become a moral commentary of some complexity on the reader's own power fantasies and the manipulative game the author has been playing with them all along (see *The Iron Dream*), and raise sci-fi to the level of literary art.

Furthermore, Card plants other clues that he fully intends the novel to be read on something deeper than a sci-fi level.

In other works, notably *Hart's Hope*, Card has shown himself to be a writer of some psychological sophistication who knows what he is doing when it comes to crafting and manipulating symbol systems to complex literary effect.

It is difficult to believe that such a writer would name the central figure in his incestuous love triangle *Valentine* (as in Be My Valentine) were he not deliberately pointing to the nature of the relationship.

Even more difficult to believe that he was unaware of the obvious sexual connotations when he named his aliens the "Buggers." That's right, the insectoid aliens who are never really described, aren't called "Bugs" or "Bug-Eyed Monsters," but *Buggers* throughout the whole novel. The little boys and girls, the desexualized adolescents, are trained by the adults to go out and fight buggers, and Ender, the hero, wins his Valentine, at least in plot terms, when he exterminates Buggery.

What is Card actually addressing in this subtext? He's certainly playing with powerful symbology! Incest, buggery, genocide, and power fantasies lurking darkly below the surface of his supposedly desexualized adolescents, and in the context of a militaristic milieu that seems to indicate that he is groping toward some libidinal equation between military power fantasies, war games, and the sublimated sexual dynamic.

Alas, all this powerfully evoked psychosexual subtext never coheres into a comprehensible thematic statement, nor does it really seem to mesh with the overt storyline in a way that adds resonance.

Ender's Game is a frustrating read. One is convinced that Card is trying to say something subtle and important about the relationship between repressed adolescent sexuality, sibling rivalry, incestuous longings, fear of buggery, power fantasies, and how society captures this libidinal energy and bends it towards military purposes. But one is also at a loss to figure out *what*.

Throw out the final chapter, which seems to exist mostly as a bridge to the sequel, *Speaker for the Dead*, and the novel reaches its proper sci-fi climax when Ender destroys the home world of the Buggers.

The hero destroys the villains and gets the girl.

But the girl he gets is his sister, and in his hour of victory what he feels is not triumphant vindication, but *guilt*.

There would be rich irony here if only the psychosexual subtext and the plot climax had come together in a thematic epiphany, if Card had successfully drawn the equation between Ender's repressed incestuous sexuality, buggery as the villain of the piece, the capture of adolescent libido for militaristic purposes, and Ender's feeling of guilt in what should have been his climactic hour of triumph.

The bulk of the novel is something of a guiltless military masturbation fantasy, nicely epitomized by the fact that all the action takes place in war-games frameworks. Only when Ender is consumed by guilt after he learns that the final game was real does Card turn the moral tables and make a perfunctory anti-war statement, a thematic turnaround that, in plot terms, seems to come from deep left field.

Why, after all, *does* Ender suffer postcoital guilt? He was *tricked* into exterminating the Buggers by the adults, by society, if you will; he was innocent of knowledge of the crime in the act of its commission, hence morally blameless. Is his feeling of guilt a product of the psychosexual subtext, an emotional awareness of his incestuous feelings for Valentine, transferred by Card onto the plot-resolution in an effort to justify it emotionally?

Ender's Game, it would seem, is two different novels that never quite come together.

The successful sci-fi novel plays the plot skeleton game to perfection, warping the reader into total identification with a hero who is himself, who wins battle game after battle game, slays the villains, becomes the savior of the human race, and gets the girl.

But the failed science fiction novel is dealing with much deeper stuff, with material whose thematic resolution is inherently at variance with the plot dynamics of sci-fi.

In *this* novel, the capture of thwarted adolescent sexuality and its transference into war-games obsession is an evil con job by society; it is an ironic comment on the very technique that Card himself has used to get the reader off.

The extermination of the Buggers should have been the point where the two strains came together to show the reader the true nature of the meal he has been happily gobbling up all along, so that Ender's guilt becomes his own.

But since Ender has no plot-reason to feel guilty, his guilt feelings, and those of the reader who identifies with them at all, can come only from the unresolved sub-rosa incest theme, another emotional con-job, since the equation between them has never really been drawn.

The trouble with SF is sci-fi, and what seems to have gone wrong with *Ender's Game* is that the exigencies of the reader-identification plotline of the sci-fi novel prevented Card from resolving the thematic material of the science fiction novel, even as the forced attempt to inject a thematic turnaround at the plot climax produced a plot resolution emotionally at variance with the thrust of the conventional sci-fi storyline.

Perhaps Orson Scott Card simply bit off more than anyone could possibly chew. *Ender's Game* could have worked on both levels only if Card had been willing to conceive the novel as a tragedy, if our reader-identification figure had attained moral insight into his act of genocide in the doing, and done it anyway, and by so doing, somehow become aware of his incestuous relationship with his sister in the process, so that the public and private tragedies became mirrors of each other, a la *Oedipus Rex*.

But adherence to the strictures of the sci-fi format seems to preclude tragedy, and while I am casting stones, I might as well throw one at myself.

In my first novel, *The Solarians*, a piece of space opera that certainly qualifies as pur sang sci-fi, humankind has been fighting an endless losing space war with the alien Duglaari. Centuries ago, Earth isolated itself from the rest of humanity, and became the legendary Fortress Sol, keeping alive mankind's hope with the promise that it will come to the rescue at the final desperate hour.

Through plot-machinations and hugger-mugger too tedious to detail, the Duglaari are conned into an all-out attack on Earth with their main battle fleet. The people of Earth then turn the sun nova, vaporizing the Duglaari, the symbol of humankind's dependence on an outside savior, and themselves, all in one unifying, bittersweet, tragic explosive image.

Pretty neat, huh? Pretty heavy stuff for a sci-fi novel? How's *that* for a unifying climactic image?

Alas, somehow, I just couldn't leave it alone. I just couldn't bring myself to really vaporize five billion heroic people in the context of a sci-fi novel.

Even as Orson Scott Card appended a chapter to *Ender's Game* that attempted to tie things up thematically after the real story was over, I tacked a coda onto *The Solarians* after that novel had reached its true tragi-triumphant climax, in which it is revealed that all those people didn't *really* sacrifice their lives for humanity's survival. They packed themselves into a fleet of giant spaceships and fled to safety, detonating the nova by remote control.

This all-too-common reluctance to bite the thematic bullet of tragedy, this fastidious unwillingness to violate sci-fi conventions, has marred many a science fiction novel far superior to something like *The Solarians* or, for that matter, even *Ender's Game*.

If SF novels in general have a characteristic literary flaw, it is that they tend to end badly, they tend to fail to come to a climax that resolves plot and thematic imperatives in a unified manner. They end with mere action climaxes that fulfill the requirements of the plot skeleton, but leave the real story unresolved. And perish the thought that the hero, the reader-identification figure, should *die* at the end of the novel, even when this is the tragic denouement that the story has been building to all along.

Case in point, Walter Jon Williams' *Hardwired*. This is unquestionably a work of true science fiction in the present context, infinitely superior on an absolute literary level to *The Solarians*, to *Ender's Game*, or even to Roger Zelazny's *Damnation Alley*, to which Wiliams pays homage in the dedication.

The cover copy compares *Hardwired* to Gibson's *Neuromancer*, and in a certain sense the novel does entitle Williams to call himself a card-carrying cyberpunk.

In this future world, the Orbitals, living in space, are the exploitative overlords of a semi-ruined Earth they deliberately keep in a state of economic depression. Cowboy, the hero, is an ex–fighter jock and present-tense "Panzerboy", a medical smuggler running the Alley (hommage a Zelazny) in his armored car, to which he is thoroughly cyborged. Sarah, the heroine, streetgirl, sometime whore and assasin, is cyborged to the Weasel, a weapon that lies coiled in her throat. Both come replete with many artificial sensory enhancements, most of the other characters also are loaded with such enhancements, there is even an electronic ghost named Reno who survives in the computer net, brand names abound, and Williams' prose style superficially resembles Gibson's.

But *Hardwired* is far from being a *Neuromancer* clone, for while the cultural ambiance of this novel, the dialog, the cyber hugger-mugger, even the surface feel of the characters' consciousnesses, do indeed seem to be in the Gibson mode, Williams gets deeper into his characters' hearts than Gibson does, and at their hearts, both Cowboy and Sarah are tender creatures, romantics, even idealists.

Sarah is motivated throughout by love for her worthless and treacherous brother, and, even as in real life, we moan at the tragic blunders this lead her into, we yearn to shake her by the shoulders and wake her up, even as we recognize all too well that we have seen the results of such misplaced love before.

Cowboy *knows* that he is a foredoomed tragic figure, fighting the good fight against forces far too powerful to defeat; he sees *himself* as an atavistic exemplar of the Western hero caught in a ruined latter-day world. Indeed it is his consciously understood desire to live out this legend to its tragic conclusion, and go out in a blaze of glory, in some magnificently futile gesture, and "win for himself a slice of immortality, a place in the mind of every panzerboy, every jock. . . ."

In the situation that Williams has set up, the resistance that Cowboy ends up leading cannot *really* hope to overthrow the overlordship of the Orbitals and rescue humanity in the time-honored sci-fi tradition. In the story that Williams has so carefully fashioned, the best that can be achieved is a single victory within the context of a struggle that must go on long after the novel is over, a spiritual victory that gives Cowboy his legendary and semi-tragic apotheosis in death as a symbol of freedom painted across his beloved sky.

And Williams takes us right to the brink. He sets up a plot situation that puts Cowboy back in his fighter plane to lead a battle to destroy an incoming Orbital ship. If the ship is destroyed, the Earth may not be freed, but a worthwhile victory will be won.

The climax of *Hardwired* is a long, well-written, aerial combat sequence, the denouement of which leaves Cowboy, his weapons out of action, as the only fighter left to take out the Orbital ship, and only one way to do it, smack in the middle of the moment the novel and his whole life have pointed toward.

"The interface demands a certain solution, and the decision is taken without conscious volition. But somewhere in Cowboy's mind there is a realization that this is the necessary and correct conclusion to his legend, to use himself and his black-matte body as the last missile against the Orbital shuttle and win for himself a slice of immortality. . . .

"Cowboy accepts the decision of his crystal. A bark of triumphant laughter bursts from his lips as the shuttle grows larger and larger in his vision. . . ."

And then—

And then a spearcarrier, a sidekick in another fighter, The Black Sidekick, fer chrissakes, appears out of nowhere, rams his plane into the shuttle, and saves Cowboy's life!

Yes, incredibly enough, after having done such a wonderful job of melding theme, plot, world building, political and economic extrapolation, and character, and bringing them all together to this textbook-perfect moment of apotheosis where they all come together in a single pivot point, Williams blows it.

He does almost exactly what I did in *The Solarians*, only worse, first because *Hardwired* is a much better novel, second because I at least gave the reader the momentary illusion of proper resolution only to yank it back, whereas Williams takes the reader to the brink and chickens out entirely.

Having thrown away the perfect tragic confluence of plot, theme, and character, Williams is then reduced to a mere sci-fi resolution, a plot-skeleton schtick, admittedly rendered as well as anything in *Neuromancer*, in which he and Reno use the interface to destroy the baddest of the baddies. And Cowboy and Sarah get to ride off into the sunset together.

Oh yes, the trouble with SF is sci-fi! Even a science fiction writer with Walter Jon Williams' plotting skills, thematic depth, sure hand at characterization, and mastery of prose style, even a novelist who gives abundant evidence that he knew where he was going all along, can't bite the bullet of tragedy in the moment of truth. He can't kill his reader-identification figure. He can't let his sympathetic hero go out in an act of philosophically, psychologically, politically, and, yes, morally justified suicide.

And if the trouble with SF writers is their adherence to the sci-fi formula even in the teeth of thematic and characterological imperatives to the contrary, then the trouble with SF *editors* is their adherence to the

marketing strictures of sci-fi publishing, even when the literary imperatives point so glaringly in the opposite direction.

Williams' error in *Hardwired* is hardly a subtle one, and it would
have been simplicity itself to fix it in the editing process. Everything was
there already except the climactic moment. One little paragraph and
then a short coda from Sarah's viewpoint would easily enough have
given this fine novel the perfect thematic resolution it so richly deserved. Surely any competent editor should have seen this on a quick
first reading.

Has the level of editorial professionalism in SF publishing really
sunk this low?

Alas, I think not.

No, from the point of view of the SF editor who knows the targeted
sci-fi audience, Williams' error as a science fiction author is Williams'
correct commercial judgment as a producer of sci-fi. Had Williams
turned in *Hardwired* with the thematic ending its literary imperatives
had called for, his editor would likely as not have called for a rewrite
bending the novel toward just the conventional sci-fi ending it bears the
burden of in print.

Kill the sympathetic hero? Eschew the scene in which he destroys
the ultimate villain? Portray instead an act of heroic suicide as his
spiritual victory? One can almost hear the savvy editor moaning.

"The fans will never buy it, Walt. They'll feel cheated. It's too
damned *literary*. The hero has to defeat the villain. You can't kill off the
reader-identification figure, he has to live to get the girl. And to star in
the sequel, which you had better set up in case this wins the Hugo."

Who knows, maybe that's just the way it happened?

Consistent critical standards? In a sense we have them already. Sci-
fi evolved out of the adventure pulps, and the pulp tradition provides
authors, editors, and critics with a template against which to measure the
commercial viability of genre SF in the form of the plot skeleton,
measured against which Williams and his editor were dead right, and my
criticism of the ending of *Hardwired* is dead wrong.

But if we, as writers, editors, and critics, dare to aspire to a vision of
science fiction in an absolute literary sense, as a subset of seriously
intended literature at large, rather than as a species of commercial pulp
writing, then we must hold SF to a higher standard, an absolute
standard, a set of critical standards *antithetical* to many of the strictures
of successful sci-fi.

We know what those standards are, too. They are at least as old as Plato and Aristotle, as Shakespeare and Tolstoi, and as contemporary as any heartfelt tale truly and courageously told according to the uncompromising demands of the story itself. If we dare to apply *these* standards, the time and place of the setting become entirely irrelevant to our judgment of the extent to which a work of fiction succeeds as literary art.

If the critical establishment should ever choose to apply these standards impartially to SF and non-SF alike, many successful Hugo- and Nebula-winning works of sci-fi will stand naked as literary failures.

But some works of *science fiction* will be revealed as worthy of taking their place in *any* literary company, and if we within the SF community should ever dare to apply absolute literary standards pitilessly to *ourselves* on a consistent basis, science fiction may yet evolve to take its rightful place in the literature of our species.

It's all a matter of what we want to be when we grow up.

Or whether we want to grow up at all.   •

Inside, Outside

If not all science fiction is sci-fi, neither, as those within the mystic circle would seem to like to believe, are SF *modes* the exclusive literary property of so-called SF writers. On the other hand, as the so-called mainstream critical establishment seems to have even more difficulty comprehending, not all SF produced by those who may be stereotyped as "genre writers" is necessarily "genre fiction."

In the past half dozen years or so we have been seeing quite a burst of SF by writers "outside the genre" and quite a bit of "crossover fiction" by so-called genre writers attempting to "break out" into "mainstream."

Two paragraphs into this piece, and we are already hip-deep in quotation marks, signifying that the meanings of the words qualified thereby would seem to be in need of more precise technical definition than Webster's provides.

If the "SF genre" is defined commercially as everything published, packaged, and promoted as "SF," then "SF genre writers" may be simply defined as those writers who regularly produce the stuff shelved in the SF racks in the bookstores.

All well and good as working definitions for commercial purposes, but the *literary* situation is a good deal more complex and growing more so daily.

For no one has come up with a generally acceptable *literary* definition of science fiction, and now that the logo "SF" has long since come to encompass both science fiction and fantasy, the essential nature of the beast has become even more elusive.

This is not so for the other genres of fiction. Mysteries are readily enough defined by their plot structures. Contemporary fiction, historical fiction, westerns, and so forth are defined by their time frames and/or their geographical settings. Gothics are defined by their ambiance and horror fiction by the horror it must evoke in the reader.

But science fiction may be and has been set in any time, past, present, or future. Indeed, it may be and has been set even in *alternate* pasts and presents, and the same work may encompass several alternate futures. One used to be able to say that science fiction could be set anywhere in the universe, but now that cosmological physics is dealing with the possibilities of multiple universes, even that limitation is no longer applicable.

Nor may science fiction be defined by characteristic plot structure, set of characters, range of themes, or evoked emotions.

Perhaps John W. Campbell, Jr., said it best when he declared that in an absolute technical sense, science fiction was the whole literary spectrum in that it was the fiction that encompassed all possibilities, past, present, and future, a fictional arena without *any* restrictions or parameters. All other fictional modes could then be readily enough defined as special cases of science fiction by referring to their temporal and spatial restrictions.

But now that the SF genre has come to encompass fantasy as well, SF modes are no longer even restricted to what is, was, or will be possible, assuming we ever really knew what *that* meant!

So in an absolute literary sense, SF *is* the mainstream, though in a commercial and general critical sense mainstream is still regarded as the mimetic contemporary-setting novel, which is to say a special case of SF.

So when "SF writers" talk about "breaking out" or "crossing over" into the "mainstream," what they are really talking about is breaking their books out of the commercial and/or critical purdah of SF genre publication, not widening their sphere of literary possibilities.

Indeed, in a literary sense, breaking out or crossing over is generally achieved or at least attempted by adopting some or all of the *narrower restrictions* of so-called mainstream, either by setting the work in some recognizable venue in the present or the historical past on the planet Earth or its immediate vicinity, or by setting the work in the immediate future, where only a few speculative elements are unfamiliar to the general reader.

Which, on the other hand, may explain why more people than one might first think have written science fiction of one kind or another in isolation from the whole genre apparatus. People who do not consider themselves science fiction writers, who turn up their noses in disdain at sci-fi, so-called mainstream writers who nevertheless are attracted to the writing of science fiction.

The roster of established literary lions who have essayed at least some science fiction or borderline fantasy since World War II is, upon reflection, quite formidable. Aldous Huxley, Vladimir Nabokov, George Orwell, William Burroughs, Gore Vidal, Thomas Pynchon, Anthony Burgess, Doris Lessing, Paddy Chayefsky, Kingsley Amis, Norman Mailer, Margaret Atwood, Don Delillo, Russell Hoban, William Golding, Lawrence Durrell, for a few quick examples.

The point being that there has always been a lot more to science fiction than sci-fi. There have long been many people writing science fiction that ignores or even knowingly defies the conventions and expectations of the sci-fi pulp tradition. There is by now a large body of science fiction that is as closely connected to the general literary tradition as it is to the SF genre.

And now, paradoxically enough at a time when SF writers have been attempting to break out of the genre and into the greater possibilities for commercial success and critical attention of the mainstream, many mainstream writers who have never labored under the commercial and critical restrictions suffered by the genre writers are attempting to break out of the *literary* restrictions of mainstream modes and into the wider literary possibilities of SF.

It's not hard to see why. On the one hand, SF now offers greater possibilities for commercial success to "literary" writers such as Russell Hoban or Mark Halperin, for so-called "serious literary fiction," which is really to say the serious mimetic *contemporary* novel, generally sells very few copies in hardcover, regardless of rave reviews from the literary establishment, and half the time has trouble even making it into paperback.

On the other hand, commercially successful and critically well-regarded writers such as Norman Mailer, Len Deighton, Doris Lessing, Anthony Burgess, and Walter Tevis are able to explore the wider literary possibilities inherent in SF modes without, for the most part, losing either sales or literary standing.

In other words, we are now in the presence of a growing body of work that is science fiction or fantasy by any reasonable literary definition, produced by writers who have developed entirely outside the SF genre and receiving wider attention from the critical establishment as such, at the same time that certain SF writers are producing at least a trickle of books in attempts to break out of the genre.

Alas, the mainstream literary establishment still, for the most part, ignores or at best looks patronizingly down its nose at most work, SF or not, produced by writers stereotyped as genre writers on the one hand, and generally displays its woeful and willful ignorance of half a century of SF when it attempts to deal with SF written by its darling sons and daughters on the other.

Take, for example, the extravagant overpraise heaped by these literary mavens upon Russell Hoban's *Riddley Walker* and contrast it with the muddled misunderstanding and consequent opprobrium dumped by the same on Norman Mailer's immeasurably superior *Ancient Evenings*.

Riddley Walker is set in a post-nuclear-collapse Britain, and the title character is a young man maturing into a kind of wandering storyteller who narrates the novel in the first person in the degenerate English of the period, meeting the usual sorts one would expect in such stories, including mutants, whom the humans hate and confine for their loathsomeness, which reminds them of man's self-inflicted fallen state, yet worship for their psychic powers.

Now as *we* all know, thematically there is absolutely nothing new in all this; it was written over and over and over again in the 1950s, it is still a staple of SF, and the greatest exemplar, the novel that any such work must be judged against, is, of course, *A Canticle for Leibowitz*. No one has topped Miller's masterpiece in the decades since he wrote it, and Hoban doesn't even come close.

Nevertheless, the literary establishment praised *Riddley Walker* not only for its prose but for its conceptual daring and hardly seemed to realize either that it was derivative of literally hundreds of previous works or that Walter M. Miller had turned the same material into an enduring masterpiece that has been conspicuously in print for about a quarter of a century.

Why?

Well first of all, to be fair about it, *Riddley Walker* is far from being a bad novel. Hoban has done a good job transmogrifying the events and lessons of the nuclear holocaust into the muzzy mythology of Riddley's future, and telling the tale in the degenerate patois of the age provides pathos, though the inconsistently-worked-out devolved orthography provides only unnecessary obfuscation.

Riddley Walker is almost a textbook example of the strengths and weaknesses of the typical "literary" writer writing SF in sublime and naive ignorance of what genre writers have done over half a century and more. Hoban concentrates on character and style, at which he is superior to most of the SF writers who have worked this theme (but inferior to, for example, Miller, Pangborn, or Sturgeon), and in the process of inventing the wheel again, he manages to avoid much of the stereotypical post-nuclear schtick while nevertheless dredging up deformed mutants with psychic powers as if no one had ever thought of them before.

On the other hand, even the journeyman genre writer would not perpetrate some of the howlers that Hoban has committed when it comes to the details of his future society. Here, for example, we have isolated British villagers at a very low technological level forever drinking tea and rolling hash in "rizlas." Hoban would seem never to have considered that the tea and hashish would have to be imported from great distances, and that in such a society paper would be far too rare and expensive to use in rolling joints. For that matter, I defy *anyone* to roll hash not liberally mixed with tobacco (which Hoban's villagers would also be unable to grow in Britain) into a tokable joint.

Now admittedly, even though there are numerous examples of such science-fictional gaffes, this would be mere nit-picking if the same lack of extrapolative rigor (indeed, I suspect, the ignorance of the concept of extrapolative rigor itself) did not infect the creation of the central core of the novel, the invented patois in which it is told.

Hoban's transmuted and degenerated English is an entirely arbitrary creation in which words are broken into fragments and put back together again for low comic effect, in which the same phoneme may have several alternative spellings, and that all too often comes off like a baggy-pants American comedian rendering British dialects (Hoban is an American residing in Britain).

Riddley Walker is to science fiction as Grandma Moses is to sophisticated gallery painting: the creation of a talented but unschooled primitive, avoiding most of the obvious cliches while reinventing some of the others, fresh and different in its freedom from genre apparatus, but hardly up to the work of true masters who have done their homework.

So why the critical overpraise? Well first of all, Hoban had something of a previous reputation as a "serious" writer and no stigma as an "SF writer"; otherwise, the overpraisers in question would never have even read his book. But once they did, my guess is that they were genuinely and sincerely moved by what they genuinely and sincerely perceived as its conceptual daring.

Stanislaw Lem's reputation in the United States was made by a long feature piece on the front page of *The New York Times Book Review*, in which Theodore Solataroff went on and on praising his inventiveness and conceptual genius in great detail, ending up by pronouncing him "one of the deep spirits of the age," never once acknowledging or realizing that the thematic materials he found so outré and revolutionary, far from springing full-blown from the brow of Stanislaw Lem, were simply the common material of middle-of-the-road SF!

In other words, while establishment literary critics may be prejudiced against genre SF, it is usually an *ignorant* prejudice. They simply haven't read the stuff. But the better ones, while regrettably ignorant and even more regrettably biased, are not stupid or imperceptive. When they are tricked into reading and reviewing even less-than-masterly SF by writers against whom they have formed no prejudgment, they frequently find themselves bowled over into excess by unexpected confrontation with a mode that suddenly evokes a sense of wonder they never even knew they had.

On the other hand, this gaping blind spot in the literary education of establishment critics can sometimes work to the disadvantage of SF or fantasy works by writers of deservedly great repute in their own circles, to wit, for example, Norman Mailer's *Ancient Evenings*.

This, as anyone at all familiar with genre fantasy instantly recognizes, is a fantasy novel set in ancient Egypt. It opens with a soul in the process of reincarnation, it proceeds to render telepathy as a fairly common given, it deals with the gods in a rather matter-of-fact manner, it has some very interesting things indeed to say about magic, and at the end, Mailer seems to be setting himself up for a sequel in a science fiction mode set in the future and in space.

Indeed, I have heard more than one SF fan complain that *Ancient Evenings* is a rip-off of Roger Zelazny's *Creatures of Light and Darkness*. While this is the equivalent of accusing anyone who has written a generation-ship story of plagiarizing Heinlein or anyone who has written an Arthurian fantasy of ripping off Malory, it does point out that even the naive and unsophisticated SF reader can easily enough perceive that *Ancient Evenings* is a *fantasy* novel.

But amazingly enough, some of the major reviews of this major novel in major critical journals entirely missed this point, and instead reviewed *Ancient Evenings* as a grossly inaccurate historical novel, taking Mailer to task for falsely portraying his ancient Egyptians as telepathic, for his twisted rendering of Egyptian mythology, for the sophisticated modernistic consciousness with which he imbued his characters, and most of all for the fascinating if unwholesome magical system he built around the symbol and psychic power of shit.

Which is to say that these ignoramuses flayed Mailer for some of the most imaginative *virtues* of his *fantasy* novel under the pig-headed assumption that they were dealing with failed historical re-creation!

If only *these* worthies were familiar with such Zelazny novels as *Creatures of Light and Darkness* and *Lord of Light*! For while Mailer is in no way plagiarizing Zelazny, *Ancient Evenings* is certainly best understood and appreciated as an evolution, deepening, and extension of the mode Zelazny more or less pioneered in such works.

Like Zelazny, Mailer takes a mythos and plays freely with it for his own modernistic purposes and gifts his prose and his characters with a certain contemporary sophistication of consciousness that may indeed be anachronistic in terms of historical realism. Why not? This is fantasy, metafiction, *not* mimesis, or, as Alexei Panshin has said in a somewhat different context, "SF that *knows* it is SF."

Where Mailer goes beyond Zelazny is in his employment of powers and virtues not generally characteristic of the genre, such as the psychosexual description (of which he is the master), psychological realism, and the willingness and ability to treat a superficially silly concept with such puissant seriousness that in the end the reader is convinced that it is no arch conceit after all.

For my money, anyway, Mailer's meditations upon the powers of shit, for which of course he has been the butt of much denigrating low humor, is in fact one of the most perceptive insights into the psychology of magic in all fantasy.

If you think not, then examine your *own* reactions to shit, which is to say the aura of taboo, fear, loathing, and yes, therefore power, exuded by the very word, let alone the substance itself! We laugh, we wrinkle our noses, we avoid the subject in polite company, but *why*?

It is precisely the courage to ask such questions, and the cold intellectual curiosity of the man from Mars necessary to try to answer them, that is perhaps the central virtue of SF, be it science fiction or fantasy, and the reason that, in the end, a writer like Mailer must perhaps inevitably be drawn to such modes in this mature stage of his career, for in this sense at least, he has always been a spiritual kinsman of science fiction writers, whether he has ever been conscious of the fact or not.

But to what extent do SF writers carry over the virtues of SF modes into mainstream fiction when they attempt to "cross over" and to what extent are they able to fuse them with the virtues of accepted literary modes such as psychological realism, irony, and ambiguity?

To what extent are the esthetic virtues of SF watered down in the attempt? And *are there* SF genre conventions and formulas, that, for the most part unexamined, tend to cross over with them to the detriment of the work?

George R.R. Martin's *Fevre Dream* and *The Armageddon Rag* have both been forthright attempts to break out into the mainstream, at least in terms of sales, albeit of two entirely different sorts.

Fevre Dream, a vampire novel set in the nineteenth century on the Mississippi, can be taken as a fantasy novel, or just as easily as a science fiction novel set in the past, since Martin has taken care to work out a very good scientific rationale and set of parameters for vampirism that are even integral to the plot.

This one is simply a fine SF novel set in the past that happens to have been packaged and marketed to appeal to a mainstream audience. As SF in a literary sense, it was entirely successful. Alas, as it turned out, in commercial terms, it was a marketing disaster that did no little harm to Martin's professional career through no fault of his own.

The Armageddon Rag, on the other hand, is something else again, a *very* ambitious novel indeed in a literary and even social sense, that paradoxically enough was packaged and marketed as mainstream, yet was severely diminished as a literary achievement by a thematically counterproductive fantasy element unnecessarily dragged in by the heels.

Novelist and former Underground journalist Sandy Blair is launched into a journey into his and our past when he is talked into investigating the brutal murder of the former manager of the Nazgul, an apocalyptic rock group whose lead singer was murdered on stage at a large rock festival, an event that Martin uses as his metasymbol for the death of the sixties and all that it has meant in his and our lives.

For perhaps the first half or so of the novel, *The Armageddon Rag* is the best fictional exploration of what the spirit of the sixties was and what its death has meant to contemporary America that has yet managed to escape from limbo into print, as Blair travels around the country, meeting old friends and acquaintances from that era, and as Martin uses this device to take us back and forth in time.

I say *escaped from limbo into print* because there has been a taboo against publishing anything that tells the truth about the sixties, as the first half of *The Armageddon Rag* does so well, for many years. One may wax sadly nostalgic about lost youth from the point of view of aging ex-hippies in the present, one may publish thrillers set in a sixties time-frame, one may now even write about the Viet Nam War, but one may *not* publish a novel directly about the Counterculture of the 1960s that deals sympathetically with the vanished spirit thereof.

I have come upon any number of unpublished novels in this vein by published writers. Upon attempting to get a contract for such a novel myself, I have been told by publishing executives and agents in words of one syllable that such a thing, no matter how well done, is unpublishable. And if you think I am just being paranoid, then try to name such a published novel yourself.

The point is that Martin either had the sad street smarts to know this on some level himself up front or was told so by his editor, for even though *The Armaggedon Rag* was marketed as a mainstream novel and, literarily speaking, would have been better as such, a deal-with-the-devil schtick is made the McGuffin of the novel, a literarily unnecessary piece of genre apparatus that destroys its thematic resolution.

Even though (perhaps *because*) Martin paints such an achingly true portrait of the lost idealism of the sixties, he has evil forces doing black magic in an attempt to resurrect the *negative* aspects of the 1960s by resurrecting the Nazgul and the murdered lead singer, so that he can be murdered again, in order to bring on the Armageddon of the title. Blair, who is being set up to be the murderer, thwarts this scheme in the end by refusing to do the deed.

Thematically, of course, in terms of what Martin has so admirably set up, this cannot make any sense. If the sixties were golden, then resurrecting them cannot be a demonic act, and preventing that resurrection is morally wrong. In order to finesse this plot flaw, Martin makes the Nazgul (i.e., the Stones and the spirit of Altamont) stand for the spirit of the times, not the Beatles or the Airplane and Woodstock. But this doesn't work, either, in terms of the rest of the novel, which tells another tale obviously closer to the author's heart, for when Blair prevents Armageddon, what he and we, alas, are left with, is what the novel began with, the death of the dream.

Alas, poor Martin was caught between a rock and a hard place. The whole esthetic and spirit of the book led toward an apotheosis in which the spirit of the sixties was resurrected, but there was no way this could be credibly done in terms of the contemporary-cum-historical mode, and even if by some act of genius he *had* found a way, it would only have rendered the novel unpublishable!

In hindsight, perhaps, he might have pulled it off by using a *different* genre convention, turning the book into an alternate-world novel, so that when Blair refrains from murder, he and we find ourselves not where we are now, but where we might have been.

But if he had pulled that off, would *The Armageddon Rag* have been published at all? Or would he and we be left with one more unpublished novel instead of this noble and heroic effort that was prevented from being entirely satisfying by the very genre ploy that allowed it to see the light of day in the first place?

Michael Moorcock's *Byzantium Endures*, on the other hand, is a historical novel entirely free from even a hint of genre conventions. This is hardly surprising since Moorcock, as editor and as writer, has been more committed than anyone else to freeing the literary modes of SF from the conventions of the SF genre. And yet, somehow, certain vigors and strengths of SF modes do seem to have insinuated themselves into this work. And this is not so surprising either, since Moorcock has also long been dedicated to breathing fresh air into the stale drawing rooms of the "literary" novel.

Byzantium Endures is the first volume of a trilogy (which may turn into a tetralogy) that will take its protagonist and narrator, Dimitri Pyanitski, from his birth in Kiev in 1900 clear through the Russian Revolution, both World Wars, and the Holocaust of the concentration camps into the present or immediate future, where he has already made cameo appearances in Moorcock's Jerry Cornelius cycle, which *is* fiction in an SF mode.

A Ukrainian Jew and an anti-Semite, an inventor, a cocaine addict, and something of a con artist, the protean and disreputable Dimitri is designed as nothing less than a literary vehicle through whose sensibility Moorcock is attempting to render, explore, and perhaps even make some sense of the entire history of Europe in the twentieth century.

Byzantium Endures takes him through the Russian Revolution and into the beginnings of the Stalinist aftermath and leaves him fleeing Russia for a future of horrors of which he is as yet unmindful but which *we* can anticipate all too well.

In another context, I once observed that "mainstream literary writers" tend to bring great erudition, psychological depth, and writing skill to bear on the detailed examination of the lint in their own navels, whereas SF writers are unafraid to tackle great themes of cosmic import, with, alas, naive triviality of treatment.

Here, however, Moorcock is bent upon taking on not one but virtually *all* of the great literary themes of the twentieth century! It is in this cosmic chutzpah that this work partakes of one of the central virtues of SF. But the first volume of this projected masterwork, at least, far from playing trivially with enormities, re-creates the world of early twentieth-century Russia and the Ukraine not only with daunting detail and political sophistication, but with a psychological depth and stylistic inventiveness that any so-called literary writer must envy, and with a mordant sense of humor to boot.

Byzantium Endures is not SF by any stretch of the imagination, and yet somehow, it is difficult to imagine any writer taking on such a task as Moorcock has herein embarked upon without a certain indefinable something that can come only from familiarity with SF modes. For this is nothing less than an attempt to write a completely rounded cycle of novels, psychological, historical, and political, that will encompass the twentieth century itself. And no one can hope to encompass both the inner and outer history of the twentieth century without absorbing the esthetic of SF.

When, however, an SF writer attempts to encompass the esthetics of modern literary theory and apply them to what is unequivocally a science fiction novel, we get something like Samuel R. Delany's *Stars in My Pocket Like Grains of Sand*.

This novel defies esthetically just description. A plot summary makes it sound quite asinine. In a galactic far future, perhaps as part of a geopolitical ploy, Industrial Diplomat Marq Dyeth is presented with Rat Korga, a former slave raised to higher consciousness by implants, the sole survivor of his destroyed home world. Korga and Dyeth have been matched as mutual ideal sex objects by computer. They meet on Dyeth's home world and have terrific sex together. But there are so many groupies bugging them that Korga leaves. Plot-wise, th-th-th-that's all, folks!

Obviously, this cannot really be what this whole long novel is about, especially since Delany neither gives their relationship an extra-sexual depth, nor really describes the nature of their perfect sexual compatibility in convincing detail.

What the novel may really be all about in social terms (Delany himself calls it a "novel of manners") is the conflict between two galactic cultures, the Family and the Sygn. The Family, simply put, believes in maintaining a culturally consistent human norm, keeping humanity human, as it were. The Sygn believes in the merger and intermingling of human and alien cultures on the deepest levels.

On Dyeth's home world, human and alien cultures have fused to the point where extended families combine both races, where the humans have adopted alien art forms, esthetics, morality, dining rituals, and sexual modes, and where even interspecies sex is common.

Since most of the novel is told from Dyeth's point of view, we are drawn into perceiving all of this as quite normal, positive, liberated, and healthy. Only at the end, when an off-world human family, which has long existed on intimate and friendly terms with Dyeth's, abruptly switches from the Sygn to the Family for apparently purely self-interested pragmatic reasons, do we suddenly get characters delivering vitriolic diatribes against what we have come to accept as a benign human-alien cultural fusion.

Still, this background, when combined with the minimal storyline, would seem to be only enough material for a short story or at best a novelette, rather than this big fat novel. Clearly, in terms of genre conventions, *Stars in My Pocket Like Grains of Sand* would have to be rated a hugely padded failure.

And yet the book *does* keep you reading along, even though in genre terms, nothing much is really happening. Clearly then, what we have here is an SF novel by an SF writer that defies genre conventions and expectations.

Since in conventional genre terms, most of the novel is padding, perhaps it is precisely the padding, or in more high-falutin' terms, the *discursiveness*, that should be taken as the focus, for along the way, Delany uses the book as a vehicle for presenting any number of artistic and esthetic theories, epitomized by a long tour-de-force sequence in which the electronically enhanced Korga "reads" centuries' worth of galactic literature in a few minutes and in which Delany manages to convey this experience and the essential content of it to the reader of *his* novel.

Padded to a fare-thee-well *Stars in My Pocket* certainly is, but with undeniably very high-quality padding. Delany has long been known for his interest in theoretical criticism, particularly semiotics, and indeed has published whole books of the stuff, and outside the genre, this sort of highly discursive, theory-based fiction is an accepted mode for the novel, for a kind of metafiction that is about fiction and the work in question itself, rather than story, setting, or character, which serve instead as merely a kind of armature.

So perhaps, in the end, what we are left with in *Stars in My Pocket Like Grains of Sand* is the currently most outré example of the strange mutations now occurring when the "Family" of "literary mainstream" and the "Sygn" of SF modes engage in interspecies miscegenation.

A miscegenation that, I would contend, has literary as well as commercial impetus for continuing. Indeed, from a certain perspective, it could be argued that the period of SF genrefication has been merely a temporary historical anomaly.

Writers who wish to speculate on modes of human consciousness or species of social or political or cultural organization that have no existence in either the past or present have only three literary alternatives—straightforward fantasy, in which anything goes a priori; science fiction, which is generally constrained by what we presently regard as the basic physical laws of existence; and that strange hybrid of science fiction and fantasy, the alternate-world story, in which one aspect of history or the environment is arbitrarily altered and the consequences worked out with science fiction's characteristic extrapolative rigor.

Fantasy, of course, is the Ur-literature of the species, since it is only rather recently in our history that we have conceived the notion that we know what is real and what is not, and in this sense just about everything written before, say, the Age of Reason partakes of the essential weltanschauung of fantasy, namely that reality is subject to capricious mutation, and anything at all may lie beyond the next hill.

Science fiction evolved at the time of the Age of Reason, the rise of the scientific world view, and the Industrial Revolution as a dialectical response to fantasy. During this period, the blank spaces on the map of the planet Earth were filled in, the exfoliating human technosphere began to divorce itself from the "natural" realm, and scientific explication of the previously mysterious pushed back the sphere of the supernatural as it delineated the physical parameters of our universe.

Fantasy requires an element of the supernatural, a transcendence of the reader's quotidian reality, a mythic dimension. From time immemorial it had addressed an audience for whom the supernatural was a pervasive reality, but now that science had severely circumscribed the realm of the supernatural, fantasy more and more required the reader's collaboration, a willing suspension of disbelief.

If, as Brian Aldiss contends, *Frankenstein* was the first true science fiction novel, it was also, apppropriately enough, centrally concerned with the very dialectic that gave the mode birth. Whereas a fantasist of previous eras could have conjured the monster as a golem with an incantation or two and gone on to tell the same tale, Mary Shelley made her wizard a scientist and concocted a scientific rationale for the human creation of artificial life.

And if she invented science fiction, she invented something far more central than the mad scientist and the android. She shifted the responsibility for suspension of disbelief away from the reader and onto the writer.

She rationalized her mythic tale of wonder with the scientific world view of her day; in terms of literary technique, however questionable the scientific speculation might have been even then, she used a scientific rationale to persuade the reader that her story took place in the realm of the possible.

And that is as good a functional definition of science fiction as any—a literary technique for re-creating the lost innocence of fantasy, for resurrecting the reader's true belief in the tale of wonder, in the possibility of the fantastic, in the notion that his universe and the universe of the marvelous may be one and the same. Through science fiction, via science and technology and not despite them, magic of a kind re-entered the mechanistic Victorian world, a magic that did *not* require the reader's willing suspension of disbelief.

If *Frankenstein* was the first true science fiction novel, Mark Twain's *A Connecticut Yankee in King Arthur's Court* created the alternate-world form and may have been the first time-travel story to boot. Twain gets his Yankee back to Arthurian England by pure fiat, but once Sir Boss gets there he proceeds to create an alternate past in which medieval Camelot acquires his modern American technology. Twain erases the alteration of history at the end; he's not quite ready to create an alternate present or play with time-travel paradoxes, but the basic technique of the alternate-world story as an offshoot of the time-travel story is all there.

So in literary terms, the basic modes of what we now publish under the logo of SF—fantasy, science fiction, the alternate-world story—had all been developed long before Hugo Gernsback published the first issue of *Amazing Stories*.

Gernsback did not invent science fiction; what he invented was only sci-fi.

Even that is questionable, for Gernsback's formula of action-adventure plotlines carrying displays of technological wonders owes much to Jules Verne, who, if nothing else, was the first hard science fiction writer, and self-proclaimedly so.

As such, he looked askance at the likes of H.G. Wells, even as his inheritors were to look askance at Wells' New Wave literary descendants. In a sense, the tension between sci-fi and science fiction began right there. Verne was not much of a storyteller and still less a master of characterization; for him, the technological extrapolation was central, and he would have found a happy home in the pages of John W. Campbell's *Astounding*.

But Wells was really the first to demonstrate the enormity of science fiction's central literary virtue. Namely, that in the modern world, with its intellectual banishment of the supernatural to the guru farms of central California, with its exponentially mutating technosphere, with its Faustian domination of nature, it is difficult indeed to deal with the interactions of your characters' psyches with the external environment, with the individual's position in the body politic, with the forces of history and destiny, with the evolving nature of human consciousness itself, *without* being constrained to write science fiction.

Well's ambition was literary and he was a committed Fabian socialist. Much of his science fiction centered on political speculation, at times on didacticism, and though in many ways he was a far more puissant technological extrapolator than Verne, his concern was almost never with the technology itself, but with the impact of technology on history and culture. He transformed the disconnected intellectual utopia into the modern political science fiction novel. Science fiction gave the literary artist in him the mode in which to speculate on history and destiny, and it gave the socialist in him the means with which to present his visions as something achievable.

And that is certainly a central literary virtue of science fiction.

In the modern context, you cannot make the reader believe in the possibility of a visionary transformation of society, environment, or consciousness *without* writing it.

This central literary virtue of science fiction is also central to the intellectual health of our society, for science fiction is arguably the only fictional mode whereby a rapidly mutating technological culture may examine its own evolutionary processes and game out its next moves.

And *that* is the main literary reason for writing science fiction in this day and age. Sci-fi may have been born in 1926 with *Amazing Stories*, but science fiction is the literary consequence of the Age of Reason, the Industrial Revolution, the rise of the scientific world view itself, and is in that sense a cultural inevitable.

That is why people with literary bones to pick in this enormous area of central cultural concern are constrained to write science fiction, even when, like Margaret Atwood, they and the publisher loudly proclaim they are doing nothing of the kind.

The Handmaid's Tale is in one sense an oft-told story, a dystopia set in a near-future United States, aka the Republic of Gilead, which has become a fascist theocratic state. We follow Offred, the handmaid of the tale, through her daily rounds as the bondservant of her master and mistress, through a forbidden love affair, and into contact with the resistance.

But you really *haven't* read this one before.

For one thing, the Republic of Gilead is the damnedest hybrid of far-right born-again Christian patriarchy and radical feminist separatism.

You've got a straightforward neo-medieval patriarchal Christian theocracy, complete with extreme sexual repression and the divine right of Big Daddy. The "handmaids" wear modified nuns' habits and are taught, indoctrinated, and bullied by "Aunts" in institutes much like schools for nuns.

But the Aunts' party line, far from being worshipful of the male lords of divine creation, promulgates the doctrine that sex is male rape and that women, who have once more become chattel, need the very system that oppresses them to protect them from the gross natures of the male beasts whose interests the system serves.

Not as loony as it seems on the surface, for this bizarre marriage of feminist separatism and born-again patriarchal theocracy admirably serves Atwood's social fascist state.

The "handmaid" is the flunky of the mistress of the house, who in turn is entirely subservient to her "Commander." But in this future, environmental pollution has severely reduced fertility, and the handmaid is chosen for her child-bearing ability. Her other job is to have sex with the Commander of the household until she gets pregnant. After the baby gets born, it becomes the official child of the Commander's wife, and the handmaid is shipped off to serve as surrogate broodmare for the next high-status stallion.

But hey guys, don't get to thinking this is male chauvinist heaven, either. Atwood has created that rarity, a genuinely new perversion, and the officially prescribed act is not much fun for any of the three participants.

Yes, the *three* of them.

The wife reclines on the bed with her legs aspraddle, the handmaid positions herself between them, and the Commander grinds away listlessly at her for as long as it takes to get his seed planted. By Talmudic legedermain, the biological exigencies are rationalized with the theocratic demands of monogamy, for psychically at least, no true act of adultery is committed, since the act is entirely dehumanized. The handmaid is reduced to the role of a marital appliance, nobody talks to anyone, and no one enjoys it.

Thus both men and women regard sex as an onerous reproductive duty, a disgusting act; indeed, it is turned into a disgusting act as a matter of official policy, and so Atwood beautifully demonstrates how tyranny's deep motive power derives from sexual repression, whatever the ideological superstructure, while daringly drawing the psychopolitical equation between Christian and feminist brands of anti-sexuality in the bargain.

This is certainly science fiction by any Wellsian criterion, and of a high order. Only at the end does Atwood reinvent for herself the pitfalls of sci-fi.

Whereas the typical sci-fi novel would run this material through a rebel-against-the-system plotline and probably have the heroine partake centrally in a successful revolution, Atwood focuses on the quotidian details of her handmaid's life for the most part, which may include involvement with a resistance, and a sojourn in a den of cynical iniquity, but which does not involve macropolitical matters, and does not culminate in triumphant liberation.

Through page 295, Margaret Atwood gives us a textbook demonstration of how a "mainstream" writer of talent, free of all sci-fi formula constraints, can renovate an old science fictional notion, not only by conceptual freshness, but by shifting the central focus away from action-adventure formulas and onto the psychological and the personal. The novel concludes, unexpectedly enough, with a "Lady or the Tiger" ending. Offred steps into a van, not knowing whether she is being dragged off to durance vile or on her way to escaping into Canada.

The way the story has been set up psychologically, this is a satisfying closure, literarily speaking; no pat demolition of what has been set up, but not entirely hopeless on a personal level. A realistic ending to a realistic and rigorous science fiction novel.

But then, as if to prove that even someone who looks down on science fiction, even while she is writing a fine job of it, is still not immune to the virus of sci-fi, or as if some editor freaked at the novel's true ending and talked her into it, Atwood appends a schlocko sci-fi afterword in a silly tone at variance with everything that has gone before, in the form of the proceedings of a congress of supercilious academics picking over the bones of her handmaid's tale in a future fuzzy ecotopia long after wicked Gilead has fallen, thus assuring us that the black hats were eventually defeated and our heroine survived to commit her tale to posterity.

Let ye among you who are without pulp sins cast the first stone.

The black hats are entirely exterminated by the end of James Morrow's *This Is the Way the World Ends*, but the black hats in question are ourselves, all of us — to wit, the human species — for this novel is just what it says it is, a tale of our terminal nuclear extinction.

God knows this has been a staple of science fiction at least since Hiroshima, but it has seldom been presented in this mode. Morrow's first novel, *The Wine of Violence*, was realistic in tone and quite well done, and his second novel, *The Continent of Lies*, was a witty Sheckleyian space romp with both humor and bite. Here he attempts to mix the two tones, or anyway that's what he ends up with.

Needless to say, you can present nuclear extinction as a comedy of assholery a la *Dr. Strangelove*, or you can render the tragic pathos, as for instance Sturgeon does so masterfully in "Thunder and Roses," but it is something else again to try for both affects simultaneously.

Morrow might actually have made it, for he dares what no one rooted in sci-fi conventions ever would: he centers the novel on a puissant piece of imagistic surrealism.

As the bombs fall, the "unadmitted" manifest themselves in

Antartica. The unadmitted are the future generations that would have been born but who will now never be admitted to life, who spring into full being with false memories of the full lives that might have been, tormented by their own unreality, destined to disintegrate shortly, and outraged at the human race for having preempted their existence.

This is where fantasy borders on science fiction and science fiction borders on magic realism, and who gives a damn as long as it works? This is true surrealism, where the power of the image is its own raison d'etre, but it is also science fiction, since the impingment of this actualized image on events is treated in a more or less rigorously extrapolative manner. Given the right image, generating the right schtick as it touches on reality, one can make a powerful emotional and thematic statement and get laughs at the same time, as Vonnegut does in *Cat's Cradle* when Bokonon lies down on the ice and freezes himself into statuary giving the finger to You Know Who.

But alas, what the unadmitted do is snatch up some of the remaining humans—military industrial types, but also the hapless and basically innocent protagonist—and stage a Nuremberg trial. This trial consumes nearly a hundred pages of a three-hundred-page book, and much of the rest of the novel is a set-up for it, too.

The endless trial sequence, like most of the novel in general, is a melange of farce and realistically portrayed existential angst, perhaps the most cogently rounded discussion of nuclear deterrence scenarios in fiction and stand-up comedy, pratfalls ending in a multiple hanging rendered in psychologically gory detail.

Well, this has to either succeed as a glorious tour de farce or fall on its face. William Burroughs might have pulled it off. Morrow doesn't. He presents his case on nuclear strategy and moral responsibility, and a complex and well-rounded case it is too, but he does it by giving us buffoon characters delivering long dissertations on doomsday strategy, intercut with humor that just isn't funny enough to sustain interest during all these speeches.

This Is the Way the World Ends is the famous exception that proves the rule, for maybe Morrow would have benefitted from some pulp-tradition strictures in this one. His protagonist is a wandering Everyman viewpoint who spends a third of the novel sitting mutely in a courtroom, and the whole middle third of the novel lacks any real narrative structure or tension.

Not only did James Morrow have things he wanted passionately to say about nuclear destiny, they were interesting and complex things, well worth saying. And in the unadmitted, he had a puissant piece of science fictional surrealism with which to concretize them into emotionally powerfully imagery.

But along about the middle of the book he got a little too passionately interested in the message and not enough in the craft of storytelling. When a political science fiction novel fails, it is usually into didacticism and even attention to a simple plot skeleton form of tensions and releases may be enough to keep the narrative focused on the story.

Notice that it is *not* the surrealistic imagery that fails even when the humor falls flat but the pace and timing and narrative tension.

No doubt there are those who would contend that science fiction and surrealism cannot cohabit, that imagistic logic and extrapolative rigor are antithetical, that surrealism is by definition fantasy.

What then would they make of Lisa Goldstein's *The Dream Years*, a science fiction novel *about* surrealism, the historical Parisian surrealist movement, and what surrealism itself means in terms of the human spirit? It draws the equation between the surrealist esthetic and the Paris uprising of May 1968, and finally generalizes its terms to equate surrealism with the revolutionary impulse and the revolutionary impulse with freedom of the spirit itself.

Goldstein does this by taking surrealists and May revolutionaries together into the future as comrades to man the barricades with yet a third band of revolutionaries fighting a far worse tyranny than either of them have yet faced.

And they succeed not by the bomb and the Kalashnikov, but by the weapon of the spirit, by unleashing the chaos of surrealist imagery into the landscape of anal-retentive order, thereby fracturing its fragile reality, and letting the sun shine in.

Is this surrealism?

For sure!

Is it science fiction?

How many fans can dance on the tip of a propeller-beanie?

Whether you choose to consider *The Dream Years* formal science fiction or not, it certainly partakes of the central esthetic thereof, yet demonstrates its unity with surrealism on the level where form follows function as well.

Dali, the quintessential surrealist, painted his dreamscape images with the realistic draftsmanship of Bonestell space art, and then some, just as the literary techniques of science fiction suspend the modern reader's disbelief in the unreal by providing convincing extrapolative detail and psychological realism.

Both surrealism and science fiction do this in order to erase the sharp border between psyche and external environment, verisimilitude and imagination, mythic imagery and the realm of the possible, and create a fictional universe in which they all interact on the same reality level. Both demonstrate how the signifying image and what is being signified can be one and the same.

Both therefore create visions that are not so much supernatural fantasies or stylized abstractions as the illusion of alternate valid realities, rendered with the verisimilitude of photographic realism, but organized along arbitrary but internally consistent world-view parameters designed to illuminate some aspect of our inner reality.

Okay, so this is admittedly the edge of the envelope of what may legitimately be called science fiction; beyond science fictional surrealism or surrealistic science fiction, we are in the realm of Latin American magic realism, where reality can mutate sentence by sentence, image by image, along *no* consistent parameters save the poetic exigencies of the moment.

What gives magic realism its "realism" — if anything does — is that all its imagistic transformations are deeply rooted in and manifestations of a deep and rich historical and cultural matrix embedded in the mind and memory of the native reader. Indeed, many magic realists consider themselves the renovators, even in a way the *inventors* of Latin American culture.

But strangely enough, when you come across a piece of *North* American magic realism like Steve Erikson's *Rubicon Beach*, you're back to something that works the border zone where science fiction and surrealism mingle.

Rubicon Beach is magic realism indeed, in that events and scenes follow poetic and imagistic rather than causal logic, many magical transformations occur, structure is emphatically non-linear, and even the resolution is almost entirely imagistic, gibberish in conventional plot terms.

But the psychic and cultural landscape is not that of Latin America but of the United States, indeed of America One and America Two, the historical American Dream, and its future decline into entropy, to put it far less complexly than Erikson does.

Past and present, America One and America Two, narrative realism and skeins of surreal tranformation intermingle quite freely here; scientific rationales for all that happens are nowhere to be found, but somehow, because this is *American* magic realism, it has the feel of science fiction, not fantasy.

This is a kind of Ballardian America, with its drowned Los Angeles, its endless railroad journeys, its Hollywood hotels, its actors and screenwriters, its Yggdrasil in the western desert: America as a metaphor, somehow, of America itself. Or America One and America Two as metaphors for each other.

But Erikson, unlike Ballard, is an American, and therefore, unlike Ballard's America, which is essentially the metaphorical America of a European sensibility, *his* surreal American landscape is that of a *product* of that inner America, not an outside observer.

Just as it is difficult to imagine a North American writing Latin American magic realism, so is it hard to imagine anyone but an American writing this sort of *American* magic realism, and for the same reason. Magic realism almost has to be written from the inside out, for the organizing principle is neither causal logic nor the generalized Jungian unconscious mythic structure, but the cultural consciousness out of which it arises.

That most Latin American magic realism is concerned with past history and has the feel of fantasy says as much about the nature of Latin American consciousness as it does about literary style or form. That most American magic realism—like *Rubicon Beach*, like Thomas Pynchon's *V* and *The Crying of Lot 49*, like most of William Burroughs, like a good deal of Bradbury—feels like science fiction says a lot about an American consciousness that somehow draws its cultural roots, its weltanschauung, its characteristic guilts, fears, hopes, longings, and inner imagery not from contemplation of the complexities of its past but from visions of its future.

And that is what ultimately connects the inner heart of this kind of American magic realism with science fiction, no matter the superficial divergences; that may also be why about 20 percent of the fiction published in this country is science fiction; and that may be why so many writers who do not write sci-fi, or wish to, find themselves nevertheless writing *science fiction* whether they are willing to admit it or not whether they even know it or not.

If there's one thing the genre insiders share with the outsiders, with those who write science fiction everywhere, and with some deep cultural tropism of the America psyche, it is a future-oriented world view.

We all know that in our bones. We know that science fiction is inextricably bound up with multiple vision of the future. Even when science fiction is set in the past, the past is seen either as something that may be mutated to affect the present (its own future), or as something that may exfoliate multiple futures, and almost never for its own sake as historical record.This is so obvious that it forms the lowest-common-denominator definition of science fiction in the public perception. Historical fiction is about the past, contemporary fiction is about the present, science fiction is about the future.

This, like most cliches, is a gross oversimplification, but like most cliches, it also contains an inner truth. Science fiction may be set in the present or the historical past, but it cannot be science fiction without accepting the mutability of history and world-lines, without relating the past or present milieu of the setting to the extrapolative principle.

And that, ultimately, is why so many writers of diverse styles, focuses, levels of literary ambition, and attitudes towards science fiction nevertheless end up writing it.

For if the statement that science fiction is the literature of the future is an oversimplification, its converse would appear to be an absolute. Literature informed by future-oriented vision *is* science fiction.

In the last quarter of the twentieth century, how can the author of fiction peer along the timelines at all without writing it?

Alternate Media:
Visual Translations

Science fiction, of course, is not only a literary mode but a sphere of discourse, not only a prose medium but a potential content for any medium. And, of course, in the real world of Hollywood and beyond, SF films have become very important indeed at the box office, for a time even dominant.

Science fiction has also had a long, if not quite so obvious, relationship with the graphic narrative, aka the comic book, aka the graphic novel, and indeed, as we shall see, the evolution of the modern graphic novel is a bit of a science fiction story itself.

My involvement with the graphic novel form has been at best tangential—I tried my hand at creating a comic once, was asked to write "Howard the Duck," and know some of the practitioners of the art—so "The Graphic Novel" is a piece of straightforward objective analysis.

"Books into Movies" is something else again. My novel *Bug Jack Barron* has been under more or less continuous film option since 1970; I have written a screen adaptation myself, so has Harlan Ellison, so has Adam Rodman. Other properties of mine have been or are under option—*Riding the Torch, Little Heroes, The Mind Game*—and at present writing I am even engaged in trying to help produce a film version of another, "La Vie Continue," myself.

So when it comes to adapting science fiction to film, I have some emotional involvement. I have been through this process unsuccessfully any number of times, which, as such things go, is par for the course. Sooner or later a film may even come out the other end. But it is foolish indeed to hold one's breath in expectation.

The Graphic Novel

In the current rapid artistic evolution of the "graphic novel" out of the "comic book," as epitomized by such diverse works as *Watchmen, Maus, Greenberg the Vampire*, and even a key transitional work like *The Dark Knight Returns*, we may be presently witnessing not merely a new publishing phenomenon but the birth of a genuine new art form, something that has occurred but rarely in the long sweep of human history.

I'm not talking about a new formal conceptualization within an existing artistic medium, such as Cubism or the symphony or the novel, nor am I talking about a new style, such as blank verse or modern dance or rock and roll, nor am I talking about new content, such as the rock opera or the underground comic or science fiction itself.

I'm talking about a whole new medium of expression, such as painting, theater, prose fiction, opera, film, or television — a new way of communicating human artistic impulses.

The further back in human history we go, the more basic and drastic such invention seems. Beating two rocks together to produce the first instrumental music. Shaping a glob of clay into a form mimicking a man or an animal. Smearing colored pigments on a cave wall to produce the first painting. The written word.

Now it would admittedly be a bit much to suggest that the development of the graphic novel in our own time is an artistic invention of this order of magnitude, but as human culture evolved and recomplicated, the nature of the evolution of new art forms changed, became more a matter of synergy and convergence than of drastic new invention.

The oral bardic storytelling tradition merged with the written word, and prose fiction and theater eventually evolved. Orchestral music merged with dance to create the ballet. Dance, song, instrumental music, theater, painting, and much more came together to create the opera.

In fact, opera is probably the best paradigm for how such synergetic art forms evolved, for in its day, grand opera was the ultimate human art form, combining as it did most of the others.

Grand opera, after all, first involves a story, which must be written down in prose. Then a libretto must be written and a score created. Dance numbers are choreographed. Sets are constructed and painted and costumes sewn together. Finally, all of this is put together inside a theater with an orchestra and actors who are also singers, and the baton comes down, and the curtain goes up, and voila, an incredibly complex art form that fuses theater with music and dance and elaborate costume and set design and even special effects, surely the crown of pre-twentieth-century artistic creation.

After that, technology begins to dominate the evolution of human art forms.

Photography is invented, and for the first time frozen moments from the real world can be permanently recorded as perfectly mimetic images. It was a brand-new art form in itself, but one that was also to drastically alter the nature of painting and sculpture away from their technologically obsoleted drive towards better and better mimesis and toward non-representational conceptualization.

The phonograph is invented and later the tape recording, eventually leading to just as drastic an evolution in the nature of music. Prior to the invention of sound recording, editing, and processing, all our musical experience was that of the live performance, with all its mistakes, flaws, spontaneity, and human limits.

Now, of course, most of the music we hear is edited, multitracked, processed, and perfected through mixing boards into something quite different from that produced by an ensemble of live performers coming together before a live audience at a given locus in space and time. Modern music is an edited and editable art form—or series of art forms—that transcends the natural capabilities of the human voice and the ranges of acoustical instruments as well as the spatial and temporal limits of live performance. So too has it been centralized from an isolated performance to be attended into an omnipresent background to our daily lives.

And then technology animates the photograph to produce the motion picture. And gives it a sound track. And full color. At which point, film supplants opera as the ultimate synergetic artform, a position from which the later invention of television has still not quite managed to displace it.

What does all this have to do with the graphic novel?

Quite a bit. For the graphic novel is precisely a new synergetic art form in the sense of opera or musical recording or the motion picture. It has at least the potential to do for the fictional narrative in book form what opera did for theatrical performance, and sound mixing and processing did for music, and the motion picture did for drama. And there are signs that it is beginning to live up to that transformational potential.

In a certain sense, there is nothing new in the graphic novel at all: the elements that have come together to create this new art form have had long separate preexistence. Painting has roots deep in prehistory and so does storytelling, and indeed both predate the written word and printing.

Indeed, it could be argued that the written word itself evolved out of something not that far removed from the graphic narrative. Look at Egyptian hieroglyphs (and the Mayan equivalent too) from a certain skewed perspective, and they can be viewed as something akin to comic books.

Hieroglyphs (particularly in earlier periods) are pictographs representing words that are recognizable stylizations of the things they represent, and they are laid out in sequential panels to carry a narrative. Later they were further stylized into a partially phonetic alphabet that broke into more recognizable pictographs for emphasis or clarity. They were even integrated with splash-panels.

Who knows how narrative writing might have evolved if the Phoenicians had not developed a purely phonetic alphabet divorced from pictographic representation of words and passed it on to the Greeks and thence to us? Or if the Egyptians had separated out their phonetic syllabary from their pictographs and started writing novels in a syntax incorporating both.

In our alternate world, however, prose and pictorial representation diverged early on, and didn't recombine into a synergetic art form until the emergence of the comic strip.

Now Egyptian hieroglyphics evolved to express the very theocratic basis of their culture, and the Mayan Codex was not exactly pop culture either, but when the graphic narrative reemerged as a consequence of cheap mass printing, it was as comic relief in throwaway daily newspapers and pulpy trash our mothers all threw away in horror, to the enrichment of future generations of comic-book dealers.

Low comedy and talking animals. Superheroes in fancy spandex long johns. Green slime and red gore. Teen-age romance and shoot-'em-up adventures. Not exactly stuff to stand beside the tomb of Tutankhamen as a peak artistic expression of its culture.

Let's face it, the graphic narrative reemerged as a vehicle for schlock, as a commercial entertainment designed to appeal to a lowest-common-denominator audience. We know what we mean when we say some boob has a "comic-book mentality," and "cartoony" is a synonym for oversimplified rendering of reality.

The function to which the graphic narrative was put long obscured the inherent potential of the form. But in retrospect, we can see that that potential was always there, waiting for more serious content to stretch it into a serious art form.

In the 1950s, that thematic deepening began to occur in the most unlikely of venues—the E.C. Comics that so horrified the adult world that Congressional hearings were held to condemn them and the Comics Code was promulgated to suppress them. The Vault Keeper, the Crypt-keeper, and their whole gang of slime-dripping ghouls and fiends were admittedly not exactly literary drawing-room company, but the horror comics at least had a moral stance and were beginning to express a cultural viewpoint.

Sure, it was all severed heads and spurting gore and horrible monsters and rotting corpses and exploding intestines, but the world of E.C. was a moral one of some complexity, if little subtlety. Villainy was punished with sadistic glee, and sympathetic characters were seldom fed to the toilet monster, but villains and heroes were not necessarily defined by the standards of Eisenhower-era adulthood. And cultural style had a lot to do with it. The shock-and-barf esthetic was that of a generation of near-pubescents who would soon enough be outraging their parents even further to the dirty beat of Elvis.

E.C. comics expressed the subculture of adolescent weirdos who delighted in horrifying adult society but who had cultural standards of their own; that was precisely why adult society eventually suppressed them. But it was too late. The genie was out of the bottle.

The E.C. horror comics, like the science fiction of the 1950s, were a commercial genre in the process of evolving into a self-conscious art form along with the generation of maturing adolescents whom they were both primarily addressing. And there were many cross-overs. E.C. did "Weird Science" and "Weird Fantasy," comics devoted to unabashed science fiction of some subtlety and sophistication, up to and including graphic narrative translations of stories by SF writers of the caliber of Ray Bradbury. Even the horror comics had a certain SF feel to them, a certain speculative logically incorporated into their storylines, and a certain hard-science realism when it came to the pictorial portrayal of the guts and gore.

The audiences overlapped heavily too. Many E.C. fans read science fiction, many SF fans read the E.C. comics, and many latter-day science fiction writers, comics writers, and artists grew up as demented kids on both.

Science fiction continued to mature with its audience, but after the Comics Code reduced the graphic narrative to that which parents found harmless to their all-too-impressionable children, comics went in the direction of Superman and Captain Marvel and Batman and eventually the mind-boggling armies of costumed superheroes churned out by DC and Marvel.

Well, not entirely.

While the E.C. generation of science fiction writers was helping to create the New Wave in the 1960s, the E.C. generation of artist-writers was helping to create the Underground Comics.

The Underground Comics were to the commercial stuff produced under the constraints of the Comics Code what underground newspapers like the *Los Angeles Free Press* were to the *New York Times* and the *Christian Science Monitor*.

They were guerrilla art, published and distributed by guerrilla companies, openly defiant of every public convention they could manage to violate, and drawing their creative energy precisely from the freedom of their self-proclaimed outlawry.

Interestingly enough, while the overground comics were almost always produced by teams of writers, artists, inkers, and letterers, the Underground Comics were usually the product of lone creators, like R. Crumb, S. Clay Wilson, and Art Spiegelman, who wrote and drew and even colored and lettered all their own stuff.

Questions of content and quality aside, it is certainly fair to say that the overground comics expressed corporate formats carried out by a collectivity in the manner of network television, whereas the Undergrounds were vehicles of personal expression for graphic narrative auteurs.

Then the wheel turned again. The Underground Press faded away as the Counterculture became history and the Underground Comics dwindled away into remnants and the corporate product of DC and Marvel prevailed. The graphic novel auteurs had few viable markets for their outré personal visions.

In the United States, that is.

In France, the auteur brand of graphic narrative flourished and moved out into new media. The magazine *Metal Hurlant* published graphic narratives alongside prose in a slick format aimed more or less at adults and with an artistic freedom reminiscent of that of the American Undergrounds. And unlike us, the French had a good name for it. "Bande desinée," they called it, literally meaning "designed band," a label referring strictly to the graphic narrative *form*, not the content, as we do in English with the term "comic book."

What's in a name? In some cases, plenty. French bande desinée is under no definitional imperative to be funny, nor to be published in any particular commercial format.

Take, for instance, a prime example of the bande desinée at the top of its form, Philippe Druillet's *Salambo* trilogy. This is Druillet's utterly transformed version of the novel by Gustave Flaubert, and it was published in full color on high-quality slick paper as coffeetable–sized hardcover books, inarguably a full-blown graphic novel in every sense of the term. And indeed the full-color hardcover "album" is a more dominant publishing mode for the graphic narrative in France than the cheap throwaway comic book, contributing perhaps in large part to the perception in French cultural circles that the bande desinée is a legitimate and serious art form.

Druillet was one of the founders of *Metal Hurlant,* certainly one of the two or three most influential figures in the development of the bande desinée, and this work is typical of Druillet at the height of his powers.

There is certainly nothing "comic" about this violent tale of conflict and revolution, not a single laugh in the whole thing. The storyline, such as it is, moves like a Ballard condensed novel or something by William Burroughs. It is very violent indeed, full of Grand Guignol battle scenes.

It is also very beautiful.

Druillet is a gallery artist of some renown, and a most painterly "comic artist." He almost entirely eschews the familiar linear comic panel layout, just as he eschews the straightforward linearity of traditional graphic narration. Every page, or in some cases, two-page spread, is laid out and designed like a self-contained diptych or triptych or tetraptych, desinée to the max, but not in relentless bande format. Druillet also turns whole pages into single complex paintings integrated thematically and psychically with the text. Other pages have an architectural design—oddly shaped panels integrated in an overall design with captions and speech balloons and incidental interstitial art.

Druillet's visual style is neither cartoony nor realistic. Many of his panels are as densely and ghoulishly populated as a Bosch painting, as complexly rendered as Dali, as brooding and involuted as Giger, as baroquely furnished as Versaille, and for want of a better term, as realistically surreal as science fiction.

Which, in the broadest sense, Druillet's work in fact is.

If the paintings of Chesley Bonestell are the visual cognates of the hard SF school of Clarke and Caiden and Benford, the graphic novels of Philippe Druillet are the visual cognates of the school of Leigh Brackett, Jack Vance, Ray Bradbury—the SF of the baroque.

Nor is he alone in this. For while Druillet is by far the best artist in a painterly sense ever to work in the graphic novel, he is a central influence on the bande destinée, not an outsider sui generis, and most of the French school is science fiction or fantasy of one kind or another.

As is almost all of the material published in the American version of *Metal Hurlant, Heavy Metal*. While *Heavy Metal* leans very heavily on translation from the French, its American contributors all do science fiction and fantasy too.

Indeed, today almost all graphic narrative is SF of one kind or another, with thematic material and storylines that would be right at home in one or another of the SF specialty magazines, from the contents of *Heavy Metal* to Superman and Batman and all the other superheroes to "Teen-age Mutant Ninja Turtles." One could even argue that there is something intrinsic to the graphic narrative form that skews it toward science fiction and fantasy, toward "SF" as it is presently pragmatically defined.

Why should this be so? True, there have been comic genres—chiefly the romance comics—that have dealt with the mundane here-

and-now. But the graphic narrative, a visual form, virtually requires story and setting scope for flamboyant art with movement and conflict and outré realities. Then too, comic art is a highly stylized and conceptualized form, inherently nonmimetic and inherently action-oriented, for there is little reason for anyone to want to see a lot of realistically rendered talking heads when prose narrative does this so much better.

In more innocent days, when the average comic reader was a prepubescent child, funny animals doing funny things would suffice (though the doings of the ducks in Carl Barks' "Uncle Scrooge" already have a decidedly science fictional flavor), and teenagers would wallow happily in gore and war (though E.C. did a lot of SF), but now that the median age of the comic buyer is twenty something, more sophisticated content is required, and about the only place to go for sophisticated content that may be expressed graphically in visually active style is fantasy and science fiction.

Sure, you could in theory go to the historical period drama, but today's readers are a lot more interested in the future than in the past, and then too, today's sophisticated twenty-year-old comic book reader probably grew up on superheroes.

After the demise of the Underground Comics, the superheroes conquered all, and of course you can't have a superhero without an SF premise. Superman is of course the template—a character with super-powers determined by his alien origin—and almost all the rest are variations on this format.

These superhero comics have, with very few exceptions, been corporate-format product, with endlessly recomplicating back-stories and interpenetrations in order to build audience loyalty, churned out episode by episode by teams of editors,writers, artists, inkers, and letterers. And if this sounds like a graphic narrative version of episodic network television, well, that's just what it is.

And like network TV, only more so, these comics are produced under censorship, to wit, the Comics Code, which limits their content and language to that which censorious adults deem fit for children.

But today's average comic reader is not a child, but a fairly sophisticated young adult with a grounding in prose SF, more often than not, and likely to be familiar with the more artistically adventurous French bande desinée school through *Heavy Metal*. And this applies in spades to the writers and artists working the form.

So by the early 1980s, the ingredients were all there for the emergence of something quite new. Talented writers and artists—refugees from the collapse of the Underground Comics market and toilers in the corporate-comics formats—looking for ways to free up the form and find a fitting audience for more outré and mature work. An older and more affluent audience who had outgrown kid stuff. Business people who saw how to put one and one together and come up with mucho dinero.

Voila, the graphic novel, which has been popping up all over of late. Long, generally self-contained graphic narratives, published in trade paperback format, generally in full color, sold in bookstores in large part, and priced accordingly. Books targeted at the sophisticated adult audience who can afford to buy them. *Books*, not comics, meaning free to operate outside the constraints of the Comics Code.

A marketing strategy that has led straight to a quantum leap in the artistic evolution of the graphic narrative from the comic book to the full-blown graphic novel.

The key transitional work—both artistically and in terms of its unprecedented commercial success as a trade item in the bookstores, that in effect vindicated the whole concept of graphic novel publication for affluent adults—is Frank Miller's transmogrification of Batman in *The Dark Knight Returns*.

Now Batman the superhero has been around for decades; he is probably the best-known superhero with the exception of Superman and enough of a cultural icon to have inspired a truly dreadful but commercially successful TV series. One would have thought that Batman, Robin, the Joker, et al, would long since have become a series of hopelessly stylized cliches.

"Wrong," sez Frank Miller, who wrote and drew *Dark Knight*, and he proves it by applying the sophisticated extrapolative vision of the science fiction novel to the material. Which is to say he dares to take Batman seriously.

Batman was perhaps the most characterologically interesting of the superheroes to begin with. A self-made superhero with no superhuman powers, driven into his crusade against crime by a thirst for vengeance, and willing to cloak himself in the morally ambiguous mantle of a night creature in the pursuit thereof.

Okay, take such a character seriously, and project him forward into his future and ours. Make Bruce Wayne a man on the verge of growing old, with his alter-ego, Batman, long since retired into legend.

Place him in a Gotham City turned into a behavioral-sink urban nightmare, Detroit or New York twenty years on, in an America on the brink of war with the Soviet Union, mutant street-gang monsters turned into media stars drooling blood on television, Mad Max out of urban jungle, and what do you get?

You get an aging Batman grunting his way back into some semblance of shape in order to bring back the legend and clean up Gotham. You get a murderous, savage, bitter old vigilante, kicking evil ass in the name of what's left of civilization, as he sees it, which ain't much.

From one point of view, that of the politicians (who seem to be mostly weak-kneed liberal boobs) and the TV commentators (who seem to be cynical social parasites), you get Batman as a Grand Guignol Bernard Goetz.

But from another point of view—that of the hapless victims of the city, that of Batman himself—you get what the situation calls for, a savage survivalist Batman with the gloves off, a guerrilla fighter for the fearful and downtrodden, a monster, yes, but a *necessary* monster under the circumstances.

It is the genius of what Miller has done with a familiar comic character like Batman that he has imbued the stock figure with such depths and portrayed the degenerate Gotham City with such passion that one can never be quite sure what moral stance Miller himself is taking. If he is taking any moral stance at all, rather than simply placing his characters in his setting and letting them and the readers try to work out their own moral conclusions.

In this respect, *The Dark Knight Returns* is very much a genuine novel, a story of character at least as much as action, and one constructed with depths that reach beyond the page to touch the ruminations of the reader.

As a *graphic* novel, it is drawn and laid out in rather conventional style. Or is it? It may be drawn and colored and laid out like a conventional comic, but there is one peculiarly cinematic quirk. Miller actually shows us very little of his Gotham City. The action is drawn as if through a camera lens in narrow focus. Close-ups. Room interiors. TV screens. Rooftops. Dark alleys. Grottoes. Garbage dumps. It would seem almost as if Miller is trying to restrict himself to a montage of fragmented tight shots, eschewing the orienting establishment shots in order to graphically portray the fragmented, isolated, paranoically narrow realities that make up his extrapolated urban environment. Or has he really succeeded in getting graphic style to mirror his Batman's own world view?

Greenberg the Vampire, written by J.M. DeMatteis and painted by Mark Badger, is in some ways an even more extreme example of the comic book mutated into the true graphic novel through the instrumentality of SF, and certainly a textbook illustration of the extent to which the contemporary graphic novel seems to require some SF or fantasy content to secure commercial viability in book form and price.

Okay, so Oscar Greenberg is a vampire, and he meets up with the demoness Lilith, who has to be exorcised in a big climactic action scene, but all this is in a sense rather pro forma, for *Greenberg the Vampire* could have worked quite well without it, at least on a story level.

Oscar Greenberg is a writer. His big problem is that he's blocked; beside which being a vampire is at worst a minor annoyance, for in this contemporary urban ambiance, vampires of taste don't bite necks, they drink animal blood at vampire cocktail parties. His long-time girlfriend is the lady who made him a vampire, but that hasn't seriously damaged their relationship; even Oscar's mother thinks she's just fine for him.

Oscar is a reasonably well-adjusted vampire until he gets writer's block and signs to do the screenplay from one of his own books, and gets involved with the aforementioned demoness in her incarnation as a starlet and. . . .

You get the general idea. *Greenberg the Vampire* is really the story of a blocked writer's brush with Hollywood, and the pressures it puts on his relationships with his family, his mother, and his lover. It could have been called *Greenberg the Writer* and been the story of Oscar's maturation as a writer and a man without Lilith or the vampirism.

Fat chance it would have been publishable that way.

Badger does as good a job as anyone could of making long conversations in interior settings visually interesting. The dialog is sophisticated and witty enough to stand up in the pages of a conventional novel, and DeMatteis lets Oscar narrate the captions himself in stream of consciousness and even gives us whole pages of his unadorned prose.

Some day, all this may be enough to carry a commercially viable graphic novel, but right now such a work would probably die on the racks. Or at any rate, no one would seem to be willing to publish a graphic novel that would appeal only to an elite audience of literati. Indeed, even in the world of conventional novel publishing, a story about a writer and his career problems is generally regarded as the commercial kiss of death.

So the vampire schtick allowed DeMatteis to get away with something he would have had a hard time publishing as a conventional novel, let alone as a "comic."

The question is whether the vampire schtick was simply a necessary commercial ploy, and the firm wedding of the emerging graphic novel to science fiction and fantasy an affair of shotgun economics, or whether that schtick adds something essential to the work and SF content is somehow inherent in the formal nature of the graphic novel.

It's not such an easy question to answer. DeMatteis *could* have written *Greenberg* without the supernatural elements and made it work artistically. But then why do it as a *graphic* novel? Or to put it another way around, would the graphic format have done anything to enhance such a story?

Maybe not. Maybe an interior-oriented character novel with stream of consciousness will always be best done in prose. And maybe the graphic novel requires something to give it scope for movement and visual invention—action, exotic setting, surreal characters, visually arresting images. One can get this from ultraviolence, historic settings, fantasy, science fiction, and not from too many other places.

And maybe one thing more. Maybe the formal potential of the graphic novel as an art form is its unique ability to give us visual images of our interior landscape that exist on two simultaneous levels—as exterior realities in themselves and as symbols for inner reality.

Which is also at the heart of fantasy and science fiction, of "SF," for if there is any esthetic congruency between these two philosophically divergent schools of literature to justify their commercially pragmatic genrefication under the SF logo, this synthesis of mimesis and symbolism that they share is surely it, a synthesis inherent in the *form* of the graphic novel, which skews its *content* inexorably towards SF.

Indeed, by making Greenberg a vampire and his temptress a demoness, and the death of his mother an act of self-sacrificing exorcism, DeMatteis concretizes the internal struggles in imagery that give Badger something more interesting to work with in the bargain.

Sometimes commercial constrictions coincide with the formal imperatives of an art form, particularly an art form that, after all, is in it childhood. There must be a *reason* to do a novel in graphic form rather than prose, and in the case of something like *Greenberg*, that reason must be more than an appeal to supposedly semiliterate comic book readers, since the work certainly requires literary sophistication to be fully enjoyed.

Perhaps that reason also has something to do with *distancing*. For what the graphic novel cannot avoid doing, unlike the prose novel, is transforming everything into scene and concrete image. The experience of reading a prose novel can often be that of inhabiting the bodies and minds of the viewpoint characters, but the experience of reading a graphic novel can perforce only be like that of watching a film, something experienced from an outside viewpoint.

This may be a limitation of the graphic novel as an art form, but it can also be a strength. Film exists as a series of scenes taking place in front of your face too, but they are mimetic images; if the film is good enough, you can imagine that you are really at the scene.

But the graphic novel is a highly stylized art form. Even the most "realistic" drawings and careful coloring and shadowing do not pretend to photographic realism. And the pictures don't move. What we see is a series of still shots; any illusion of motion is created by the layout, and by artistic conventions like speed-streaking that we have been conditioned to accept. And the pace of the story is the pace at which we read it. When we read a graphic novel, we accept speech balloons and captions and thought balloons, and we understand the stylizations that make the difference.

The graphic novel is a heavily stylized form of necessity, but while in certain respects that may be a limitation of the medium, it does permit us to accept stylizations of reality that in some cases can allow us the distance necessary to view emotionally charged material with an engaged heart but a detached eye, which sometimes gives us a truer vision that a literal mirror of reality.

Take what Art Spiegelman has done with talking animals in *Maus*.

Maus is nothing less than the story of the destruction of European Jewry during the Holocaust, or rather the volume that has so far been published is the first installment of this dark epic, ending in one of the most ghastly cliff-hangers of all time at the gate to Auschwitz.

Maus may be nothing *less* than the story of the Holocaust, but it is something *more* as well. The story is narrated from two viewpoints, one inside the other. In the present day, we have an artist son extracting the tale of the past from his survivor father, with whom he has a very complex and ambiguous relationship that is quite fully rendered. In the past, we have the viewpoint of the father, Vladek, narrating the events to his son, Artie. So what we have is the immediate story of the young Vladek's travails in Nazi Europe, framed by the story of his older self's relationship with his son, a portrait of him as both an acting survivalist and an old survivor in America. Vladek the active survivalist is a sympathetic character, but old Vladek the survivor, from the point of view of his son, is something of a whinning, crotchety bastard.

And that isn't all, by a long shot. The fathers' full name is Vladek *Spiegelman* and the son's full name is Art Spiegelman—the writer and artist of *Maus* is telling the story of his father and himself, with all the problems and moral ambiguities, even with a certain ruthlessness of insight.

Imagine for a moment that Spiegelman had written this as a conventional prose novel. Difficult, isn't it? One cringes at the thought of reading such an emotionally charged true story of father and son from the point of view of the son, who is frequently openly contemptuous of the doings of a father who is a Holocaust survivor. Imagine how difficult it would have been for Art Spiegelman to attain the artistic detachment, not only from his father, but from himself, to write such a prose novel.

But the graphic novel form makes it all possible. In *Maus*, the Nazis are cats, the Poles are pigs, and the Jews, including Vladek and *Art Spiegelman* himself, are all mice!

The book is done entirely in black-and-white line drawings in a layout and style more reminiscent of a newspaper comic strip than a comic book. This subtly associates Vladek's story of the Holocaust with newspaper coverage of the historical events and gives Artie's present-day frame story the feel of a soap newspaper strip like the old *Mary Worth*.

The story is told in cold, chilling detail; the Jews of Poland are not simply presented as innocent victims, but are honestly shown as flawed humans doing what they think they must to survive. Artie and Vladek have a tempestuous present-day relationship; at times, the son even expresses hate for his father. The dialog is as complex, subtle, and realistic as anything in a novel.

But the characters we see are all pigs and cats and mice.

It's hard to imagine a better example than this of the power of the graphic novel to give the reader—and in this peculiar instance the writer and artist as well—insight into thematic material through distancing. It's even harder to imagine Spiegelman being able to face creating such a thing without this device. It's hard to imagine *Maus* in any other form, for what Spiegelman has done here is possible *only* in the graphic novel.

And what he has done points to the heart of the synergy between SF content and the graphic novel form, even though there is no science fiction or fantasy in *Maus* at all.

Well, not exactly. Talking animals, after all, are not exactly mimesis of contemporary reality. They are a well-established graphic narrative convention that serves the same purpose through *form* as science fiction or fantasy would have through *content* in this context while being neither—a distancing device that enables the writer-artist to render inner symbolism concretely and visually and give his graphic narrative a personal style beyond the slavish visual mimesis of photographic realism.

Neither science fiction nor quite fantasy perhaps, but also partaking of the psychoesthetic angle of attack of "SF."

For by distancing his gut-wrenching story into the convention of the talking-animal strip, Spiegelman enables the reader to deal with it emotionally with some kind of balance. We're used to *laughing* at talking animals; we certainly don't laugh at these, but we do have a breathing space between ourselves and their anguish. Even as science fiction and fantasy, via the convention of altered reality, allow us a truer mirror of our own through the distancing effect of concretized symbolism.

Maus demonstrates what a mature creative sensibility can make of the graphic novel; to anyone who demands the proof of a masterpiece before they are willing to grant the graphic novel the status of a serious art form, here is one.

And *Watchmen*, written by Alan Moore and drawn by Dave Gibbons, is surely another, albeit of an entirely different kind. Whereas Spiegelman comes out of the Undergrounds, Moore and Gibbons come out of the world of commercial comic publishing, and the art and layout of *Watchmen* stick pretty much to the superhero visual style and format, so that *Watchmen*, unlike *Maus*, is quite conventional, formally speaking.

Except for one thing, which we have seen before in *Greenberg the Vampire*—Moore integrates pages of straight prose into the narrative. Well, not exactly *straight* prose. What Moore gives us is a kind of media montage—newspaper stories, magazine interviews, excerpts from books, etc., laid out as they would appear in their actual forms of publication, complete with drawings that we accept as stylizations of the accompanying photographs.

This prose montage illuminates the inner lives of characters, in some cases carries the story forward, gives back-story, and establishes the alternate world not only in historical details of its divergences from our own but in the details of its divergent popular culture, down to alternate histories of the Counterculture, rock music, and yes, comic books.

In Alan Moore's alternate America, costumed superheroes of a kind were a reality in pre–WW II America, rather gay-hearted innocent vigilantes who masked themselves and dressed up in costumes to fight crime. As a consequence, superhero comics never made it (even Superman was a flop); a dark kind of pirate comic took their place, of which we are given an intercut example, a pirate-reality symbolic displacement of the inner lives of the characters in the main story of *Watchmen*.

You can see the influence of Frank Miller's *Dark Knight* here. Moore takes the costumed-crime-fighter convention seriously and views it through a science fictional eye. His first-generation costumed heroes hang out together, have affairs with each other, even have children together. Second-generation costumed heroes inherit the personas of retirees. It's all almost like some kind of fandom, except that the masquerade takes place in the streets, and crime-fighting superhero fandom battles real criminals.

But in 1960, an experiment goes wrong, or perhaps too right, and Dr. Jonathan Osterman is given a blast of radiation that turns him into a *real* superhero, or more precisely, gives him extraordinary powers. He can control his atomic structure as well as the structure of other matter. Change his size. Walk through walls. Teleport. Direct energy. Control or dismantle machinery and weapons by act of will. Devastate whole continents, perhaps destroy the world. Or save it.

The government turns him into a superhero. They design him a fancy costume (which he later discards in favor of going bright blue nude), name him "Dr. Manhattan" to cash in on the vibes of the Manhattan Project and the atom bomb, and launch him with a big TV campaign, seeing him as the ultimate weapon against the Russians in the Cold War.

What raises *Watchmen* to the state of novelistic art is that Moore takes this character *seriously*, views Dr. Manhattan through a true science fictional eye. He has a sex life; he has a stormy love life; his powers affect his personality, making him more and more alien, distancing him from ordinary humanity, turning him stepwise into a creature whose alienness derives not so much from his superpowers as from their effects over time on an ordinary human psyche.

And there is more, much more. Rorschach, a retired costumed superhero, always demented, comes out of retirement to seek out the murderer of the Comedian, a costumed superhero type who became something of an Oliver North in spandex underwear in the postwar era. The Owl comes reluctantly out of retirement. This, mind you, after the government has passed a law banning costumed superheroes, except for those in its own employ.

In the meantime, the geopolitical situation is deteriorating around Afghanistn. Adrian Veidt, the smartest man in the world, another superhero, who had retired into the marketing of the merchandising tie-ins of his own image, concocts a crazy plan to save humanity from itself by simulating an alien invasion.

Just when he is needed most, Dr. Manhattan finally decides he has had it with humanity and teleports to Mars, from which vantage he plans to sit out the impending cataclysm while contemplating the universe.

There is no real point in trying to detail the plots and subplots further. *Watchman* is a real novel, and a complex one at that.

Formally, it is a lot more complicated than it seems at first. Various viewpoint characters narrate sections. Time moves forward and backward. The pirate comic — drawn in a different style — provides one fugal counterpoint to the main line action, and the media montage provides another.

And there are many, many characters, all quite realistically portrayed. There is the bitter editor of a right-wing yellow rag and his dummkopf flunky. Moore even seems to take a schtick from Dickens or maybe Shakespeare and intercuts street-level commentary from an old newsdealer and the kid who is reading the pirate comic at his newsstand.

Then too, Moore has a political viewpoint (see his British comic *V*), though it never becomes an ax to grind, and what it does is give his extremely detailed cultural and political extrapolation texture and cutting edge.

One example must be given. We see a newspaper headline that says "RR TO RUN IN 1988?" A little later, the right-wing editor's flunky suggests maybe they should run a piece on Robert Redford, who's running for president. "This is still America!" his boss screams. "Who wants a *cowboy actor* in the White House?"

Watchmen is full of little bits like this that integrate historical speculation with popular culture and that make perfect use of the graphic narrative form to do it. It is a full-sized novel, a complex one, a sophisticated one, and Moore and Gibbons bring it all together in a manner which makes *Watchmen* to the graphic novel what *Don Quixote* was to the prose novel—the first full-scale demonstration of the mature potentials of a new art form in its adolescence.

It will be interesting indeed to see what it becomes when it grows up.

Books into Movies

A new stage in the evolution of the relationship between the literature and the cinema of SF would now seem to be under way.

With the release of *Blade Runner, Dune, Altered States, Enemy Mine*, and *2010*; with *The Stars My Destination, Bug Jack Barron*, and who knows what else in various nebulous stages of production for theatrical release; with at least two TV anthology series, *Amazing Stories* and the revived *Twilight Zone*, having broken the ice, with SF film making having consolidated its position of dominance at the box office and with TV trying to play catch-up, it would seem that too many people have seen too many SF films and gotten too sophisticated, and too much new product is needed for the film and TV people to rely on their own questionable genius anymore.

So they're doing what every other major-league commercial film genre has long been doing, they're looking for literary properties to adapt.

One would think that such a course of action would have been self-evident to any form of life of sufficient sapience to chew gum and sign checks at the same time. One would be wrong.

For while as early an SF film as Melies' silent turn-of-the-century *Voyage to the Moon* may have been science fiction, as was Fritz Lang's later silent masterpiece *Metropolis*, the American so-called "science fiction film' emerged as a B-movie commercial staple from the Cretaceous swamps of the 1950s as a giant reptile slinking towards Tokyo and Hollywood to be born and didn't even evolve into primate form until *Planet of the Apes*; only in the past few years has the creature learned how to read.

As to *how well* it has learned to read, that we will get to later.

Suffice it to say that in this stage of the relationship between the literature of SF and sci-fi movies, the two genres were quite separate; indeed about the only thing that they did have in common was that the monster movies of the 1950s happened to be marketed as "sci-fi" (a term coined by Forrest J. Ackerman, long-time editor of *Famous Monsters of Filmland*), which unfortunately tended to equate "sci-fi" novels with those self-same slimy reptilians in the perception of the public at large.

Even the dominant imagery had little in common. SF novels of the 1950s tended much more to spaceships and nuclear holocaust than to giant ants and killer carrots. Most of the exceptions only proved the point.

How many people who watched James Arness do his killer-ape act as the vegetable monster from outer space in *The Thing* knew that in the original, John W. Campbell's *Who Goes There?*, the alien thawed from the ice was of sufficient puissance and malign intelligence to perfectly mimic any life-form, including the human characters?

When "sci-fi movies" *did* involve spaceships and other planets, they tended to be travelogue primers like *Destination Moon* and *The Conquest of Space* or monster movies transferred to an unearthly venue.

Of course there were the occasional honorable exceptions like *The War of the Worlds, Forbidden Planet, The Day the Earth Stood Still, When Worlds Collide, This Island Earth, The Circus of Dr. Lao, The Power*, but more of these than not were the creations, one way or another, of a lone individual, George Pal, who kept the notion that a science fiction film might *really* be science fiction alive during the long dark night.

But generally speaking, before the advent of *Fahrenheit 451, 2001, Star Trek*, and *Star Wars*, sci-fi movies did not use the literature as source material, and greatly harmed the general public acceptance of the literature by equating it in the eyes of the uninitiated reader with giant apes, crazed reptilians, flying saucers, and Creatures from the Green Latrine.

With press agents like these, who needed enemies?

About the middle of the 1960s, this situation began to mutate drastically for the better. Truffaut's *Fahrenheit 451* might not have been exactly his masterpiece nor a box-office success, but it *was* an adaptation of a major work of science fiction literature by a director with front-line international cachet. And Kubrick's *2001* was not only a collaboration of sorts with Arthur C. Clarke, it *was* generally greeted as *Kubrick's* masterpiece and showed a profit on a budget, gargantuan for the time, of $11 million. And most important of all, *Star Trek* had three seasons in prime time and then became the world champion of syndication.

Far too little attention has been paid to Star Trek as the pivotal work in the growth of SF cinema into a dominant force, and the concurrent growth of SF publishing into what it is today. Without *Star Trek*, *Star Wars* would never have been a viable project, let alone the unprecedented box office bonanza that launched a thousand kit-bashed spaceships. And without the emergence of a dominant SF film genre spawned by *Star Wars*, there probably wouldn't be half so many SF novels on the best-seller list.

The creation of the *Star Trek* concept (as opposed to the wildly uneven quality and level of intent of the episodes) was a cunning and audacious stroke of genius that changed the relation of SF to popular culture forever.

By setting his series aboard a wandering starship whose sets could be endlessly reused, Gene Roddenberry was able to keep his budgets within the realm of TV practicality and still do an SF anthology series, wherein the mandatory running characters could each week confront a new story and setting that was entirely self-contained.

While *Star Trek* limped along for three years in the Nielsens before expiring, *over twenty million people* watched the Starship *Enterprise* on its five-year mission to explore the galaxy every week, and a whole generation grew up on the endless reruns. More people saw *Star Trek* every day than read a work of literary SF in five years.

Star Trek imprinted the imagery of science fiction on mass public consciousness, where it had never been before, opening, thereby, the languages and concerns of science fiction to a mass audience for the very first time. And *Star Trek*, whatever the show's artistic shortcomings, at least imprinted the imagery and schtick of *real* science fiction onto popular culture, so that years and a generation of Trekkies later, George Lucas could confidently begin *Star Wars* with a full-bore space chase and take the largest film audiences in history with him from the opening shot.

And so stage two began, in which SF film making boomed to dominance and SF literature broke the bonds of its little pocket universe to conquer the best-seller list.

It's science fiction time now. A general audience will now accept any science fictional premise. Two whole generations of viewers and readers have grown up on *Star Trek* and one on *Star Wars* and the new SF cinema.

Sure, most of it has been pretty primitive stuff by the critical standards within science fiction's literary realm. After all, most of it has been aimed squarely at an adolescent audience, the audience that demographically dominates the box office, kids who were weaned on Mr. Spock and underwent puberty rites with Luke Skywalker.

So rather than look to the literature for source material, second-stage SF films have tended to be inspired by *Star Trek, Star Wars*, Superman Comics, arcade games, and the rest of the simple SF imagery that has long since become the lingua franca of American adolescence.

The thing of it is that until rather recently, big-time cinematic SF has been a relentlessly commercial genre demographically targeted at this huge adolescent audience and supplied, for the most part, with simple good-versus-evil action-adventure plotting designed to show off special effects, and no adult artistic intent at whose fulfillment to succeed or fail.

Second-stage cinematic SF was at the same artistic stage as the early SF pulps, turned out by professionals from other commercial genres for an adolescent audience, the big difference being that *this* adolescent audience was a *mass* adolescent audience.

For this, you do not need to adapt science fiction novels, indeed just about the only way you *can* adapt them is by reducing them to your perception of the demographic target, a la the execrable film version of *Damnation Alley*, where Hell Tanner was given a bath and a shave and stripped of his Hell's Angels colors.

But as the *Star Trek* and *Star Wars* generation matures, a good many of however many of these kids start reading for pleasure at all naturally turn to reading science fiction, and by now there is a generation of American *adults* who grew up on SF, as witness the fact that we now have *hardcover* SF best-sellers, and at $18.95 a pop, not too many of these are being bought by kids with their lunch money.

By now the mass audience for SF, both literary and cinematic, spans all ages and levels of sophistication, and even adolescents are more blasé about primitive SF than they once were, so that the current stage of the relationship between cinematic literary SF has been attained, wherein the film and TV makers are now looking at adult science fiction novels and stories to adapt for films aimed at adult audiences.

Such adaptations are not without precedent; George Pal adapted such novels as *The War of the Worlds* and *When Worlds Collide*, Truffaut adapted *Fahrenheit 451*, and there were others, but for a variety of dialectical reasons, Stanley Kubrick's *2001* is the most important ancestor of the *artistically ambitions* SF film.

For one thing, Kubrick was at the time unquestionably a world-class director on a roll after *Dr. Strangelove*, he used his clout unmercifully when it came to budget, and he quite consciously set out to "make a science fiction film this time," not realizing he had already done so the last time out.

At the time, I happened to work in the literary agency that put together the deal, and the inside story is quite instructive. All Kubrick knew was that he wanted to make a science fiction film and that he wanted to collaborate on the screenplay with a science fiction writer. Among the things he looked at was Arthur C. Clarke's short story "The Sentinel"; something clicked, and that's how the collaboration between Clarke and Kubrick began.

And what an intimate and complicated collaboration it was! The book and the screenplay were written more or less simultaneously, with Kubrick doing more of the screenplay work and Clarke really writing the novel, so that *2001*, the novel, was neither a novelization of a screenplay nor the novel from which the screenplay was adapted, but Clarke's novelization of a Kubrick-dominated storyline, which in turn had been generated by a couple of Clarke's own stories. It is not likely that there will ever again be a cross-fertilization between SF cinema and SF literature quite as intimate and convoluted as this.

Unless, of course, you count this union's ultimate progeny, *2010*. Whereas *2001*, the novel, was a kind of symbiote of the screenplay, *2010*, the novel, was written before there was any movie project, though Clarke must surely have known full well that the film sequel would then become inevitable. Working with Peter Hyams, Clarke was much more in control than he had been with Kubrick; indeed *2010*, the novel, was written in part to clarify some of what Clarke felt was the murk at the end of *2001*, and he consulted with Hyams, who wrote and directed, throughout the writing of the screenplay, so that *2010* should certainly serve as the ideal test case for how far the art of adapting SF novels to film has and has not come since its illustrious ancestor opened the way for the major SF film made for adults.

In the book, as in the film, nine years after HAL does his dingo act and Bowman metamorphoses into the Star Child, a mixed crew of Americans and Russians goes out to the Jovian sattelites on a Russian ship, the *Leonov*, to find out what happened. In the film, as in the book, they see evidence of life on Europa, are warned off by the force of the giant monolith, and then go on to rendevous with the *Discovery*, orbiting Io.

In the film, as in the novel, HAL is reactivated and cured of his insanity, and Bowman somehow reappears both on Earth and in the *Discovery*, where he warns them to depart within two days, as war on Earth seems imminent. This leads into the climactic plot schtick where the *Discovery* and HAL are expended as a first-stage booster to kick the *Leonov* into emergency escape trajectory. The off-stage forces of the Monolith then turn Jupiter into a second sun, leaving the message that all the Jovian satellites are now given as worlds to men, save Europa, which is declared off-limits.

Plot element for plot element, the film follows the book, and the special effects, the visuals of the Jovian satellites, and particularly the scenes of Earth with two suns in its sky at the end, admirably convey that hard-edged sense of the transcendental reality of space that we associate with Clarke's vision.

Yet the film ends up being only a pale shadow of the book, perhaps not for lack of intent or even lack of skill, but because of a fundamental translation problem with adapting literary SF to film.

Namely, that it is virtually impossible to use point-of-view stream of consciousness in film—either as narration, where it is deadly, or as camera's eye pov, which quickly becomes tedious, or anything but a series of visual images. You can do a lot of things in film that you can't do in prose fiction, but one thing you *can't* do is put the audience inside a character's head.

But the novelist, and the science fiction novelist in particular, does this all the time, in order to smoothly combine needed exposition with characterization, in order to portray the alterations in consciousness produced by external events. This is not only a primary means whereby prose science fiction conveys the psychic core of character, but an important technical means for advancing exposition without falling into didacticism. And film has no easy equivalent.

In the book, the revived Bowman is a viewpoint character, and through the filter of his alien-altered consciousness, we get Clarke's considered explication of the nature of the galactic culture behind the events of the plot, and we get a grand tour of the ecospheres of Europa, and we see that Jupiter is being turned into a second sun at least as much for the benefit of the future evolution of the bioforms of Europa to sapience as for the benefit of man. In the book, the disembodied Bowman prevails upon his mighty alien masters to grant the consciousness of the dying HAL the same sort of discorporate immortality they have granted him. All this is really the heart and soul of Clarke's novel.

And none of it is in the film.

Without it, we have a film without a raison d'etre, we have pretty pictures and a more or less standardized plot, and a plea for detente, and all the phenomenological events of the novel, but where the intellectual and emotional core of the novel should have been, we have only the same mystification with which Kubrick faked his way out of the impossibility of presenting a true vision of what lay out there in the galaxy at the anticlimactically abstract end of *2001*.

God or the Great Monolith only knows how Hyams might have solved this problem. Clearly an act of creative inspiration on the part of the screenwriter was required, for the inherently novelistic heart of Clarke's book cannot simply be literally translated to film, and indeed, that may be what makes the book a real novel as opposed to a time-warped novelization.

Hyams was neither right nor wrong in leaving out what he did; he really had no choice, he had to leave it out because there was probably no way to put it in.

So he followed the path of least resistance along the plotline and made a film that was faithful to the story and characters and respectful to the ambiance, but that seems intellectually and spiritually empty when judged against the book.

This, admittedly, is not merely a problem peculiar to the translation of science fiction novels to film, it is a problem inherent in the translation of *any* novel to film. Most novels are of sufficient density and complexity that a complete film version would have a running time of ten hours, and most novels have elements such as stream-of-consciousness, first- or third-person narrative viewpoint, which simply do not translate to film.

Science fiction novels present a further difficulty in this regard, because another thing you cannot even attempt in a film without rendering audiences irately comatose is naked *exposition*. You cannot, or at any rate should not, have a voice-over narrating the relationship of history to the timeframe, the society to the characters, the scientific extrapolation to the culture, the individual to the body politic.

Science fiction novelists, though, do all of this all of the time; we have evolved a huge bag of tricks for integrating necessary expository lumps into a storyline, and, in common with all novelists, for making the story resonate with larger social, esthetic, and spiritual concerns not immediately inherent in the skein of events alone, no matter how puissantly visualized.

Indeed, it is arguable that this is most of what people read science fiction novels for, this speculative fusion of intellectual extrapolation and analysis with a good tale well told.

Does this mean that serious film makers should give up the attempt to adapt science fiction novels? Are all such adaptations doomed to be cinematic Classic Comics by the very nature of the medium?

Indeed, there are some exemplary arguments for the case that films in general, and SF films in particular, are more artistically successful when they are conceived originally for the medium to start with. Certainly most of the artistically successful SF films of the psst few years were the original visions of the film makers, notably the films of David Cronenberg and Larry Cohen, *Liquid Sky*, and so forth.

But the trouble is that original SF films require a creative genius who understands both science fiction and the art of filmmaking, and such rare creatures seem likely to remain in short supply. And the opportunity is that during half a century, a vast body of science fiction novels and stories have been published that could be translated into wonderful films.

It can be done.

It has been done.

But not the way most people seem to think it should be done.

Let us therefore contemplate the current most perfect example of precisely how *not* to translate an SF novel to film, *Dune*.

Admittedly the De Laurentiis organization set itself a formidable task. Not only are the plots and subplots endlessly recomplicated, but the novel is very long indeed; a good deal of it takes place inside people's heads, and the theme and storylines are inextricably bound up in the extrapolative details of two complex civilizations, that of a galactic empire and that of the desert Fremen. Giant sandworms to get in the can without looking ridiculous. Three planetary ambiances. Formidable!

Dino and Raffaella stride boldly in where Maxim Jodorowski fell flat on his face and Hollywood angels fear to tread.

The tragedy of *Dune*, the movie, is that it *is* a tragedy, a noble attempt at a heroic task that produced an artistic and box-office catastrophe.

What a waste!

Here was arguably one of the great science fiction novels of all time, a book that over the years rose to bestsellerdom on its own merits, a book woven into the psyche of more than one generation, and a project therefore that millions of potential ticket buyers desperately wanted to see succeed.

And Dino De Laurentiis seemed to have set the project up with a proper balance of high style and prudent business practice. He paid Frank Herbert big bucks and virtually insisted, by making an offer no one could refuse, that Herbert at least be the first to try writing the screenplay. By shooting it in Mexico, he leveraged his budget by a big factor, meaning that dollar for dollar he could put more pizazz up on the screen, and the large amount of capital he was leveraging in the first place meant that the money was there for effects and sets that would be state of the art.

When Herbert's script bombed out, De Laurentiis hired David Lynch to write and direct, and Herbert, with no ego-attachment to his own script, became Lynch's friendly consultant.

Which, in retrospect, can be seen to be the moment when things began to fall apart.

While Lynch's previous films *Eraserhead* and *The Elephant Man* were evidence of his undeniable talent as a film maker, what made De Laurentiis think this sensibility synced with that of Herbert's novel must forever remain a mystery to those who have seen either one of them.

While one may admire De Laurentiis' daring in bring in a talented young director of real artistic depth and subtlety rather than the best available Lucas clone, the installation of such a director, who had no familiarity with or demonstrated understanding of literary science fiction, would certainly seem to mandate that he be handed a script by someone who did.

Instead, quelle horreur, Lynch wrote the script while Herbert cheered him on!

The very first shot of the film reveals what is to come: as the audience, groaning and fidgeting, is subjected to the literal talking head of the Princess Irulan babbling back-story for what seems like several centuries.

But there is worse, much worse, in store. As scenes play out, we often hear the voice-overs of the characters speaking their thoughts while the camera holds close up. If their thoughts were true stream of consciousness or ironic commentary on the dialogue, this attempt to include Herbert's use of shifting viewpoints just might have worked, but instead, the characters' thoughts serve as lame attempts to explain to the increasingly befuddled audience what the hell is going on and why they should give a damn about any of it.

Right away, you know what's gone wrong with this film. Any time a film relies on voice-overs reading deathless prose from the novel, you know that either the writer failed to translate the story to cinematic terms or that the director has developed a stupefying, literal-minded faithfulness to the book.

Here, since David Lynch was both the writer and director, we end up with the worst of all possible worlds, which is to say *both*. Lynch genuinely wanted to be faithful to Frank Herbert's novel, but he didn't understand what the *story* of *Dune* was at all, and his faithfulness took the form of trying to get in all the characters and subplots and using Herbert's words generously. And Herbert, seeing how Lynch was trying to follow his book scene by scene as best as was humanly possible, and already having failed at adapting it himself, couldn't see what was wrong either.

What was wrong, of course, is that a film is not a novel, and it cannot simply reproduce the multiple plotlines of the novel, first because it would run ten hours if it did, and secondly because it would be a tendentious bore. A film must abstract the essential story and spirit of a novel, and then structure itself cinematically in a manner that conveys that story and spirit truly. One would think that it would go without saying that before this is possible, either the screenwriter or director preferably both, should know what the real story of the novel is.

But Lynch, who was both, had no idea what the real story of *Dune* was, and Herbert, who saw him attempting to be so faithful to the detail and plot of the novel, apparently couldn't tell him.

It shouldn't have been so difficult. The plot of *Dune* is quite complex, but the *story* is archetypally simple. An orphaned young prince flees into the desert from the usurpers of his rightful throne, and there among the mystic rebels, by courage and destiny and psychedeli visions, he is transformed into the warrior prophet of the people, and leads them to a victory that crowns him with the godhead.

That's the heart and soul of *Dune*, and it can hardly be said to lack power, compression, or coherence! This primal-level Jungian fairy-tale at its core is why the novel lives as a classic, and it's also why, by the way, all the subsequent sequels that do not have Paul Atreides at their center are pale shadows.

Had Lynch found that core, he could have freely embellished any of his own glosses he liked upon it, thrown out as much plot-complication as did not define it, and still have been truly faithful to the novel.

Indeed, even if Lynch didn't understand the story, at least he should have been able to read the title, which clearly indicates that the essential story takes place on Arrakis. Instead, *Dune*, the movie, takes about half its running time getting to Dune, the planet, and the real story is chopped up and compressed into meaningless action scenes in the second half.

Nor does Lynch have any feeling for the desert planet and what it stands for ecologically and mystically. On his planet of sun and sand, everyone wears dark clothing and huddles indoors in windowless gray castles, which almost would have worked, had not the Fremen been seen to live in caves done up by the same depressive junkie decorator, who also took away their flowing desert robes, designed to blend in with the color and spirit of the, ah, Dunes, and stuffed them into skintight black rubber fetish suits to broil and sweat in the blazing sun.

Enough! Do we really need to contemplate the Baron Harkonnen's pustules or the love story between Paul and Chani, which is detailed in a couple of breathless voice-over narrations, or the climactic scene, which doesn't quite make clear that Paul is now emperor?

Rather than contemplate this fiasco further, let us seal up the body-bag and draw the lesson of *Dune*'s failure. Which is that the way to translate a novel to film is not with literal-minded doggedness, but by understanding the inner story and spirit, and then creating an original work of cinematic art with that inner story at its heart.

So finally, rather than end this essay on a note of despair, let us consider a film whose writer and director did seem to understand this, *Blade Runner*, and see how it can be done.

For various reasons, I avoided seeing *Blade Runner* for as long as I could. Philip K. Dick's novel *Do Androids Dream of Electric Sheep?* was one of my personal favorites, Phil was a close personal friend, and Phil had made it quite clear in public and private that he considered the first-draft screenplay an atrocity.

What was more, Riddley Scott, the director, the previous intellectual high point of whose career had been *Alien*, was making a boor and a fool of himself in public by declaring his intention not to read the book upon which his film was to be based, lest he contaminate the purity of his vision.

Then Phil died, and the film came out, and it died at the box office, and people said it was nothing like the novel at all, and I had no desire to see what an arrogant pinhead action director had done to such an intellectually and spiritually subtle novel, so I had to be practically conned into seeing it.

I had somehow managed to forget that a new script had been written by Scott and David Peeples, and that Phil, at the end, had declared that screenplay a work of genius, which captured the spirit of the world he had created. Maybe Scott had just been shooting his mouth off for the benefit of the studio, who wanted something they could market to the *Star Wars* audience of adolescents, or maybe, just maybe, he had really been serious.

Maybe all Scott wanted to know was the essential story of the novel and to hell with the plot details, maybe he trusted Peeples enough to abstract this from the book, so that the two of them could then develop it into cinematic storytelling without getting bogged down in literal-minded mechanical faithfulness to the apparatus of the novel.

However they did it, Scott and Peeples did precisely right that which Lynch did so precisely wrong.

Lynch had been mechanically faithful to Herbert's apparatus to the point of excruciation, and so he ended up with everything but the real story, whereas Scott and Peeples threw out most of Dick's novelistic apparatus, replaced it with creative cinematic apparatus of their own, and so, by chopping down the necessary trees, attained a clear vision of the forest.

In the film as in the novel, we have Deckard, the android hunter (though in the film he is called a Blade Runner and the androids replicants), and the runaway androids, their short life-spans running out, wanting only to live, but lacking any human sense of caritas, having absolutely no concern for any life other than their own. If they ruthlessly kill humans to survive then the humans, in the form of Deckard, are also engaging in exactly the same moral behavior in regard to them.

The question upon which the story then revolves is that of who is the human and who is the android, and Dick's criterion is a moral one. A human is a being possessed of caritas; we define our humanity by our ability to see the mirror of that humanity in others. An android is a sentient being devoid of caritas, a psychopathic creature of pure survival mechanism, incapable of empathy.

There is much more in Dick's novel—a whole post-catastrophe world, a religion, wonderful minor characters, humor—that is not in the film, which no doubt is why people complain that it is not faithful to the novel.

But when the dying replicant Roy Batty, who moments before was relishing the slow, sadistic death he had been inflicting on Deckard in vengeance for Deckard's cold extermination of his comrades, reaches out his hand and saves Deckard's life after visible consideration at death's door, *Blade Runner* achieves the ultimate in true faithfulness to the novel.

In a scene that was not in the book, it poignantly and forcefully manifests Dick's true meaning in entirely cinematic terms, that "human" and "android" are moral and spiritual definitions and not a matter of protoplasm. That by achieving empathy, a manufactured creature can gain its humanity, just as by losing it, a natural man can become a human android.

And indeed, as we can see, this lesson is applicable to the true translation of the science fiction novel into film.

For just as we forgive Roy Batty his monsterhood when he attains moral humanity in the epiphany of the film, so can we forgive *Blade Runner* its free play with the plot and characters and ambiance of the novel in the magic moment thereof.

For, warts and all, *Blade Runner* proves in that moment that it is no cinematic android like *Dune*, no Disneyland simulacrum of a great science fiction novel with nothing but a vacuum where the heart of the novel should be. By its empathy with the spirit of *Do Androids Dream of Electric Sheep?*, *Blade Runner* attains the humanity of the novel, and so successfully translates Dick's true vision to film.

All else is Muzak.

Modes of Content:
Hard SF, Cyberpunk, and
the Space Visionaries

It is not so unusual that science fiction has from time to time spawned literary movements like the New Wave and Cyberpunk along with their passionate detractors, for such is the history of literature in general.

But one thing about such factionalism that is perhaps unique to science fiction is that so much of the heat in both controversies has centered on the philosophical relationship of the human spirit to science and technology and the proper literary stance for science fiction and science fiction writers to assume when addressing this thematic core of SF.

Interestingly, there has always been general agreement that this relationship is the central thematic core of science fiction. The controversies have always concerned angles of approach, moral and spiritual implications, esthetics, political consequences; never the centrality of the relationship of man to the technosphere, but always what that relationship is or should or could be.

And while the conclusion is far from unanimous that humanity has or could or should have a future in space, it is certainly fair to say that this is an overwhelming consensus in the science fiction community, a consensus that not only spawned the space movement but, some would content, inspired spaceflight itself.

And indeed, as we shall see, even the hard science advocates and the cyberpunks can agree on that, for there are visionary space dreamers in both camps, though the nature of the human future in space is something else again.

"The Hard Staff" and "Dreams of Space" appear as published in my column in *Asimov's* with only minor revision, but "The Neuromantic

Cyberpunks," which originally appeared as "The Neuromantics," has been retitled and revised to acknowledge my complete and utter failure to rename the "Movement" after Gardner Dozois has already stuck its present handle on it.

The Hard Stuff

Some have identified it with the "nuts and bolts" school. Some have credited John W. Campbell, Jr., with its editorial invention. Some trace its origins back to Jules Verne. Some define it in terms of exemplary practitioners alone—Arthur C. Clarke, Hal Clement, Robert W. Forward, Poul Anderson, Gregory Benford, et al. Benford himself has likened all *other* science fiction to "playing tennis with the net down" and therefore deemed it the form's esthetic core.

I'm talking, of course, about "hard science fiction."

Hard science fiction has been generally recognized as a subcategory of the genre about as long as the genre itself has been the subject of its own internal literary criticism, but after all these decades, a "hard definition" of "hard science fiction" remains ironically elusive.

In a sense, it seems to have been generally defined by its dialectical opposition to a changing series of antitheses, and the meaning of the term has mutated accordingly.

Though not precisely in those terms, Jules Verne castigated H.G. Wells for writing less than the hard stuff, to wit, the *scientific romance* that Verne deemed to be his own creation.

During the so-called Golden Age of the 1930s and 1940s, hard science fiction was identified with what John W. Cmapbell, Jr., was publishing in *Astounding* as opposed to the interplanetary adventure tales tht were the mainstays of "less serious" SF magazines.

In the 1950s, when the center of the field shifted towards *Galaxy* and *The Magazine of Fantasy and Science Fiction* and a school of SF whose thematic material was drawn from such "soft" sciences as psychology and sociology, hard science fiction was generally defined as fiction grounded in the "hard" sciences of physics, astronomy, chemistry, and (perhaps with a grudging nod) biology.

During the New Wave period of the 1960s, hard science fiction, rightly or wrongly, came to be identified as the exemplary anti-New Wave SF by the New Wave school and its opposition alike.

In the 1970s, when science fantasy came into vogue, hard science fiction was seen as the bastion of pur sang SF against the bastardization of the form.

And now, in the 1980s, some, primarily and most coherently Gregory Benford, have championed hard science fiction as an antithesis to cyberpunk, though some of the cyberpunks themselves insist that *they* are writing in the hard SF tradition.

So what *is* hard science fiction? And who is writing it? And are they all writing the same thing? And to what extent is hard science fiction really the esthetic center of science fiction itself?

It is easy enough to dispose of the obvious. Fantasy, whether high fantasy, sword and sorcery, or contemporary, is obviously not hard science fiction. Science fantasy, with its amalgamation of science fiction image systems with the supernatural, with its swordfights in spaceships, with its deliberate disregard of scientific and technological verities in the service of thematic and plotline imperatives, is the opposite pole from hard science fiction, to the extent that they are really extremes of the same form at all.

But beyond the obvious, the picture becomes murky indeed. If hard science fiction is defined as SF that operates within the reality constraints of the best currently available scientific world view, then why is Larry Niven considered a hard SF writer and not J.G. Ballard? Why Arthur C. Clarke but not Frederik Pohl? Why Hal Clement but not Theodore Sturgeon? Why Gregory Benford but not Bruce Sterling? Why Poul Anderson but not William Gibson?

Niven makes free use of faster-than-light travel as a literary convention, as do Clement and Anderson, which is hardly playing the game with the net of Einsteinian relativity firmly erected in the center of the court. Clarke has declared that any sufficiently advanced technology will appear as magic, and his best works partake heavily of mystical transcendence. Even Benford has dabbled in a kind of time travel and is as much a transcendentalist as Clarke.

The Ballard of the disaster novels, on the other hand, postulates a single geophysical transformation of the climate and proceeds to its specific effects with considerable scientific rigor. Frederik Pohl's worlds are generally portrayed with lapidary scientific and technological verisimilitude and detail. Sturgeon's works display a formidable grounding in psychology and biology. Gibson brings high technology down to a quotidian and pervasive street level, and Sterling, the main cyberpunk dialectician, places the transformation of humanity *by* science and technology at the thematic heart of his work.

Clearly then, neither scrupulous adherence to the parameters of the current best scientific world view nor the centrality of science and technology to the lives of the characters and the driving imperatives of the story define hard science fiction.

Those unsympathetic to hard science fiction have at times opined that, far from being central to the genre's esthetic virtue, it may be defined as SF's characteristic literary flaw. Namely, that by placing the focus on scientific speculation and technological extrapolation, the hard science fiction esthetic produces a fiction short on characterization, human feeling, stylistic excellence, and thematic depth.

Indeed, some devotees of the form turn it inside out but are really saying very much the same thing when they declare tht science fiction, being a "literature of ideas," is exempt from general literary standards in regard to character development, style, and emotional depth.

Well, this does define a certain kind of hard science fiction. Clement, Forward, Clarke, Niven, and many other generally recognized successful hard science fiction writers are not read for their memorable characters or emotional subtlety or singing prose, but for the fascination of their scientific notions and technological extrapolations.

This is not to say that such fiction need be subliterate or lacking in narrative tension or emotionally flat. Take *West of Eden* and *Winter in Eden*, the first two volumes of a trilogy by Harry Harrison.

If there is such a thing as hard science fiction at all, surely this is it. Harrison accepts, for the purpose of science fictional argument, the still-controversial theory that an asteroid strike about sixty-five million years ago altered the Earth's climate and thereby caused the extinction of the dinosaurs.

So what would have happened if that asteroid had never hit?

A classical hard science fiction premise, from which Harrison extrapolates and exfoliates his alternate Earth with rigor and care rarely matched.

The dinosaurs survive and continue to evolve; the pinnacle of their evolution is the Yilane, a race of intelligent saurians. The Yilane in turn evolve a high technological culture based on genetics and biology. Boats, submarines, guns, microscopes, medical instruments, even whole cities, are developed by genetically altering living organisms beyond all recognition. For the Yilane have never harnessed fire, they know it only as a natural calamity and a bizarre laboratory phenomenon.

Unlikely as this may seem, Harrison makes it credible. He shows how such a weirdly skewed technology arises out of the Yilane life-cycle and biology, out of their birth and maturation in the ocean, out of their saurian cold-bloodedness. (These are *not* the warm-blooded dinosaurs of current revisionary vogue.)

Harrison also develops a complicated and variegated Yilane society, which also is seen to be squarely rooted in the biological parameters of their being. He develops a Yilane language, incorporating gestural signs and a grammar unlike that of any human tongue I have ever heard of.

And he has secured the collaboration of three scientists—a linguist, a biologist, and, apparently, an anthropologist, in the creation of this fully rounded Yilane world. It's difficult indeed to imagine harder science fiction than this!

But what of the story?

Here Harrison resorts to a technique at least as old as Hugo Gernsback's "scientifiction formula" and probably as old as Verne—an action-adventure plotline to walk us through his world. Here too, perhaps, he must fudge the science a bit in order for his story to exist.

In Harrison's alternate Earth, North America has been isolated long enough for a mammalian ecosystem to have evolved there, up to and including a Homo sapiens hunter-gatherer culture and another human culture with early agriculture, plus the humanlike Angurpiaq, basically furry Eskimos.

Since in *our* Earth, the dinosaurs are known to have been dominant before the asteroid strike in North America too, and since genus *Homo* evolved on the African savannah, and since the rest of the science here is so carefully done, it may be safe to assume that Harrison set this up of necessity, and with a sidewise wink.

For what it does is allow him to play human protagonists against Yilane antagonists in a more or less classic action-adventure format. An encroaching ice age exerts pressure on the Yilane to seek new territory across the sea in warmer climes. They establish a colony in North America, and the first two books of the trilogy, at least, chronicle the human-Yilane conflict.

But it's not all thud, blunder, and lizard-bashing by cardboard characters. Kerrick, the main hero, is captured by the Yilane as a boy and brought up Yilane under the tutelage of Vainte, an important Yilane leader. Under her patronage, he becomes something of a Yilane Prince, like Moses in Egypt. Like Moses, blood wins out when push comes to shove, and he escapes to become a leader of the humans in their battle to survive against the technologically superior Yilane. Vainte, stung by this betrayal, conceives a vicious vendetta against all humankind, and becomes the champion of anti-human Yilane genocide.

While this story runs tautly along a good-guys-versus-bad-guys plotline, there is some characterological depth. There are the Daughters of Life, a Yilane reform movement in conflict with their own culture. And Kerrick himself remains half-Yilane in a certain psychic sense, for he has made some real friends among the saurians, exercised some power in their society, and at times pines wistfully for the higher Yilane civilization.

The trilogy is only two-thirds done, but it would seem that Harrison is moving toward some kind of eventual detente and even cultural cross-fertilization between human and Yilane cultures, embodied and epitomized by Kerrick, the man of both worlds. The humans acquire some Yilane technology. Two Yilane males (Yilane society is overwhelmingly female chauvinist) more or less defect to the human side. At the end of *Winter in Eden*, the climactic battle ends not in a one-sided bloodbath but in something of a negotiated settlement.

West of Eden and *Winter in Eden* are exemplars of a certain species of hard science fiction. The scientific and technological extrapolation are certainly front and center, the reader is propelled through it by an action-adventure plotline, the prose is straightforward and transparent, and the inner lives of the characters are not really central nor intended to be.

But there *are* real characters, the novels *do* integrate their personal tales into the plot dynamics of the war story, and Harrison *would* seem to be moving towards a thematic climax of some depth and subtlety.

These books are in a sense science fiction as a literature of ideas, with the extrapolation at the core and the character development at the periphery, but a certain balance between them is maintained here. This is hard science fiction that knows it is hard science fiction, and if it is not great literary art, that doesn't seem to be what it is intended to be. Harrison's ambitions are extraliterary here; these novels are forthright, traditional, hard science fiction, but they also demonstrate that hard science fiction does not *have* to be subliterate, that a literature of ideas can and should pay some attention to general literary virtues, even if they may properly be subsumed by the ideational content.

On the other hand, *Japan Sinks*, the classic disaster novel by Sakyo Komatsu, like Ballard's disaster novels, reverses the relative balance of scientific speculation and general literary concerns, which may be why neither Ballard's disaster novels nor *Japan Sinks* are generally accepted into the hard science fiction canon, even though Komatsu's scientific speculation, in particular, is quite rigorous.

Komatsu destroys the entire Japanese archipelago in this one through a series of geological events, each one entirely credible, each one flowing out of the other. Komatsu has the geology of all this down cold, and the story unfolds through multiple viewpoint characters, several of them scientists studying the events, as the islands of Japan are stepwise broken apart by a disastrous shifting of the fault in the Japan Trench and the resultant volcanic eruptions and sink into the sea.

Japan Sinks is virtually a textbook lesson in how to write this stuff, geophysics certainly qualifies as a "hard science," and yet this is really no more hard science fiction than Ballard's disaster novels, and for much the same reason.

Komatsu's central concern here is *not* the scientific speculation but the impingement of the resultant disaster on the lives of his characters and, in particular, on how it impinges upon the character of the Japanese people as a whole as seen through them. The Japanese, long isolated from the international mainstream by geography and language, must come to terms with the fact that their ancient and rich culture, so intimately an organic outgrowth of their beloved Home Islands, can now survive only in a geographically rootless diaspora.

When Fujiyama itself finally turns on the Japanese in a disastrous eruption, one feels that symbolically at least, the novel has reached its thematic climax, that a great people, shorn irrevocably from the very wellsprings of their culture, from the geographical groundings of Shinto itself, must now change radically in order to survive as a refugee nation.

In other words, Komatsu, even more than Ballard, centers his novel not on the speculative science but on the political, social, psychic, and spiritual consequences. Even though his science is as hard as basalt, it is not the *central* concern of the novel, it is merely the McGuffin and if *Japan Sinks* is *not* hard science fiction, only this can be the reason.

Reversing Harrison, Komatsu, like Ballard, uses the hard science content primarily to set up an altered psychic landscape and emphasizes the general literary concerns over the scientific speculation.

Yet hard science fiction *can* seek to maintain a careful balance between scientific speculation and the general literary concerns at its core and still remain hard science fiction, or so it would seem from something like Greg Bear's *The Forge of God*.

This is another disaster novel, but on a far grander scale. Alien invaders, apparently from a machine civilization fundamentally inimical to organic life, destroy the Earth, and the means by which Bear has them do so is repellently fascinating in hard science terms, all too credible, and quite original.

Two dense masses, one composed of neutronium, the other of anti-neutronium, are dropped onto our planet. They are so dense that they sink right in and establish decaying orbits *within* the mantle and the core. The anti-neutronium "bullet" interacts with the Earth's matter and its orbit decays more rapidly, so it comes to rest at the center of the planet first. When the neutronium "bullet" reaches it and they are fused together by the pressures at the Earth's core there is an enormous total annihilation reaction and the planet is blown apart from within.

Just for good measure, the aliens drop automated machinery into deep sea trenches which extract deuterium and/or tritium from the water and/or rock, releasing vast quantities of hydrogen and oxygen in the process of manufacturing thousands of hydrogen bombs that are timed to go off as the neutronium and anti-neutronium bullets come together, splitting the crust along its deepest fault-lines and enhancing thereby the efficacy of the internal explosion.

There is much speculation in here as well on the matter of the evolution of life and machine civilizations in the galaxy, and the main viewpoint characters, Arthur Gordon, former National Science Adviser, Edwin Shaw, geologist, and Trevor Hicks, scientific journalist, are placed at the heart of the scientific unraveling of the mystery of what is really happening and also close to the seat of presidential power, attempting to deal with the situation militarily and politically.

This, of course, is a classic hard science fiction structure. Begin with a series of seemingly isolated scientific mysteries that slowly converge on an outré enormity, building narrative tension as your viewpoint characters become deeply involved in the scientific effort to uncover the truth, then convert the scientific mystery into a problem to be solved by a neat technological fix whose nature you have carefully but not obviously foreshadowed in the previous scientific speculation.

But Bear is after something more literarily ambitious here.

Once the neutronium and anti-neutronium bullets enter the Earth, and they enter fairly early in the novel, the outcome is inevitable. The Earth is doomed, humanity can do nothing to save it, and all the characters move through the story under a sentence of impending death, an impending *species* death, of which the whole world eventually becomes aware.

The Forge of God approaches tragedy.

Both Shaw and Gordon have a love for the land, and through their eyes we see and feel what is to be lost. Gordon has a family from whom he is separated for much of the novel, and we get a feel for that, too. Gordon's friend, scientist Harry Feinman, is under his own personal sentence of death from leukemia and dies before the novel is over, nicely mirroring the macrotheme.

Greg Bear makes an earnest attempt to balance a novel of hard science fiction with a novel of character and to unite the two thematically in a tragedy. He seems to be doing all the right things. And yet, somehow, he doesn't quite bring it off.

The characters are real, they have deeply felt emotions, they have networks of friends and family, they care, they suffer, they would seem to fulfill all the standard literary criteria, yet they, and their personal stories, are simply not as *interesting* as the scientific speculation and enormous events. They are intelligent, feeling, but basically rather ordinary people witnessing extraordinary events, and their personal stories seem like an overlay on the main event, not a thematic extension thereof.

Then too, Bear cannot quite bring himself to fully bite the bullet of tragedy. The Earth *is* destroyed, and Bear *does* render its destruction with power and even poetry, but there is a second alien machine civilization at work in the solar system, a literal deus ex machina, which terraforms Mars and Venus and rescues a remnant of humanity, including Arthur Gordon and his family.

Yet if Bear does not quite succeed in marrying hard science fiction to the novel of character in the form of a tragedy, he *does* come close enough to demonstrate that it *can* be done, that hard science fiction *can* rise to the state of literature by any reasonable criterion, that *humanistic hard science fiction* need not be a contradiction in terms. And indeed, in a previous hard science fiction novel, *Blood Music*, Bear himself *has* pulled it off.

Nor—despite the general impression that hard science fiction is the uncompromising core of the SF genre and its enjoyment thereby limited to the sophisticated cognoscenti thereof—is that unlikely hybrid, a hard science fiction *best-seller* aimed at a general audience of science fictional naifs, an inherent impossibility.

Michael Crichton, himself a physician, has made quite a successful career for himself writing just such novels. *The Andromeda Strain* was a hard science fiction thriller about a deadly plague brought back by a satellite, and the narrative tension resided almost entirely in the unraveling of the scientific mystery and scientific attempts to solve the problem, with a bit of physical derring-do thrown in at the climax. *The Terminal Man* concerned control of human behavior by a sophisticated version of the so-called Del Gado box.

Sphere, his latest, begins with the discovery of a huge ancient spaceship, or so it first seems, buried deep on the southern Pacific seabed. Psychologist Norman Johnson, the viewpoint character, is sent down to a seabed habitat as part of the investigating team. Most of the novel takes place within the deep-sea habitat, the crashed spaceship, and the undersea complex between.

As in *The Andromeda Strain*, and to a lesser degree in *The Terminal Man*, Crichton has done his homework, and he renders the nuts and bolts of the habitat with accuracy, skill, and verismilitude. More important, perhaps, for a general audience, he does a fine job of portraying the *psychological* ambiance of this constricted technosphere through its effects on characters not at all accustomed to such a venue, as seen through the eyes of a man who is not at home there, either, but who is a skilled psychologist, an Everyman in terms of the environment, but possessed of special scientific knowledge.

Sphere progresses much like a traditional hard science fiction novel as the scientific team investigates the mystery of the spaceship, though more than the usual attention is paid to the psychic states of the characters. But the spaceship turns out to be other than it seems, an American spaceship from the *future* rather than an ancient alien visitor, and this is where, just as the story really starts to pick up steam, Crichton begins to abandon the scientific rigor of what has gone before.

His description of the futuristic American spaceship is fascinating and puissant indeed, particularly in its cunning use of brand names and familiar quotidian touches in the midst of all the futuristic technology, but as it turns out, it got there by flying through a black hole, and Crichton must justify this by a rather silly explication of wonky relativity theory for the masses that, while it may successfully justify time travel to a general audience, can only embarrass the scientifically literate. That is, Crichton removes the net from Benford's tennis court in the middle of the match.

From there, the psychological thriller plotline takes over. The mysterious sphere of the title is found inside the spaceship. It turns out to be some kind of artifact snatched from the universe beyond the black hole. It gives anyone who enters the power to actualize imagery from his subconscious. There is a menacing giant squid, as well as many other such manifestations.

But before the cognoscenti begin to sneer, let it be said that *Sphere* nevertheless holds up quite nicely as a novel. The narrative tension does not at all slacken when the net is removed, and the denouement—in admirable fashion—derives directly from the psyche of the protagonist as manifested through the powers of the sphere, though to say more would ruin the novel for the reader.

What we have here is something more common than some people would like to imagine—the hard science fiction novel of apparatus. Or more properly, perhaps, the novel of hard *technology*.

The *scientific* speculation is, well, basically bullshit. But the description of the technological artifacts is so realistic and convincing that the *illusion* of scientific verisimilitude is maintained for the reader even while the net of scientific plausibility is torn to shreds in the service of the story.

This is not necessarily a bad thing. *This* is in a sense arguably the true esthetic center of science fiction. Every science fiction novel or story that utilizes such standard SF tropes as faster-than-light spaceships, time travel, or parallel worlds partakes of it. *Most* of what we call "hard science fiction" is really "hard *technological* fiction."

Indeed, it can be argued that if the science is 100 percent faithful to the best available knowledge, then a piece of fiction isn't science fiction at all, since scientific *speculation* is then entirely absent, and what we have is mimetic fiction with futuristic technological trappings.

In other words, most of what we think of as hard science fiction is a literary illusion—not a matter of scientific accuracy but of literary technique. As long as the description of the *technology* has the hard edged plausibility of a Chesley Bonestell painting, we will swallow great gobs of scientific baloney as long as the story holds up and be convinced that we are reading hard science fiction in the bargain.

And why not? All fiction, as Kurt Vonnegut has pointed out, is lies. So why not this one, if we can be made to enjoy it?

Which is not to say that true hardcore hard science fiction cannot exist or cannot rise to the literary heights. Indeed, to be entirely paradoxical about it, one can also argue that the highest form of hard science fiction, that hard science fiction that indeed may be said to be the essence of the genre itself, is fiction that applies all the available literary techniques to preserve the illusion of verisimilitude, while it pushes the edge of the best known scientific world view just far enough to enter terra incognita without actually *contradicting* known scientific fact, and does this in the service of a story centered on the human heart.

And no one has done this better than Gregory Benford, who indeed plays the game with the net up, but plays it with a net of rubber.

Benford is a working astrophysicist of some repute, but he does not write like the typical scientist dabbling in science fiction.

For instance, his novel *Against Infinity* was rather foolishly attacked for quasi-plagiarism because of its similarities to William Faulkner's story "The Bear," when what Benford was actually doing was rendering literary homage to Faulkner while giving his own novel additional resonance through the time-honored technique of literary reference.

Benford, a native Alabamian, also engages in a subtle and self-conscious attempt to bring Southern rhythms and speech patterns into his prose, feeling that the voice of most science fiction is perhaps a bit too relentlessly Yankee.

Benford's novel *Timescape* was in part a literary response to C.P. Snow's "two-culture problem" down to some of the English settings, a character-centered novel, but a character-centered novel about scientists actually doing science that admirably portrays the scientific *esthetic*, the scientific *passion*, as no one has really done before. Ironically enough, or perhaps not so ironically, he resorts to a certain amount of rather rubbery science as the McGuffin.

Benford has traveled widely, and he spent time in Japan in his youth; some of his stories and notably his novel *The Stars in Shroud* stretch themselves beyond Western esthetics and social and psychological patterns to project futures with heavy Eastern influences.

Artifact was a straightforward thriller of sorts, but with a hard science McGuffin at the core and a complex and controversial political subtext exploring the beginnings of the breakup of the NATO alliance.

The point of all this is that Gregory Benford, scientist or not, self-declared hard science fiction purist though he be, is by far the most complete and literarily sophisticated novelist ever to have declared himself a hard science fiction writer. And while he can speculate scientifically with the best of them, the scientific speculation is, as often as not, *not* his central concern. Nor is he such a purist that he will not bend his science a bit in the service of his other literary concerns.

When Benford the polemicist extols hard science fiction over the more rubbery stuff, what he really may be championing is nothing more recondite than *good science fiction* over *bad science fiction*, at least to judge from his own best fiction, which is purely and simply the former.

A prime example is his latest, *Great Sky River*, a tenuously thematic sequel to *In the Ocean of Night*, which in turn has a tenuous thematic connection to his collaboration with Gordon Eklund, *If the Stars Are Gods*.

In *If the Stars Are Gods*, mankind has its first contact with extraterrestrials. In *In the Ocean of Night*, humans begin to venture out among the stars in a slower-than-light vehicle—FTL being one of Benford's prime examples of "playing the game with the net down" and something he for the most part eschews, even when it would be literarily convenient.

What humans learn, to their dismay, in *In the Ocean of Night* is that machine civilizations dominate in the Galaxy and, moreover, are engaged in the general extermination of organic sapients.

This theme has gained considerable prominence of late (see *The Forge of God, Rendevous with Rama*, etc.) and seems to have entered science fiction via its currency in contemporary scientific circles. The temperature of most of the Galaxy is far more suitable to metallo-silicon life-forms than to frail carbon-based organics, so the theory goes, really advanced machines could be virtually immortal, unfazed by the light-speed limitation on interstellar travel, and machine civilizations could last for millions or even billions of years. And sooner or later high organic civilizations will produce self-replicating, self-programming machines who will supersede them.

All of this has a hard science plausibility, but the notion that such high machine civilizations would seek to exterminate lower organic forms seems to owe more to the anthropomorphic projection of our own unfortunate xenophobic imperialism than to the Cold Equations.

Be that as it may, *Great Sky River* takes a long, long jump-cut from *In the Ocean of Night*, several tens of thousands of years, in fact, for Benford simply *will not* resort to FTL no matter how much more difficult his literary problems may be when he eschews it.

Humans, apparently via automated starships with stored germ plasm and/or embryos, have reached the galactic center, an area of densely packed stars around the great central black hole, only to find the area dominated by advanced machine civilizations. These civilizations are to the humans as humans are to cockroaches, and their attitude toward such bothersome vermin would seem to be rather similar to our own.

The humans build Chandeliers, cities in space. The machine civilizations treat them like bothersome wasp nests. Humans descend to the planet Snowglade and build great Arcologies. Machine civilization eventually lands on Snowglade, too, and begins the long, slow, inevitable process of "anti-terraforming" the planet, cooling it and drying it out to suit machine needs and making it unsuitable to organic forms in the process.

The machines force the humans out of their proud Arcologies. The humans build more modest Citadels. The machines sack the Citadels, and finally the last few remaining human tribes are constrained to wander the organically dying planet in a permanent state of flight and dread.

All of the above, amazingly enough, is back-story, which emerges in bits and pieces throughout *Great Sky River*, which begins with the last humans fleeing across Snowglade and focuses down on a single viewpoint character, Killeen.

On the one hand, this could be seen as a demonstration of the literary constrictions Benford forced on himself by excessive scientific scrupulousness. He could only have written the long epic back-story as a real-time saga either by hopping cavalierly from character to character down the timeline like Olaf Stapledon and losing all semblance of emotional involvement or by giving us main characters who somehow lived through it all.

And that would have required the acceptance of either immortality or faster-than-light starships.

And that, chez Benford, would be playing the game with the net down.

So Benford kept the net up and accepted the literary consequences, and on the other hand, what he has done in *Great Sky River* is also an example of how adhering to the scientific restrictions can sometimes *enhance* the literary art.

The restrictions Benford placed on himself prevented him from writing *Great Sky River* as a vast parsec-spanning saga of the spaceways. It forced him to focus down on a single small band of humans at the tag end of the story and the consciousness of one man and to channel all of his huge thematic material through this lens of emotional reality, to make the novel as much a novel of character as a novel of galactic speculation.

Then too, really advanced machine civilizations in the centers of their higher flowering would be entirely beyond human comprehension, which is part of Benford's thematic point, and Benford, being human himself, would have had to either reduce their grandeur to sci-fi conventions or lapse into babblement, had he attempted to depict Chandelier-humanity confronting their full-blown manifestations.

Instead we have the widowed Killeen, his son, and a small band of humans fleeing and fighting for brute survival at the tag end of the long historical process across the surface of what, from the point of view of the machine civilizations, is a boondock planet. We have the Mantis, a kind of machine artist and curator of organic forms, representing the alien spirit of the machines.

And it works admirably. The human-level story centers on Killeen's relationship with his maturing son Toby and with Shibo, a refugee woman from another band, and it blends nicely with the over-story, which itself enters realms of deep psychic imagery, thanks to the powers of the Mantis.

Further, while portraying humanity as bands of poor, small creatures trying desperately to survive at the margins of machine civilization, as a species that in some ways really *is* inferior, Benford manages to turn *Great Sky River* into something of a celebration of the human spirit under extreme physical and psychic pressure.

He does this in a number of ways. He keeps the story squarely focused on the personal for the most part, making us care for and admire his characters. He gives us everything through the consciousness of Killeen, and renders that consciousness with skill and depth and compassion. He gives us a human culture-on-the-run that still retains a rather touching dignity. Through "Aspects" and "Faces"—avatars of dead humans recorded on chips within Killeen—he frequently evokes the bygone grandeur of humanity's greater days and connects his people with the stream of human history and thereby with ourselves.

He even cunningly connects our remote cyborged descendants with ourselves by very subtle larding of their somewhat mutated English with familiar and homey Southern speech patterns.

Finally, he rings in nonmaterial beings existing as magnetic patterns in the accretion disc of the central black hole, or perhaps somehow within the event horizon as well, whom the Mantis regards rather worshipfully as far above machines as machines are above humans. And he hints at a kind of immortal afterlife for humans in this arcane realm of patterned energy.

Here we have Benford the scientific transcendentalist, who seems to be saying that the metallo-silicon matrix need not contain the highest endpoint of the evolution of galactic consciousness. That there may be no such endpoint, no such innate superiority of matrix, that consciousness itself may have a certain independence from the matrix in which it has arisen, that all consciousness is on the same journey. That each matrix of consciousness—flesh, metal, magnetic—contains a spirit that in that ultimate sense is equally valid, equally precious, even though hierarchies of relative physical and intellectual superiority are also quite real, and sometimes tragic.

Alas, he does use these magnetic beings as a kind of deus ex machina to produce a happy ending. The humans are led to an ancient spaceship, which, with the aid of the Mantis, they renovate, and in which they leave Snowglade for the great unknown, and perhaps a sequel.

This ending is a double-edged sword—psychologically satisfying since we care for Killeen and this remnant of humanity and feel they deserve to survive with dignity, intellectually annoying since it is something of a pat ending that violates the thematic unity of what has gone before.

Still, if we can forgive a certain amount of bending of the laws of science in the service of story—as we so often do—perhaps we can also forgive a certain bending of thematic logic in the service of emotional satisfaction.

In a sense, Benford was caught in a bit of a bind. If he followed the cold logic of the tale to its relentless conclusion and had his people fail to survive or be crushed spiritually by the machines, the novel probably would not have had an emotionally satisfying ending. Having chosen to satisfy our hearts, he leaves our intellects somewhat put off.

In a certain sense, Benford the humanist and Benford the transcendentalist won out over Benford the hard science fiction writer at the conclusion of *Great Sky River*. And perhaps that is one of the things that makes him the novelist he is.

The strictures of hard science fiction do not define a separate category of fiction exempt from general literary standards and imperatives. Scientific accuracy and technological verisimilitude are *additional* strictures overlaid on those who would wish to write literarily ambitious science fiction. They make such stuff harder to write successfully, not easier, at least for a writer like Benford, who aspires to produce true literature.

Ultimately they are a means, not an end, part of a certain literary equation, not the controlling factor, part of the full spectrum of human literary technique. The best so-called "hard science fiction writers" like Benford know in their heart of hearts that the must give and bend a bit in the service of total literary concerns, whether they are willing to admit it in polite company or not.

And *that* is the hard science fiction that is central to the genre. That is the genre's highest form.

Hard science fiction?

Maybe not.

Maybe just *good* science fiction.

The Neuromantic Cyberpunks

The Cyberpunks are the first new literary movement within the SF field since the New Wave of the 1960s, or at the very least the first to have a collective label pinned on them. For reasons that will become apparent, I tried to rechristen them "the Neuromantics," and while that attempt was entirely unsuccessful, the reasoning behind it, I believe, remains valid.

For while some of my reasons for wanting to change the nomenclature may have been trivial, others cut to the heart of the matter.

For one thing, everyone agrees that William Gibson's *Neuromancer* started it all, including the "Movement" writers, who, unlike the writers of the New Wave movement who habitually insisted that no such thing existed, openly proclaim themselves a Movement with a capital *M*.

The New Wave, according to most of us labelled New Wave writers, was a post-facto critical description of a more complex and anarchical phenomenon, but there is or at least was a core group of "Movement" writers quite willing to declare their mutual literary kinship, most of whom appeared on the now-notorious Cyberpunk Panel at the 1985 North American Science Fiction Convention in Austin, Texas.

The panelists in question were Bruce Sterling, John Shirley, Lewis Shiner, and Rudy Rucker. William Gibson was certainly there in spirit and reference if not in the flesh, a state of being quite appropriate to a Neuromantic, as we shall see.

Also on the panel, however, was Greg Bear, openly denying membership in any cyberpunk tribe and openly wondering what he was doing on any such panel. And that is why I will more or less stick with the Neuromantics as my label for the literary phenomenon as opposed to the Movement, for as we shall see, Greg Bear was quite wrong. For in literary terms, he did belong on the panel, for when it comes to the actual fiction being produced in what I call the Neuromantic vein, there is more to it than the work of the writers who are mirror-shades-carrying Cyberpunks.

The logical place to begin this discussion, is, of course, with William Gibson's novel *Neuromancer* the archetypal template for the core group of writers, and the book most accurately described by the term cyberpunk.

Case, the "hero" of *Neuromancer*, certainly has what one might fairly call a punk sensibility in the current extended meaning of the term. He is an ex–speed freak—ex not as a matter of his own choice, but courtesy of "therapeutic" tampering with his brain against his will. He is a marginal man living on the razor edge of the underworld of his future, and his sometime lady-love is a mercenary killer with permanently implanted mirror-shades.

So far we could be dealing with a not terribly atypical Harlan Ellison protagonist of a certain period. And indeed, a strong Ellison influence underlies at least one aspect of the core Neuromantic sensibility.

For it was Ellison, writing SF and contemporary "gang" or "street" fiction simultaneously, who did the most to bring the sensibility, style, rhythm, and characters of the demimonde of the street into the clean while middle-class worlds of 1950s SF, though it would seem that William Burroughs might have been at least as direct an influence on Gibson. Certainly the Ellison oeuvre abounds with punk protagonists, in the 1950s sense of the word.

But by the end of the 1970s, punk had taken on new meanings, though curiously enough, black leather jackets and defiantly artificial hairdos had once more become the trappings of a kind of rebellion.

The black leather and DA punks of the 1950s were rebelling against Mom, Apple Pie, sexual repression, intellectuality, and the America of Dwight Eisenhower and Norman Rockwell, and their libidinal marching music was, interestingly enough, already primitively electronic, to wit, early primary-stage rock and roll.

These punks disappeared into history in the 1960s, their fate being sealed when Bob Dylan and the Beatles began the transformation of rock and roll from the ass-kicking music of Elvis and street gangs into the music of the politically conscious transcendental revolutionary utopianism that spawned the Counterculture.

So the "punks" or "new wavers" who emerged towards the middle of the 1970s were not at all the same as the punks of the 1950s, despite the superficial trappings, for these *nouvelle* punks were in rebellion against the countercultural sensibilities of the *1960s*, not the long-gone innocent ennui of the 1950s.

What *they* were in rebellion against was the self-conscious artsiness of early 1970s rock, the failed laid-back utopianism of the Counterculture, mysticism, and the naive supposition that the future would be better if youthful idealism kept the faith. If the punks of the 1950s really *were* anti-intellectual hoods, the nouvelle punks of the 1970s were *intellectual* anti-intellectuals; not naive natural nihilistic rebels without a cause but *self-consciously* nihilistic pessimists capable of raising cynicism to a more or less coherent philosophy and sophisticated enough to know they were doing it.

Case, the hero of *Neuromancer*, is a punk in the nouvelle mode, an intellectual punk rather than a simple greaser, and it is the "cyber" half of the equation that informs his intellectuality. This is precisely what makes *Neuromancer* a watershed book, what distinguishes the Cyberpunks from the New Wave, and what begins to define what this new esthetic means to science fiction as a whole.

Although the Neuromancer of the title is technically the name of an Artificial Intelligence, Case is the true Neuromancer of the story, in more ways than one.

The word Neuromancer is of course a pun on *necromancer*, meaning magician, and *neuro*, meaning pertaining to the nervous system. The Neuromancer is a contemporary (or in this case intermediate future) magician whose wizardry consists of directly interfacing his protoplasmic nervous system with the electronic nervous system of the computersphere, manipulating it imagistically (and being manipulated by it) much as more traditional shamans interact imagistically with more traditional mythic realms via drugs or trance states.

Now of course as a science fictional idea, this is not exactly new. I did something like this myself in *Riding the Torch*; there is Vernor Vinge's *True Names*, Alfred Bester's *Golem 100*, and the recent endless spate of stories and novels in which human protagonists find themselves acting and living in some kind of "cyberspace." The Disney studio even did it in a special-effects extravaganza called *Tron*.

But "neuromancer" is a pun on "necromancer" in another sense, too, for the narrowest meaning of the latter word is "raiser of the dead," and the spirit underworld in which Case and Gibson dabble is also magic of a black kind, where electronic means are used to raise neural ghosts in the software.

What's critical here is that Gibson's Neuromancer, Case, is not a Faustian scientist but an outlaw, not a computer *wimp* but a computer *punk*. A *cyberpunk*, if you will. An electronic necromancer in a black leather jacket and mirror-shades.

While certain hard science fiction writers have complained that Gibson's computer science is somewhat less than expertly rendered, what *really* upsets the hard science types about the book, aside from the scientific quibbles, is that *stylistically* and *characterologically Neuromancer* is unlike any previous novel to poach on their territory.

Yes, by any contentual criterion, Gibson writes hard science fiction.

But he doesn't write it like Heinlein or Poul Anderson or Hal Clement or even Gregory Benford.

Stylistically, philosophically, esthetically, and in terms of the consciousness-style of his protagonist, Gibson is instead a kinsman of Ellison, William Burroughs, the Michael Moorcock of the Jerry Cornelius stories, and the Spinrad of "The Big Flash," *Bug Jack Barron*, or "Street Meat."

Neuromancer is that seeming contradiction in terms, a *New Wave* hard science fiction novel.

Neuromantic, you might say.

Neuro-romantic.

But also *new* romantic.

When Bob Dylan appeared at a Newport Folk Festival in the early 1960s playing an *electric* guitar, the assembled beats, bohemians, and folkies were scandalized. This was a folk festival, these people were intellectuals, Dylan was their hero, and his lyrics spoke for what was later through this very instrumentality to become the spirit of the Counterculture.

But the electric guitar was the instrument of *rock and roll*, the music of pinheaded greasy hoods in black leather jackets, in British terms, of the Rockers (the lumpenproletariat skinheads), not of the Mods (nascent countercultural types).

Yes indeed, kiddies, difficult as it is to believe now, once upon a time, rock was regarded as *antithetical* to the spiritual, cultural, esthetic, and class values of the elitist bohemian realm that rock itself, transmogrified by Dylan and the Beatles, was to transform into the shared values of an entire generation in the form of the Counterculture!

And there remained a strange contradiction at the heart of the Counterculture throughout the 1960s and well into the 1970s; to wit that its antitechnological ideology, the neo-Ludditism, the suspicion of the works of science and technology, the bucolic mysticism, the back-to-the-soil movement, the ecological awareness, the whole tie-dyed ball of candle wax, was characteristically expressed by *rock and roll*, a musical mode whose dominant instruments were the electrically amplified guitar and the entirely electronics-based synthesizer.

New Wave science fiction was also to a certain extent a counter-cultural phenomenon, and the strident conflict between the New Wavers and SF's old guard mirrored and to some extent was only a literary aspect of the polarization and generational conflict going on in society at large.

We all know the litany. The New Wave stood for sexual liberation and cultural pluralism, and the old guard for traditional moral values. The New Wave stood for stylistic experimentalism, and the old guard for a good tale told in simple transparent prose. The New Wave was anti-Establishment and anti-war, and the old guard supported Our Boys in Viet Nam.

And the old guard was forever accusing the New Wave of being nihilistically against science and technology, while the New Wave chided the old guard for its naive assumption that the upward evolution of science and technology led ipso facto to the improvement of the human condition.

The point being that the political polarizations of the time led to the entirely false perception on *both* sides that there was an irreconcilable dichotomy between the things of science and the things of the spirit, between hard science fiction and stylistic experimentalism, between logical positivism and streetwise sensibility, between a science fiction grounded in rigorous scientific extrapolation, and a science fiction grounded in characterological realism, between computer hackers and hippies, between the scientific world view and the romantic impulse.

It has taken us a long time to begin to understand that this dichotomy is an illusion. Yet we should have seen it all along, or rather heard it, for the expression of the romantic impulse through high-tech instrumentalities is the heart of rock and roll.

Rock has always been the music of libidinal anarchy and the romantic and transcendental impulses; without this message, it just ain't rock and roll. Yet rock has also always been by definition *technological* music, for without the electric guitar and the synthesizer, it ain't rock and roll either.

The ideological politics of the 1960s and early 1970s obscured this obvious truth, obscured our perception of the possibility, and indeed the actual existence, of high-tech romanticism and cyborged transcendentalism. On one side, long natural hair, ecology, organic food, bucolic back-to-nature romanticism, Eastern mysticism, and doing your own thing. On the other side, the uptight, morally righteous, militaristic, coldly rational realm of science, technology, and the technocratic servants of Amerika with a *k*.

But in the middle 1970s the nouvelle punks rebelled against the anti-artificial anti-technological esthetic of the Counterculture, against what was seen as the reactionary wimpish denial of the esthetic possibilities of the technosphere. Out went flowery tie-dyed earth colors, and in came shiny black leather and high-tech, high-gloss chrome. Out went rose-colored granny glasses and in came mirror-shades. Out went long natural hair and in came defiantly artificial spiked, color-frosted, and sculptured hair-dos.

A new, forthrightly high-tech, romanticism.

The nouvelle punks are not nose-to-the-grindstone technocrats but anarchistic rockers in the old romantic tradition. But they are rockers who have finally come to embrace wholeheartedly the real world that science and technology have made, the technosphere, the cybersphere, the reality of the last quarter of the twentieth century and as far ahead as the visionary eye can see.

So too the Neuromantics.

Some, like Gibson and especially John Shirley, *are* cyberpunks, in that much of their work is directly informed by the trappings and surface texture of contemporary rocker style. Others, like Bruce Sterling, Lewis Shiner, and Greg Bear, are writing stories set in milieus from which any sort of punk esthetic is entirely absent. Gibson, and even more so Sterling and Bear, are into scientific extrapolation quite as thoroughly as recognized hard SF writers like Larry Niven or Hal Clement, and then some.

But one way or another, none of the Neuromantics would seem to view scientific speculation as the be-all and end-all of their work, as the thematic core of what they are about. And while few of the others attempt quite the idiosyncratic edge of Gibson's prose, all of them focus directly on character with an intensity and subtlety that we do not associate with the virtues of traditional hard science fiction.

Nevertheless, the Neuromantics *are* writing hard science fiction by every positive definition of the term, just as they are also writing stories of character. For what they share is a general subject of discourse intrinsic to both hard science fiction and characterological science fiction, and therefore arguably the core subject of all really ambitious science fiction, period.

Namely, how our increasingly intimate feedback relationship with the technosphere we are creating has been, is, and will be altering our definition of what it means to be human itself.

John Shirley's latest novel, *Eclipse*, is as forthrightly and specifically political as any SF novel published in the past decade and a half and then some. Set fairly early in the next century, it uses multiple viewpoints to tell the complex story of a complex resistance to a complicated fascist conspiracy to take over the United States and Western Europe. Over the past few years, Shirley has spent quite a bit of time in Europe, and he has been writing political action thrillers under various names, and *Eclipse* shows it. One may argue with Shirley's politics, and no doubt many people will, but no science fiction writer has really dealt with sub rosa and not-so-sub-rosa international terror politics any more realistically than Shirley has here, for the simple reason that you just can't get much more realistic about future politics than this. Shirley may not actually name names, but the movements and conspiracies in *Eclipse* clearly derive from movements and conspiracies already under way today; *Eclipse* is that current rarity, an angry, politically committed science fiction novel, and Shirley makes no bones about it.

Shirley has always proclaimed his identity as a card-carrying Cyberpunk, but aside from that, what, you may ask, makes a novel like *Eclipse* a Neuromantic novel in a *literary* sense?

Well, for one thing most of the characters in *Eclipse*, at any rate most of the sympathetic ones, derive from the same marginal underbelly of high-tech society we see in *Neuromancer*, and Shirley's overall stylistic sensibility is even more self-consciously streetwise than Gibson's, punker than the Pope, as it were.

But here we see this punk sensibility applied to very subtle and sophisticated political analysis, so that if we accept political science as a science, *Eclipse* is a hard science fiction novel quite literally with a vengeance.

More to the current point, perhaps, while there is plenty of conventional combat and action in *Eclipse*, the key arena of the struggle between the forces of religious-corporate fascism and the amorphous resistance is what Shirley calls the Grid, the international media net that permeates the planet. The fascist forces use it subliminally and subtly. Soviet society simply cannot cope with its existence. The resistance fights to gain a measure of access. The point being that what is perceived via our extended electronic senses has more psychic reality than actual events in the so-called real world and hence *determines* political reality more certainly than the outcome of physical combat.

At the climax of *Eclipse* (alas, it *is* the first book of a trilogy), the fascist SA forces literally crunch the Arc de Triomphe, the ultimate symbol of the resistance, under the treads of their juggernaut. But Rickenharp, rock musician resistance fighter, has occupied the top of the arch with instruments, microphones, and amplifiers, and his final performance unto death before the world via the Grid transmutes the fact of the fascist triumph into a symbolic apotheosis of resistance, and Shirley makes you believe it.

This is about as romantic as the Neuromantics (read New Romantics) can get, and it is entirely appropriate that the technological instrumentalities of this triumph of symbol over raw physical reality are the microphones, amplifiers, and electric guitar of rock and roll.

Eclipse may be more of a cyberpunk novel than a full-blown Neuromantic work, in that the hard science content is marginal, but the absolute thematic centrality of rock and roll to its climax is critical to a kind of Ur-Neuromantic core sensibility. For Rickenharp's triumph at the end is a *cyborged* triumph made possible at all only through the electronic augmentation of his fleshly musical powers, and what it demonstrates in words of one syllable is that cyborgs, romantic cyborgs, *Neuromantic* cyborgs, have in fact been using technological augments for transcendental purposes ever since Dylan picked up that electric guitar. When it comes to the characteristic music of our times, we have all been accepting Neuromanticism as a given for a quarter of a century.

And *Eclipse* does one more thing. Rickenharp is a devotee of a drug called blue mesc, and it is shown to enhance his musical creativity, though not without psychic cost. Throughout the book Shirley draws the connection between electronic amplifications and alterations of the naturally evolved human being and chemical amplifications of same, reminding us of something else that we already know, that chemical alteration of consciousness is technology too, that it already permeates our culture, and that it is no accident that drugs and rock are so intimately intertwined. Electronic amplification and consciousness-altering drugs have *already* changed the parameters of the human sensorium, and altered, thereby, our perceptual and psychic definitions of what it means to be human.

Other Neuromantics carry the technological alteration of our definitions of humanity much further, and indeed it is precisely the *acceptance* of the technological evolution and alteration of our definition of our humanity, the *romantic* acceptance of the technological alteration of the species, rather than the more traditional posture of cautionary warnings against the dangers of same, that ultimately defines the Neuromantic sensibility, and defines it in terms far broader and deeper than the title of Bruce Sterling's Movement anthology *Mirrorshades*.

Greg Bear, who wouldn't be caught dead in black leather and mirror shades, wondered aloud what a square hard science type like himself was doing up there on a panel with these cyberpunks in Austin. He then unwittingly answered his own question when he rather stunned all present, including yours truly, with the most radical Neuromantic statement uttered during the whole proceedings.

"How many of you think people will look recognizably human fifty years from now?" he asked the audience.

A forest of hands.

"You're all wrong," Bear declared with his usual calm geniality.

In the short-story version of Bear's "Blood Music," an experiment with biochips, that is with using DNA as read-write computer memory, goes awry. The altered molecules become *sapient*, that is, consciousness descends to the pre-cellular level. These "noocytes" spread like a plague and infect the human populace. People evolve (or devolve, depending on your point of view) into colonial organisms, each molecule of which is possessed of human-level intelligence. The noocytes end up dissolving the human forms into their constituent molecules, and humanity disappears, replaced entirely by the new form of intelligent life. Something of a scientific horror story.

But somehow, in the process of turning the short story into the novel *Blood Music*, Bear turned around philosophically and transformed himself into a Neuromantic. While the short story ends with the replacement of humanity by the noocytes, the novel goes on to explore the new world the noocytes make. The personalities of the vanished humans are replicated, multiplied, and stored on the noocyte level; they are treasured by the noocytes as obsolete but revered ancestors, achieving a kind of multiplexed immortality, among other things. We see the intelligence of a slightly retarded girl amplified by the translation of her personality to the "Noosphere." And the Noosphere itself becomes a kind of transcendent software reality, a realm of illusion, perhaps, but also a higher state of being, ultimately detaching itself from the physical universe in a mystical apotheosis.

In the novel, Bear's attitude towards this supersession of humanity as we know it by this higher form of sapience, indeed this higher form of spirit, is approving, positive, romantic, *Neuromantic* in the extreme, for here we have an ultimate expression of the fusion of hard science and romantic transcendentalism, the transcendence of the physical universe itself through the instrumentality of science and technology.

But even *Blood Music* is not quite *the* currently ultimate expression of the Neuromantic enthusiasm for mutagenic technology. While Bear brings human evolution to a convergent, transcendent endpoint in which human form is subsumed by a higher consciousness, which then transcends the physical universe, this is a notion with plenty of antecedents, ranging from the works of Olaf Stapledon to Arthur C. Clarke's *Childhood's End*, to, for that matter, Hindu and Buddhist scriptures.

But Bruce Sterling's novel *Schismatrix* does something quite different and in its way even more radically disturbing to our cozy definitions of humanity.

Schismatrix is the somewhat picaresque story of diplomat and "sundog" (a kind of footloose, high-level space hobo) Abelard Lindsay's wanderings through the space and history of the solar system. From circumlunar space colony, to the asteroid belt, to the outer satellites, Lindsay meanders and machinates through a series of entirely artificial environments, conveniently giving the reader interior access to a long stretch of history in the process.

The historical dynamic of Sterling's solar system is the long, sometimes hostile, sometimes interpenetrating, dialectic between the Mechs and the Shapers. The Mechs are devotees of the arts and sciences of cyborging humans, and the Shapers are genetic engineers and biological transformers. Their endless conflicts are occasionally military, but mostly economic, diplomatic, technological, and esthetic, and as the fortunes of either side wax and wane, waves of defectors and refugees, including Lindsay, pass back and forth between them.

What finally begins to emerge out of all this is the Schismatrix of the title, a solar system of bewildering human complexity, in which the key concepts are *post-humanism* and *moving in clades*.

Post-humanism is basically the situation that evolves in the Schismatrix after decades of genetic engineering, cyborging, cloning, and combinations of the two lines of species-altering technology. The original human form has been so diversely transmogrified by these technologies that it persists mainly in a circumlunar colony set up as a kind of nature preserve.

Alteration of the human body by technology has been viewed as less than horrific before, notably by John Varley, in many of whose stories and novels people change sexes as casually as they would go to the hairdresser, and in Delany's *Nova*, where people have bizarre cosmetic surgery.

But Sterling's "Post-humanists" go much further. Both the Mechs and the Shapers who merge into the "Post-humanism" of the eventual Schismatrix have always agreed that the human form should be mutated technologically; their whole long struggle concerned only *how*. And the Post-humanist answer ultimately satisfies both of them—by any means convenient, to anything the heart desires.

And the concept of moving in clades takes it one radical step further.

Moving in clades is the current most extreme statement of the Neuromantic concept of human evolution through science and technology. Bear has humanity evolve first into a *singular* post-human physical form and then to a transcedence of the physical universe. But Sterling introduces the concept of evolutionary *multiplexity* through technology.

Evolution, chez Sterling, moves in clades or daughter species; it does not move linearly, it *radiates*. Successful species do not evolve in a straight line into a *single* daughter species, they radiate into a *multitude* of successor species.

The fully developed Schismatrix contains a vast complexity of post-human species, all the product, not of natural selection, but of technological development. "Lobsters" so cyborged into their spacesuits that they abhor atmospheres. Humans biologically adapted to methane oceans. Even an entire space colony whose interior structure is the altered protoplasm of a single woman, Lindsay's sometime lover, who retains her human personality.

Schismatrix is a thoroughgoing hard science fiction novel, in that all the scientific and technological extrapolation and all the descriptions of space habitats (and there certainly are plenty of both) are executed with a rigor and attention to detail of which a Heinlein, Niven, or even Benford could be proud, and then some. But while the prose follows the straightforward transparent line we have come to expect from the hard science mode, Sterling uses it to ground his novel with equal attention to psychological depth and details. The characters, Lindsay in particular, no matter how weird their physiognomies become, are believably human on a psychological level.

And that, perhaps, is what makes *Schismatrix* even more radical and distrubing than *Blood Music*. Whereas Bear's singular daughter species, the Noosphere, is a mystical transcendent endpoint with precedents in Stapledon, Clarke, and perhaps most directly Teilhard de Chardin, and one that ultimately confronts primarily our spiritual definition of humanity, Sterling's nontranscendental rendering of the relatively ordinary and indisputably human psyches of all these physically transmogrified human clades forces us to confront the inevitable alteration of our *body images* by science and technology.

Strangely enough, it is Sterling, not Bear, at least at this juncture, who has gone furthest in the Neuromantic direction proposed by Bear in Austin. For the people in *Schismatrix*, or more properly the peoples, while rendered as our psychic brothers and sisters, are, physically speaking, anything bur recognizably human.

Through science and technology, we will meet the aliens, and they will be us.

Only at the very end does Sterling lapse into a somewhat vague transcendental denouement at variance with the hard-edged structure he has so carefully constructed, bringing Lindsay to an evolutionary endpoint in which we, and perhaps the author himself, cannot quite believe. For the whole thrust of the novel has been that there *is* no endpoint to the evolution of our species through science and technology, only an endless process of radiation.

Thus, perhaps, do the Neuromantics themselves shrink back, at least at this stage, from the ultimate consequences of their explorations of the frontiers of technologically based human evolution. Beyond this point, perhaps, even the visionaries of our species are not yet equipped to travel.

Evolution moves in clades. So does science fiction. Perhaps there will always be a point beyond which further explorations must be left to daughter species.

Dreams of Space

The French critic Michel Butor once suggested quite seriously (or at least in perfect deadpan) that science fiction writers get together, agree on a desirable consensus future, and then, by setting all their stories and novels in this collective dreamworld, imprint it upon the public consciousness and thereby call it into being.

It seemed rather silly at the time, though, in a sense, the flip side had long been practiced in the Soviet Union under the esthetic rubric of Socialist Realism.

There, instead of *writers* getting together to agree on a consensus future, the parameters of that future were supplied by the Communist Party, and anything that violated them too egregiously, anything that might tend to warp the collective dreamworld of the masses beyond the theoretical bounds of official Marxist reality, was simply not published. Soviet science fiction writers certainly do not set all their stories in the same consistent future, but they are forced to set all their stories in futures that are consistently Soviet, which is to say, at least not *inconsistent* with the long-range utopian goals of Party ideology.

We in the West may shake our heads ruefully at the constraints under which our Soviet colleagues must labor, for while science fiction extolling the virtues of Communism or the USSR may not exactly be overflowing our racks, works critical of our own society and its official reality certainly are, and their authors do not find themselves chopping rocks in a gulag—at least, not yet.

On the other hand, a certain "Butorism" *has* crept into American science fiction over the past decade or so. It all seems to have begun with Gerard O'Neil.

O'Neil, of course, is the Princeton professor who set his students the task of designing a space colony and ended up so convinced of the result's practical viability that he became dedicated to getting the "L-5 colony" built.

By now, the L-5 colony concept is probably understood in considerable detail by just about anyone who reads much science fiction and by many people who do not. A large cylindrical canister, perhaps ten miles long, stabilized at Lagrange Point 5, one of the gravitationally stable libration points between the Earth and the Moon, where it would maintain a fixed position in relationship to both bodies. Rotated about its long axis to supply artificial gravity. Powered by solar collectors. Supplied with a self-contained, more or less closed ecology. Built out of lunar material flung up to the vicinity of the L-5 point by a "mass-driver" or monster "rail gun" driven by a nuclear reactor. An artificial world with the population of a major city.

Needless to say, most of the L-5 colony concept had been anticipated in science fiction. Space stations had long been a staple of the genre. The huge self-contained artificial world, at least in terms of the powered "generation ship," is a concept at least as old as Robert A. Heinlein's "Universe." Putting the thing at an Earth-Moon libration point instead of in a conventional orbit about an astronomical body may be new, but it was foreshadowed by George O. Smith's "Venus Equilateral" series, in which a space station is placed in stable position at a Venusian Trojan point. Even the lunar mass driver and its economic and political consequences were described in great detail in Heinlein's *The Moon Is a Harsh Mistress*.

In a sense then, O'Neil's L-5 concept was cobbled together out of decades' worth of science fictional space colonies, or to put it another way, decades' worth of science fiction had explored so many possible variations on this piece of macrotechnology, that just about anything O'Neil could have come up with would have been anticipated somewhere in the literature, itself, just as Project Apollo, though long anticipated by science fiction in its generality and scattered detail, never quite appeared in the literature in its actual nuts and bolts and systems form.

And when the L-5 Society was founded as a lobbying group whose political goal was to get a space colony actually built, a strange new thing began to happen.

The dream of space has always been thematically central to American science fiction, and more, dear to the hearts of most of the people who wrote and read in as a vision of the future much to be desired in the real world. Science fiction, in point of actual fact if not by theoretical definition, could hardly be science fiction without it. If there is one collective value held by the science fiction community as a whole, it is a belief in our destiny as a space-faring species.

But of course far from agreeing on a consensus future in space and setting all these stories and novels in it, science fiction writers followed their own individual stars and created not a collective dream but a rich profusion of alternate futures and multiplex realities.

This view of "the future" as a multiplexity of possibilities, rather than a collective dream castle awaiting only its construction to be moved into, is of course science fiction's greatest strength as a visionary literature, without which it would long since have devolved into its own didactic version of Socialist Realism.

Nor did science fiction's refusal to champion a collective prescription for a space program vitiate its successful social role as a major spiritual and even mystical inspiration of Project Apollo.

For while science fiction never did predict the details of Project Apollo, let alone champion anything so apparently ludicrous as going to the Moon via brute-force rocketry directly from the surface of the Earth without building an orbital space station first, many were the astronauts and space scientists whose careers were set in motion by its multiple visions of space-faring futures.

But many science fiction writers supported the goal of the L-5 Society, some were active in the organization itself, and science fiction fandom, of course, was the most fertile ground for space lobby recruitment.

Space lobbyists became part of the SF convention scene, the L-5 proposal became a popular panel item and topic of barroom conversation, and while M. Butor's proposal was never to my knowledge seriously advanced, he would no doubt have smiled contentedly at what evolved out of this general process.

The L-5 Colony became a collective consensus image.

The science fiction genre had evolved plenty of consensus images before. The interplanetary rocket. The robot. The wheel-shaped space station. Hyperdrive. The ray gun. Hive mind. The list, though not endless, is quite extensive.

But never before had a specific engineering proposal injected itself like a virus into the species DNA of the genre, replicating itself in stories by many writers. Instead of frontier technology mirroring science fiction, science fiction was emulating and promoting the program of the L-5 Society.

L-5 colonies abounded in stories and novels, and they were called just that, when they were not called O'Neil Colonies. The place of Gerard O'Neil himself in future history became a given. Generally speaking, these fictional L-5 colonies were all very much like each other, and were all pretty much as described by O'Neil.

Was this merely a matter of science fiction writers' staying au courant with space science and adopting the L-5 design as the obvious form of the large space colony?

Perhaps a certain intellectual laziness was indeed involved. It was easier to do a quick rewrite of O'Neil's detailed description than to reinvent the wheel from scratch. But on careful retrospective consideration, the L-5 design is far from the optimum inevitable in space colony design.

For one thing, living around the interior circumference of a huge spinning cylinder in order to enjoy Earth-normal gravity means that most of the enclosed volume of your colony is useless empty space.

For another, I took considerable ribbing as a science fiction writer on the subject of "artificial gravity" from astronaut Wally Shirra at the Global Vision seminar in Tokyo.

Centrifugal force is *not* the same thing as artificial gravity because your head is rotating somewhat slower than your feet and subject therefore to the Coriolis force, Shirra pointed out. And if you think the effect is negligible, try some of the actual experiments I took part in and find your sense of balance quite destroyed.

The shorter the axis of rotation, the greater the gut-wrenching effect; the greater the length of the moment arm, the closer centrifugal "gravity" approaches the real thing. Therefore, in terms of both geometrically efficient enclosure of *usable* space and achieving maximum rotation diameter with minimal mass, the good old wheel-shaped space station makes more sense than the cylindrical L-5 colony. Two discs tethered together by a kilometers-long cable and rotating about a common center makes even more sense.

As with Project Apollo, all those old SF stories were right and the engineering designs were wrong.

Why then did the L-5 colony achieve, at least for a time, the status of a consensus image a la M. Butor?

Precisely, I believe, for M. Butor's reason.

A future for the human race in space had long been the central collective dream of science fiction. Project Apollo had validated the vision and given science fiction writers a perhaps exaggerated sense of their ability to propel the national psyche towards its destiny in space. But Project Apollo had been a false first step, not our vision at all, and it had turned out to be a dead end in terms of our expansion into space.

The L-5 proposal, however, whatever its possible design flaws, had real-world plausibility. Here was a developer's detailed blueprint for a city in space that could be built without real technological breakthroughs, a dream castle that those already born might expect to be able to move into. Timothy Leary even concocted a perhaps sardonic scheme to finance the building of the space development by pre-selling lots inside it.

Then too, this was the first time that the science fiction community had been subject to real lobbying, lobbying for a cause, at least in general, to which it had long since already been converted.

The Butorism seemed relatively subtle. Readers were mercifully spared a flood of science fictional Socialist Realism depicting the heroic struggle of the scientists, workers, and SF fans to build utopia in space. Comparatively few of the stories and novels directly *concerned* the construction of an L-5 colony. Writers simply tended to write in O'Neil's projected artifact whenever the tale called for a colony in space. It was as innocent as the time-honored employment of "Tuckerisms," the injection of names or persons of real SF figures into fictional futures.

Or was it?

In retrospect, as we shall soon see, maybe not.

For as science fiction writers began to use the L-5 colony as a consensus setting, a kind of thematic consensus began to accrete around the artifact, a collective vision of the future of the solar system at least halfway to becoming an ideology.

Indeed, in certain quarters, that ideology was preexistent. The American myth of the frontier is older than American science fiction, and long before the L-5 concept was even a gleam in O'Neil's eye, it had been moved to the Asteroid Belt by science fiction writers of a laissez-faire libertarian bent.

The asteroids (colonial America or the Old West) were seen as the free frontier, the future of economic (and sometimes political) freedom, colonized by rugged individualists who were usually fighting for economic and/or political independence from wicked, degenerate, collectivist, played-out Earth (old Europe or the effete East). Out there in the Belt, with its limitless mineral resources, its low gravity, and its wide-open spaces, was the future of the species, and as for poor old polluted, overpopulated, screwed-up Earth, well, tough shit.

In part, this myth of the Free Asteroids served as a venue for laissez-faire libertarian political fables, but it was also in part a reflection of a certain viewpoint within the SF community, the one that divides the species into free-thinking, future-oriented SF fans (the Belters of the free frontier) and "mundanes," the rest of humanity (poor played-out old Earth).

Not all of this stuff had a right-wing political message, and not all of it limited the frontier to the Asteroid Belt, but all of it displayed much the same attitude towards Earth and what it stood for. Poor old Earth was unsalvageable and at best must be left to stew in its own juices while the best and the brightest headed in the direction of Pluto. In John Varley's *The Ophiuchi Hotline* and related stories collected in *The Persistence of Vision*—by no means laissez-faire screeds—powerful aliens have evicted humanity from Earth and forced the species to make its way as best it can in the solar suburbs.

The advent of the L-5 proposal and the lobbying efforts of the L-5 Society within the SF community pushed these tendencies to their logical extremes.

The L-5 colony would be built with material from beyond Earth's gravity well. It would have its own self-contained ecology and draw its energy from the sun. It would be a brand new world entire, a new start, fashioned entirely by the hand of man, completely self-sufficient, a society independent not only from Earth but from reliance upon the resources of any planetary surface, from geology, weather, the natural realm itself.

"Planetary chauvinism" became a buzzword, meaning that the future of the species lay in self-created artificial worlds, that while the mundanes were left to stew in their own self-created mess on Earth, star-faring man would conquer not so much other planets as the tabula rasa of space itself. In his novelette *Tricentennial* and his novel trilogy aptly titled *Worlds*, Joe Haldeman fits propulsion systems on his space habitats and sends them towards the stars, artificial worlds independent of even the sun itself.

What was more, what was *much* more, SF writers and readers felt that this was a dream world they could actually build for themselves precisely as Michel Butor suggested. Detailed engineering plans for the L-5 colony existed; given the money and political commitment, it could be built well within the lifetimes of those now living; a lobbying effort to build a constituency for the funding was already under way; science fiction had helped inspire Project Apollo, and so, if the SF community, if SF writers, did their bit, why, we might actually get to *live* in our collective vision, we might actually be able to leave the mundacity of Earth and move into our dream castle in space, become the heroes and heroines of our own science fiction stories.

Had the collective image of the L-5 colony merely been adopted as a convenient hardware convention within which to explore the diverse possibilities of social and political evolution that might take place in such independent enclosed pocket universes, the genre might have suffered no worse than a certain circumscription of technological extrapolation in the service of its collective idealism.

But fiction, even science fiction, is not written in a political and social vacuum, and in the 1970s and early 1980s, when the bulk of this stuff was being written, America was sliding into economic decline, the prosperous middle class was under financial and social pressure, and the collective utopian dream of the L-5 colony reflected the longings of the beleaguered middle class.

There was a sameness to most of these L-5 colonies, a sameness of more than technological framework, a sameness mirrored nicely in the title of Sumtow Sucharitkul's Mallworld series, a uniformity of social vision epitomized, with weird appropriateness, by the closed society of *Todos Santos*, the huge self-contained habitat in *Oath of Fealty* by Larry Niven and Jerry Pournelle.

Weird because *Todos Santos* is not an L-5 colony, but a kind of Festung Los Angeles, a giant self-contained suburb-cum-fortress plunked down in the festering midst of a socially, politically, and economically degenerate future L.A., Mallworld with a vengeance. Appropriate because *Oath of Fealty* quite openly and with sophisticated political consciousness depicts the middle-class vision of beleaguered technocratic utopia surrounded by lumpen-proletarian social degeneracy that other writers placed in outer space.

It's all there in words of one syllable. *Todos Santos* is bright and clean and shiny and technologically up to date. It is a corporate utopia run with tight but unobtrusive security by dedicated technocrats. It is entirely self-contained, a pocket universe that, if fitted with artificial gravity and a life-support system and boosted out of the gravity well, would be rather indistinguishable from a space colony. No slums. No sleazy red-light districts. Openly designed as a safe, secure, rather antiseptic middle-class fortress. Even the name, Spanish for "All Saints," declares that lesser social beings need not apply.

Thus the outcome of this stage of science fiction's affair with Butorism—a collective vision of bright, clean, ecologically, economically, and socially self-contained technocratic, middle-class suburbs in space, with no poor people, no street gange, no cockroaches, and no dogshit on the streets. Vast spanking shopping malls and neat housing developments and not even freeway gridlock between. Floating airily unconcerned above a Third World favella called Earth.

> "The street finds it own uses for technology."
>
> —William Gibson

> "If you want to imagine what an L-5 Colony would *really* be like, picture a Worldcon in a submarine forever."
>
> —Norman Spinrad

Then came the cyberpunks.

While much has been written about the central cyberpunk ethos and about the paraphernalia of "cyberspace," "wetware," "implants," and "interfaces," including some by yours truly, no one, including yours truly, seems to have noticed something rather important that so-called cyberpunks like William Gibson, Bruce Sterling, and John Shirley share with their supposed antitheses, the so-called humanists like Kim Stanley Robinson, Michael Swanwick, and John Varley—a new collective vision of space colonization quite different from that of the L-5 enthusiasts.

I have before me eight rather recent novels—*The Memory of Whiteness* and *Icehenge* by Kim Stanley Robinson, *Eclipse* by John Shirley, *Voice of the Whirlwind* by Walter Jon Williams, *Neuromancer* and *Count Zero* by William Gibson, *Schismatrix* by Bruce Sterling, and *Vacuum Flowers* by Michael Swanwick—all of which, viewed together, converge on quite a new conception of space colonization.

Sterling, Shirley, and Gibson are card-carrying cyberpunks (though Gibson has lately tried to burn his), Williams is writing in a similar mode, Robinson and Swanwick probably wouldn't be caught dead in mirror shades. Yet all of these novels are set in somewhat different versions of the same solar system, and somehow, Toto, I don't think we're in Mallworld, let alone *Todos Santos*.

All of these works are set a century or three in the future. In most of them, the action wanders about a thoroughly colonized solar system. Gibson, Williams, and Swanwick emphasize artificial habitats; Robinson places a bit more emphasis on asteroids and satellites; and Shirley sets most of the action on Earth, but in all of these books, the terraformed surfaces of major planets do not hold the bulk of humanity's extraterrestrial population.

In some of these novels, the solar system is a patchwork of independent states, in some a patchwork of corporate fiefdoms, in others a complex political melange of both, but in *none* of them does a system-wide government of any coherent sort prevail, nor does Earth dominate its far-flung sons and daughters.

Indeed, in most of these novels, Earth is either a backwater, a degenerate mess, a corporate battleground, or, in the case of *Vacuum Flowers*, even the homeland of a hive mind hostile to space-going man. In most of these novels, Earth's gravity well is something to escape from, and most of the characters would prefer to live in a low- or zero-g environment, rather than reproduce a one-g field artificially.

Who wrote what first and who influenced whom could be the subject of endless inconclusive debate, since all of these books were published within a four-year span, and what with variable publishing lead-times, there's really no way of knowing who had already read what when they sat down to produce their own novels.

Of late, certain of the cyberpunks have been complaining that the purity of the Movement has been compromised by derivative work, and one can certainly see the influence of Gibson on Williams, and particularly of Sterling's *Schismatrix* on Swanwick's *Vacuum Flowers*. But on the other hand, Swanwick was beginning to work this area in novelette form before *Neuromancer* or *Schismatrix* was published, and the novellas that Robinson cobbled together into *Icehenge* predate them too.

Furthermore, aside from the shared vision of space, these are very different books by very different writers.

Eclipse is a forthrightly antifascist novel set mainly on Earth and intimately involved with rock and roll.

The Memory of Whiteness and *Icehenge* bop around the solar system; the latter is concerned with how lengthened life span affects character, and the former, while thematically centered on music, is concerned with the classical variety and its relationship to metaphysics.

Count Zero is a sequel to *Neuromancer*, and its focus is on Gibson's "Cyberspace." *Voice of the Whirlwind* is also supposed to be a sequel, to Williams' *Hardwired*, but this seems to be mostly a marketing ploy, since it is set further in the future, moves off the surface of the Earth, and includes no repeat characters or even references to same.

Schismatrix and *Vacuum Flowers* are the most similar to each other in terms of setting and straightforward style (and neither of them has what one could rationally call a punk sensibility), but the former is centered on the radiation of humanity into biologically disparate but psychically rather similar daughter species, whereas the latter leaves the human form more or less as is but rings complex changes on the very concepts of "personality," "identity," and "being."

So in terms of style, theme, focus, politics, and esthetics, these novels are about as similar as say, *Dr. Strangelove, Bug Jack Barron, The Handmaid's Tale, Fail-Safe*, and *On Wings of Song*, all of which are set in the United States in the relatively near future.

But since *their* similar future venues are all entirely imaginary, they reflect not extrapolation from a shared real political geography but the outline of a new emerging collective vision of the human future in space, an alternative Butorism that seems to be gaining ascendancy within the genre.

In all of them, the action takes place at least in part in artificial space habitats in the next two or three centuries, and what they have in common is first, the politically balkanized solar system in which these space habitats exist, and second, and most central to the present discussion, the nature of the space habitats themselves.

These space colonies are emphatically *not* spanking clean Mall-worlds; well-run, technocratic, middle-class bastions in space, a la the collective vision inspired by Gerard O'Neil and the L-5 movement.

The one space habitat that Shirley shows us has a rigid class structure, a prerevolutionary atmosphere, and all the neat, clean, well-maintained, middle-class stability of Jersey City or Beirut. Gibson extends his corporately balkanized Earthside culture seamlessly into space, along with its streetwise outlaw underbelly, and Williams does something similar.

Robinson seems to be painting a superficially different picture. His solar system is thoroughly colonized and politically balkanized too, and what he gives us are no middle-class housing developments in space either, but *Icehenge* and particularly *The Memory of Whiteness* present a more positive and prosperous vision, economically and especially esthetically, a richly complex and baroque version of solar man, more like the worlds of Jack Vance or the Second Starfaring Age of *The Void Captain's Tale* and *Child of Fortune* than the decaying space city of Shirley or Gibson's corporate social Darwinism, perfectly epitomized by the baroque musical style at the thematic core of *The Memory of Whiteness*.

Swanwick's solar system in *Vacuum Flowers* lies somewhere in between. Once again we have political balkanization and a profusion of space habitats—moons, asteroids, artificial worlds in clusters and clouds, even "dyson worlds" in the Oort Cloud. But while a good many of them are fetid slums, and the majority of them are literally barnacled with the irksome vacuum flowers of the title, and none of them runs with the antiseptic perfection of the ideal L-5 colony, there is room inside for Robinson's high cultural style, too.

And Swanwick's space habitats have a decidedly organic flavor. The vacuum flowers were originally designed to soak up the inevitable leakage of air and garbage for efficient recycling but grew out of control, so that hulls need continual scraping. Giant mutated trees fill the interior spaces of many of them by design, forming complex three-dimensional mazes, forests with winding trails, and unplanned peripatetic villages. These habitats really *are* little worlds in space, with all the chaotic unplanned complexity of living ecologies.

But it is Sterling's *Schismatrix* that was the earliest novel to present this new vision of space in its maximum diversity, it is the only novel to date with this very vision at its thematic center, and because Sterling is the theoretical guru of the Cyberpunk Movement, it is the reason why there have arisen certain complaints that "non-Movement writers" are aping the "true cyberpunks," even though *Schismatrix* is light-years away from Gibson and Shirley in terms of style, sensibility, theme, and superficial trappings.

Once again we have a profusion of diverse artificial worlds and fragmented political complexity, though here the ebb and flow of the fortunes of the two main human factions, the Mechs (cyborgers) and the Shapers (genetic engineers), give the politics a certain overall coherence over the novel's long time-span, while the constant shifting of sides in any given venue and the cross-currents of refugees finally create a melange not merely of cultures but of daughter species so complex that almost any somatic variation is possible.

And that is Sterling's thematic point, a point that may not be central to *Vacuum Flowers* or *Icehenge* or *The Memory of Whiteness*, but that is taken as a given by Robinson and Swanwick in the construction of their settings, and that has even been picked up by Gregory Benford and David Brin in *Heart of the Comet*.

Namely, that given time, technology, and the human impulse toward diversity, the habitats we construct for ourselves in space—be they terraformed comets, asteroids, and moons or new man-made worlds entire—will sooner or later evolve into environments as ecologically complex, politically fragmented, and recomplicated as the so-called "natural realm," the mosaic of ecospheres, cultures, social classes, and ways of life we presently see on Earth.

If this new collective vision is a form of Butorism too, it is Butorism of a peculiarly paradoxical sort, different in kind, not merely in specific content, from the earlier version with its cookie-cutter O'Neil colonies, and a vision at least partially extrapolated from a key element of the cyberpunk social ethos. And yet, strangely enough, it also serves to renovate science fiction's hoary romantic vision of our solar system as the venue of the infinite possible.

Way back when the Soviet and American space programs were only gleams in SF's collective eye, in the days of Edgar Rice Burroughs, Leigh Brackett, Jack Vance, Ray Bradbury, C.L. Moore, & Co., the solar system was an Arabian Nights fantasy, replete with dying Martian civilizations, Venusian jungles, space pirates, Elder Races, open-ended sense of wonder, and the promise of the infinite possible in our own stellar backyard.

The pictures and data from real planetary probes banished all these baroque possibilities from our solar system in terms of science fictional plausibility and relegated the wonderful worlds just beyond our gravity well to the far stars, to a literary dreamworld not even our children were likely to reach.

Gerard O'Neil and his L-5 proposal gave us a new vision of our future within the solar system; a reachable, attainable vision of bright, clean, well-ordered artificial worlds in space, an escape from the ecological pollution, resource depletion, poverty, collectivism, and unseemly, unplanned natural chaos of poor old Earth.

But it was a pale shadow of what we seemed to have lost, a middle-class, controlled, relentlessly suburban collective vision of our space-faring future—technocratic, enclosed, antiseptic, socially mean-spirited, reminiscent, somehow, of the bleak unadorned architectural futurism of the Bauhaus school, from which the romantic impulse and the organic sense of cultural ornamentation and social richness had been banished, along with ghettos, underclasses, countercultures, and interesting nightlife—a future in which pallid order reigned triumphant over tasty chaos, Velveeta on Wonderbread, rather than a ripe runny brie messily smeared on crusty pumpernickel.

Cyberpunk was, among other things, a reaction against this well-ordered, denatured, inorganic, white-middle-class, essentially social-fascist vision of the future, of high technology as inherently the property of the ruling power structure, as an instrumentality of social and political control, as the servant of order.

Uh-uh, says Gibson in *Neuromancer* and *Count Zero*. "The street finds its own uses for technology." Nor will technology eliminate the sensibility of the street, of underclasses, ghettos, countercultures, and class struggle, say Shirley in *Eclipse* and Williams in *Hardwired* and *Voice of the Whirlwind*.

And it's not just a matter of street culture, Robinson demonstrates in *Icehenge* and *The Memory of Whiteness*. As technology advances, as we not only move out into the solar system but attain the ability to mold worlds entire to our own desire, our cultures, even on the highest levels, will become *more* baroque, not more simplified, more chaotic in a positive esthetic sense, not more predictably ordered and boring.

Nor must we necessarily lose our oldest source of environmental surprise, recomplication, and unpredictability even in artificial space colonies, as Swanwick demonstrates in *Vacuum Flowers*, to wit, ongoing organic evolution itself. We may genetically engineer the elements of artificial ecosystems, but precisely to the extent that they cohere as self-contained ecosystems, so will they develop the ability to mutate and adapt to the conditions of space habitations in ways we never predicted or intended. Even our designer organisms will find their own uses for technology, as Swanwick's vacuum flowers so puissantly demonstrate.

Indeed, as we see in *Schismatrix*, the advance of technology, the colonization of the solar system, the ability to construct worlds of any idiosyncratic design out of the void itself, and ultimately the power of human consciousness to redesign its own biological matrixes to whim and fashion, will in the end make us both the masters and creations of a new kind of evolution—human-created, faster, more diverse, and infinitely more complex and baroque than anything that has presently come into being on the surface of the Earth.

"The universe is not only stranger than we think, it is stranger than we *can* think," J.B. Priestly once declared.

How wrong he was! The endless diversity of environments we can create in space and the endlessly diverse self-created mutations of humanity we will turn ourselves into when we inhabit them will be stranger and more varied by far than anything in the so-called natural realm.

Thus do the thesis of "cyberpunk" and the antithesis of "humanism" unite in the synthesis of this new "Butorism," science fiction's new collective vision of our *multiplex* futures in space.

Thus too its happy paradox. In a sense, many science fiction writers do seem to be taking Michel Butor's advice. They have come together to create a new collective dream of space. But this collective dream is not a vision of uniformity but of infinitely multiplexed diversity, not of order and control but of chaos and romanticism reborn.

A vision that gives us back the dream of the solar system as an Arabian Nights fantasy of the infinite possible, of marvelous and terrifying lands just beyond Earth's gravity well, ours not merely to conquer but to create. A literary creation achievable not by the willful disregard of the scientific realities but through their imaginative ultilization.

The street finds its own uses for technology.

So does science fiction.

Psychopolitics and Science Fiction: Heroes — True and Otherwise

As we have just seen, science fiction is a literature with a rather complex feedback relationship with the real world. Like all fiction, it mirrors the context in which it is written. But unlike other fiction, it deals with the possible future evolution of the society in which it is written, and so, to one degree or another, influences that society's vision of its future and thereby tends to influence that future evolution itself.

This effect can be one thing when it leads to things like Project Apollo or the exploration of the planets, but it can be something else again when it leads to things like the Manson family or the Strategic Defense Initiative, though of course there are plenty of people who would contend that science fiction's key role in promulgating SDI was a service to the Nation.

Political opinions aside, left, right, and center can perhaps agree on one thing, namely, that science fiction *does* have its effect on society for good or ill, however those terms might be defined. Therefore, we should at least be aware that this effect exists, and perhaps even ponder the social morality of what we are writing.

Much science fiction, indeed much of the best science fiction, openly addresses questions of social morality, but unfortunately the majority of science fiction novels published are action-entertainment formula stuff in which the major moral conflict is simply between the good guys (us) and the bad guys (them), itself a paradigm that does not exactly promote peace and understanding.

There is something deeply disturbing in the congruence between the commercial pulp action-adventure formula and the Übermensch in jackboots, something I have pondered at novel length in *The Iron Dream*, and something I ponder again here from a different perspective.

137

Must There Be War?

Some of us may champion the cause of hard science fiction, others may promulgate the ethos of cyberpunk, and still others may declare that science fiction should be more humanistic or sytlistically inventive or better at characterization, and these Platonic ideals are well worth serious consideration.

But when it comes to describing what has long dominated the science fiction that actually gets written and published in the realm of maya, it is no longer a matter of genteel literary discourse.

For what really dominates on the racks is neither ideational content nor emotionally complex characterization, but rather the rendition of violent action undertaken against physical jeopardy.

This centrality of violent conflict to the mainstream of science fiction is so primordial to the genre, so pervasive, so self-evident, that we hardly even notice it in these terms. But it *is*, after all, what is really meant by such diverse terms as *"action-adventure," "sword and sorcery," "military SF," "galactic conflict," "alien invasion,"* and more often than not, even Hero and Villain, Good versus Evil.

How many science fiction or fantasy novels have you read lately in which no one got punched, shot, stabbed, vaporized, lased, clawed, devoured, or blasted? I'm staring at a great big stack of books right now, and for the life of me, I can't fine *one*.

More than half of them have stories in which violent action dominates in terms of both plot dynamics and word-count. Even the ones that fulfill the ideal of speculative content expressed through the emotional lives of complex characters in morally ambiguous circumstances, like Jack Dann's *The Man Who Melted*, Lisa Goldstein's *The*

Dream Years, and James Tiptree, Jr.'s *Brightness Falls from the Air*, are not exempt from a bit of bovver.

David Brin's *The Postman*, an earnestly Jeffersonian treatise on democratic communal idealism with a bit of guilty male feminism thrown in on the side, still expresses these noble ideals through page after page of detailed description of physical combat.

Gregory Benford's *Artifact* is arguably the most thrilling hard science fiction novel ever written, in that Benford is able to keep the reader on the edge of his chair describing the science itself and the doing of it as well as the best action writers can puissantly describing scenes of mortal combat. But even Benford feels constrained to factor in subplotting that will justify a violent climax.

Most of the rest, good and bad, are structured along plot skeletons with combat of one form or another at the tension peaks, the physical outcome of which serves as story resolution.

Does it begin to seem that I am overstating the obvious?

Then let me overstate another obvious: life ain't like that, kiddo!

Most of the turning points in our lives are not determined by our prowess with fists, guns, swords, or knives. Most of the emotional apexes and nadirs of our existence take place in bed, or at work, or in the presence of great art, or attempting to balance the checkbook, not in physical combat.

I mean, even what fights we do get into are usually random intrusions, which seldom settle a philosophical, cultural, or political point, and which almost never are satoric moments that permamently alter our personalities.

And yet when we read fiction, and not just science fiction by any means, the protagonists with whom we identify are not only regularly involved in combat, but are required to be able to handle themselves like Bruce Lee when the time comes if we are to accept them as exemplars of moral virtue.

How many times does a sympathetic hero get the crap kicked out of him by the villain in a fair fight? Even when the hero takes his lumps as a result of violation of the rules of fair combat by the bad guys, we can generally anticipate with relish a scene in which he punches them out before the tale is over.

But of course life is not like that either. In real life, other factors being equal, a mean psychopathic son of a bitch will usually be able to use a virtuous man as a punching bag in a mano a mano. For he feels no empathy for his victim, he *enjoys* hurting people, he's practiced at it; that's why he's *evil*. Whereas the virtuous man, by definition, fights only when he must, to defend himself or others, and therefore lacks both killer instinct and experience by comparison.

So rarely do we see this unfortunate fact of life rendered realistically in science fiction that it is really striking when someone does it right, as Benford does in *Artifact*. Here mathematician John Bishop, the admirable and sympathetic hero, twice gets beaten up by Colonel Kontos, the thoroughly unpleasant villain, and is even bested, one-on-one, by a woman, without getting to kayo either of them later on. Indeed, even when he has Kontos at machinegunpoint, the proficient colonel manages to disarm him because Bishop hasn't remembered to take his piece off safety.

On the other end of the spectrum, we have Gordon R. Dickson's *The Final Encyclopedia*, an admittedly extreme exemplar of what, in less naked form, is all too common. We know that Hal Mayne is the "hero" of this novel because he and Dickson continually remind us, and because he receives the unquestioned obedience and wide-eyed worship due such a figure by most of the other sympathetic characters most of the time, and, of course, because he's a genius military tactician who can handle his dukes.

But actually, were we to encounter Mr. Mayne in the real world, we would probably deem him an arrogant, high-handed bully and braggart, given to long-winded, self-glorifying rapping; a monster of ego demanding our allegiance to his wonderfulness by divine genetic right.

Clearly then, the level and frequency of physical violence in science fiction, the prevalent equation of moral virtue with fighting skill, the manner in which story outcomes are so often determined by prowess in combat, and indeed the clean dualistic razor edge between good and evil, hero and villain, are so out of sync with the realities of our lives that we cannot be dealing with a plethora of failed attempts at realism.

Moreover, in literary terms, it is quite possible to write good novels, and even masterpieces, that follow these parameters faithfully; while many literary atrocities have been committed in this vein, the action-adventure parameters themselves are not necessarily a foolproof formula for crap.

After all, great writers from Homer onward have used these

parameters to noble effect, and in the SF canon, writers like Bester, Herbert, Moorcock, Dickson, and even Delany have from time to time worked this vein successfully with high literary purpose.

So what may at first glance seem like an embarrassing mass misperception of reality on the part of generations of science fiction writers can sometimes really be something else, namely self-conscious anti-realistic stylization; the adoption of certain literary conventions that the author knows full well do not mirror the quotidian reality of the readers but that instead draw their emotional effectiveness from their manipulation of the readers' inner dream landscapes.

After all, since we all consider ourselves the virtuous heroes of our own stories, we would certainly all *like* to have right make might so that we can give that mugger, or the boss, or the Russians, or any other bully with the nerve to kick sand in our faces, the proper thrashing they so richly deserve.

And while few of us experience daily physical combat, most of us know all too well what it feels like to face fear and frustration and injustice, so we can empathize endocrinely with the hero surrounded by enemies and triumph justly in the pages of a book when he finally kicks their asses as we so seldom do to our persecutors in the mundane world.

In the hands of a cynical hack, these action-adventure parameters can be responsible for pornography of the most obscene species, the masturbatory manipulation not of our sexual arousal, which at worst may result in compulsive onanism, but of our *violent* arousal, which at best results in a catharsis of suppressed rage, and which at worst results in war.

But in the hands of a master, the very same action-adventure morality can be used to write fables, or even archetypal dramas, that, by allowing us to inhabit a more cosmically just universe for the duration, imbue us with the courage to attempt to champion justice in our own.

After all, this *is* the mythic structure of the western, and the samurai film, and the war story, and great swatches of folk myths of numerous cultures, and so too of much of the folk myths of the future we call science fiction.

Dune, after all, is the story of the dispossessed young prince who flees from his mighty enemies into the mystic sea of the people, returning as their god-hero at the head of a popular juggernaut to defeat the forces of evil and become emperor of the known worlds.

No one has ever told this one better than Herbert did in the original *Dune*. It's all there, and in its higher form. Paul's virtue is the product of genetics to an extent; he, like our own dream image of ourselves, is one of destiny's darlings. But when he sheds tears over the man he has just killed in fair combat, he convinces both the Fremen and the reader that he is an exemplar of more complex virtues, a man we may admire for what is in his heart, a true hero in a deeper sense.

And—unlike Perry Rhodan, Feric Jaggar, Mung the Barbarian, or Hal Mayne—Paul Atreides, like Poul Anderson's Dominic Flandry, has a sense of irony about his works and himself. He ends up being Emperor of Everything, but in the process brings on precisely the presciently foreseen jihad he has spent the book trying to prevent. He triumphs over his human enemies, but not over his fated destiny.

It is this masterly telling of the myth we all keep telling ourselves and the moral justice and sophistication that Herbert brings to it that make *Dune* a masterpiece that has sold zillions of copies and has probably inspired the spirit of many successful lives.

It is the absence of Paul as the hero of the readers' spirit from the subsequent installments that makes the rest of the series so dim by comparison.

Lewis Shiner has given us a more modern version in *Frontera*, a well-written first novel in the action-adventure vein, principally set in a lost colony on Mars. *Frontera* rises to literary art, first because several viewpoint characters are rendered with skill and sensitivity as complex people, and second because Kane, the central combat-capable figure, is a poor bastard who's had his head screwed with in various unpleasant ways, so that he is both hero and victim, doing his deeds of derring-do as best he can with a headful of broken glass.

Here we are getting closer to the intersection of myth and reality. Much beyond this point and we are looking at science fiction that *examines* the effect of the myth of the mystic warrior on events in a psychologically realistic world with a somewhat jaundiced eye. Mandela, in Joe Haldeman's *Forever War*, is basically a competent grunt who was drafted into a permanent conflict whose higher political content, such as it is, he views with indifferent contempt. The protagonist of Harry Harrison's *Bill, The Galactic Hero* was conned into enlisting in an imperial army run by mental defectives and time-servers keeping an endless war and their jobs going against the Chingers, fearsome lizard-monsters who turn out to be about eight inches tall. In *The Iron Dream*, I attempted to say it in words of one syllable by making Feric Jaggar the wish-fulfillment alter-ego of a hack SF writer named Adolf Hitler.

Mysterious, isn't it? The dominance of this stylized action-adventure myth in science fiction produces masterpieces like *Dune* that speak to and inspire our noblest spirits, earnest attempts at same like *The Postman*, and at the same time, hundreds of novels in which violent combat lovingly described for its own sake is the unwholesome raison d'etre.

Thus, perhaps, our fascination, both as a species and as science fiction writers, with war.

War is where the dualistic nature of the action-adventure myth intersects with reality. The battlefield is where we regularly commit our most vile atrocities as a species, and yet the battlefield is also a venue of transcendently selfless heroism.

Moreover, while such moral vices as ruthlessness, psychopathy, blind obedience to power, and sadism can be put to telling use as military virtues, such moral virtues as courage, cooperation, and self-sacrifice for the common good are hardly without their military practicality either. Indeed, in the Battle of Britain, the American Revolution, Viet Nam, and endless science fiction novels, they have enabled militarily inferior forces to prevail.

Small wonder then that science fiction, like the species itself, is fascinated with war. The field of combat is both a butchershop of horrors and the arena of courage and honor, for war is what occurs when irreconcilable opposites clash both on the battlefield and within the heart of each of us.

Those of us who have never known combat secretly wonder whether we have missed a human peak experience. Those who have either tend to view their survival through a rosy haze of glory as the time of their lives or are marked by the horror forever, and occasionally both.

So, since war is a central subject of the dreamtime of our species, like it or not, perhaps there is something positive after all to be said for war as a central subject of fiction. Particularly of science fiction.

Most of us, let us hope, will never know combat, and perhaps the fulfillment of that hope will not be so ill-served by science fiction that allows us to contemplate war in all its glory, terror, horror, heroism, and moral complexity without having to risk actually *dying* in one.

Of course I'm not talking about military wet-dream fantasies like *Starship Troopers*, Perry Rhodan, or *Star Wars*, in which righteous ingenues guiltlessly slaughter faceless gunfodder in alien or robot gooksuits. Nor merciless satires of things military like *Bill, The Galactic*

Hero or *The Iron Dream*, though these certainly have their place as warnings for the innocent.

If we are to survive as a species to reach the stars, or even for that matter much past next Tuesday, we are going to have to come to terms with Mars. As Pogo so aptly put it, "We have seen the enemy, and he is us."

As a species, we love war because it is the ultimate drama of life and death, selfless transcendence and egoistic vengeance fantasies, highest heroism and deepest sadism. And in the twentieth century, it is also the cutting edge of wondrous technology, force-fed by grotesque military-industrial banquets at the public trough.

So science fiction that explores this dark conundrum at the heart of our cultures and psyches can certainly be as artistically and morally valid as scientific speculation, sensitive characterization of sensitive characters, or the exploration of civilian political realities, democratic or otherwise.

We have a need as a species for novels like *The Forever War* and *Bill, The Galactic Hero*, which illuminate the sheer assholery of war, and novels like *The Men in the Jungle* and *The Red Magician*, which illuminate the butchery of war, but perhaps we also need novels like *Janissaries* and *Hammer's Slammers* and *Killer* and even the Conan books, which portray the warrior psyche on its own terms.

That much being said, however, it should also be said that what we *don't* need, and what we do have, is the pervasive permeation of the stylized action-adventure combat formula into so many science fiction novels where it does not belong.

For, political morality aside, this leads directly to a prevalent literary vice: the degeneration of sophisticated storytelling into a stylized plot skeleton based on escalating sine waves of tension and release, in which stirring scenes of physical combat at the peak points of the plot replace thematic and personal epiphanies as dramatic resolutions.

In *Killer*, by David Drake, author of high-tech military SF, and Karl Edward Wagner, who comes to the Rome of the tale from sword and sorcery and dark fantasy, we have an honest rendition of what it might have been like for a professional warrior, trying to keep himself covered politically, to confront an alien intruder who is even more ruthless than he is. Lycon and the alien are both the *Killer* of the title, as the denouement bring home in words of one syllable. Believably, Lycon, professional soldier and beast catcher, succeeds through his prowess at the arts he has practiced all his life. Just as believably, he does it by instigating the butchery of an enemy as a tactical diversion.

Lycon is a warrior, but he is a real warrior in a real Rome; he suffers real domestic tragedy; he knows real love, both carnal and paternal; and with his balls to the wall, he is an amoral killing machine.

Killer tells his story with the pain and the sorrow as well as abundant blood and gore. You may not like Lycon by the end, but you will probably come to some empathetic understanding of his viewpoint.

Killer is very much *about* the action-adventure hero and legitimately so, but since its action-adventure hero is a morally ambiguous creature, it becomes in part a meditation on the difference between fantasy heroes and the professionals who really do the dirty work.

Gordon R. Dickson's aforementioned *The Final Encyclopedia*, on the other hand, is what happens when action-loops are almost entirely substituted for story, and philosophical expostulation for character development. Long, boring speeches and didactic, stream-of-consciousness meditations upon destiny and history are more or less regularly relieved by combat sequences that do little to advance the story, possibly because what little story there is to advance ends abruptly in a cliff-hanger after 696 pages.

Good God, Gordon Dickson knows better than this, as he has proven over and over again, and indeed even in most of the previous books of the Dorsai cycle. Dickson has always been able to render his heroes of destiny believable by grounding their virtues in cultural specificity and by the sheer subtlety of his psychological descriptions and portrayals of mystical states. While plenty of battle scenes were often de rigueur, the Dickson hero previously rose to apotheosis along a curve of evolving consciousness, so that the conclusion of a novel of derring-do was also the conclusion of a novel of spiritual development.

Here there is no conclusion; we find at the end that this whole thing has been a set-up for a sequel, and Hal Mayne, the protagonist, is, well, a prick. He's a *parody* of previously three-dimensional Dicksonian heroes. He expects people to follow on pure Fuhrerprincip, on one occasion even airily declaring that an explication of his plan should not be required by true believers. He enlists in various causes and fights for them as long as it serves his own ends, and then he splits to the next gig in medias res.

As a portrait of egoistic swinishness, Mayne might have achieved three-dimensionality, but the people in the novel pop to, click their heels, and acknowledge his wonderfulness.

What happened here?

What seems to have happened here is that Gordon Dickson had a long series of speculative philosophical and political theories he wished to explicate in a novel. What he did not have was a story. So what he did was construct a cardboard character who exemplified and proclaimed the thematic material at exhaustive length, in dialogue, stream of consciousness, and author exposition, and ran him through a series of standard combat scenes in a problematic attempt to hold the reader's attention.

The first section of *The Final Encyclopedia*, where the young Mayne is exiled for years on a mining planet, is vintage Dickson; the boy grows through adolescence to manhood under extreme and outré pressures, but once Mayne's maturity is attained and he marches off into the action-adventure formula, spouting somewhat inchoate profundities, it is as if another writer took over, one with not half of Gordon Dickson's skills.

Dickson, it would appear, was primarily concerned in this one with summing up a vast social historic schema he had been following in many books, to bring this cycle to a valedictory conclusion, to create a masterpiece that would express his grandest visions on the grandest scale.

Like others before him, he may have become so enthused with his philosophy that he failed to notice that he had not crafted a story to exemplify it, and so he contented himself with stringing his lectures along the old action-adventure plot skeleton.

Let *The Final Encyclopedia* serve as a warning to all science fiction writers, for potentially, we all have a book like this in us, the novel that will lay out the full brilliance of our thought in exhaustive detail, and the better the writers we are, the more tempting it is to try and write it. Moreover, consciously or not, we observe our colleagues getting away with formula action-adventure manipulations instead of story, without even attempting our depth of philosophical thought.

Surely, we can therefore stop waiting for this mother lode of wisdom magically to cohere into a proper story with complex characters which will render it self-evident, and get on with enlightening the world by sugar-coating the symposium with well-written action-sequences.

Surely, we had better not.

Surely, we should realize that this impulse means we've *really* gone over the top. For when our philosophies take over to the point where they lose their grounding in the psychological complexities and moral ambiguities of the human heart, when we are so convinced of the wisdom of our insights that we seek to impose them by literary main force, why then, we ourselves are behaving just like the righteous mighty warriors we tend to create under the influence.

Just like all the heroes of the One True Way who from time out of mind have led us into the gory glory of war.

Emperor of Everything

Don't stop me if you've read this one before, because if you do, about half the science fiction and about two-thirds of the fantasy on the racks will disappear in a flash of ectoplasm.

Our story begins out on the edge of civilization, where a seemingly ordinary youth is undergoing the alienated travails of adolescent angst. Unbeknownst to the bumpkins around him (and perhaps to himself), he is in fact the exiled rightful heir to the throne of Empire, or a closet mutant superman, or possessed of dormant magical powers, or one hell of a cyberwizard, or maybe just a natural .400 hitter with the double-edged broadsword.

But the Dark Forces are ascendant, a climactic Armageddon between Good and Evil is building, and our hero-in-hiding is destined by genes or bloodline or plotline imperatives to become the champion of the Armies of the Light. Sinister characters are sniffing around Podunk after him, and maybe come close to snuffing him by the end of chapter one.

'Long about now, a stranger from the central worlds shows up, possessed of advanced knowledge, a sense of political history, and a mission to seek out Destiny's Darling, inform him of his birthright, and train him up to take on Darth Vader for the heavyweight championship of the universe.

Thus begins our hero's wandering education under Merlin the Mutant, developing his full powers on a tank-town tour of the galaxy as he fights his way out of the boonies on a slow spiral trajectory inward towards the Seat of Empire.

Along the way he is spurned by the Princess, accretes a colorful satellite system of doughty lieutenants and top sergeants, puts together a People's Army, saves the Princess from a fate worse than Gor, winning her love in the process, then reveals to her his Secret Identity as the rightful Emperor of Everything, and converts her to his cause.

The People's Army battles its way to Rome, and fights its way through toward the Presidential Palace for about 60 pages of heavy-duty derring-do. But the Dark Lord ain't the Master of Evil for nothin', kiddo. He slips a horseshoe in one glove and a neural disrupter in the other, and he and the hero go fifteen founds, mano a mano, for the fate of the universe.

Well Uncle Ugly he ain't never heard of the Marquis of Queensbury and he's got the ref on the pad, and so our boy takes his lumps for about fourteen rounds, two minutes, and forty seconds. Black Bart is way ahead on all the judges' scorecards and he's about to kayo the White Light Kid anyway, so it looks like creation is in for a million years of red-hot claws.

But just as he's down and about to go out for the count, his magic powers surface, the Princess blows him a kiss, Obi Wan Kenobi reminds him that the Force is with him, his mutant intellect allows him to slap together a particle-beam pistol out of toothpicks and paperclips, and a lowly spear-carrier whose life he once saved shoots him up with about 100 mg of sacred speed.

He rises from the canvas at the count of nine, delivers a stirring peroration. "Hey bozo," he tells the Ultimate Villain, "yer shoelace is untied." As Ming the Merciless looks down to check it out, the Hero of the People lands a haymaker that knocks him clean out of the ring, out of the novel, and into the next book in the series.

Good triumphs over Evil, justice prevails, the hero marries the Princess and becomes Emperor of Everything, and everyone lives happily ever after, or anyway till it's time to grind out the sequel.

Sounds familiar, doesn't it? The SF racks are groaning under the leaden weight of these cloned "epic sagas of the struggle between Good and Evil," these "mighty heroes" in skintight space suits and brass-bound jockstraps, these "stirring action-adventure tales." With a decent find-and-replace program in your computer, the above can serve as a marketing outline for the majority of SF published, and probably has.

If there could be such a thing as a foolproof formula for crud, this would be it. This is the time-honored equation for the commercial SF plot skeleton with all the variables cranked up to their theoretical limits.

The identification figure isn't just a sympathetic hero, he's the ultimate wank fantasy, the reader as rightful Emperor of the Universe, indeed as the Godhead. The stakes are nothing less than human destiny for all time, and the Princess to win is always the number one piece of ass in the galaxy. The villain is as close to Satan as you can come without awarding both horns and the tail, twirling his black moustache as he feasts on the torment of the downtrodden masses, performs unspeakably vile sex acts, and squashes cute little mammals in wine glasses so he can drink the blood.

Ah, but there is no such thing as a *foolproof* formula for crud, not even the outline of *The Emperor of Everything*. For while it is certainly true that the diligent application of this formula has allowed armies of hacks to pile up mile-high mountains of adolescent power-fantasies for the masturbatory delection of wimpish nerds, wonder of wonders, it is also true that many of the genre's genuine masterpieces fit comfortably within its formal parameters.

Dune, Neuromancer, The Book of the New Sun, The Stars My Destination, most of Gordon Dickson's Dorsai cycle, *The Lord of the Rings, The Three Stigmata of Palmer Eldritch, Lord of Light, Nova, The Einstein Intersection*, Philip Jose Farmer's *Riverworld* books, *Stranger in a Strange Land, Three Hearts and Three Lions*, and many, many more novels of real literary worth are brothers between the covers, at least in plot summary terms, to the Ur–action-adventure formula.

So too, for that matter, are the Book of Exodus, the New Testament, the Bhagavad Gita, the legends of King Arthur, Robin Hood, Siegfried, Barbarossa, and Musashi Murakami, the careers of Alexander the Great, Napoleon, George Washington, Simón Bólivar, Tokugawa Ieyasu, Lawrence of Arabia, and Fidel Castro, not to mention *Atlas Shrugged, An American Dream, The Count of Monte Cristo, David Copperfield, The Man Who Could Work Miracles*, and Superman.

Clearly then, we are looking at something far deeper here than a mere commercial fiction formula, a cross-cultural archetypal tale that would seem to arise out of the collective unconscious of the species wherever stories are told, and that indeed, some have argued, is even *the* archetypal story, period.

Joseph Campbell's *The Hero with a Thousand Faces* is probably the most exhaustive, subtle, sophisticated, and spiritually aware explication of this thesis. Read this one if you really want the inner meaning with copious cross-cultural specifics.

Campbell's Hero, like the hero of *The Emperor of Everything*, begins the tale as a naif, acquires a mentor and a mission, fights his way to the center or the underworld, wins a climactic battle that gains him the object of the quest, often wins himself a Princess, and rises in triumph as a Lightbringer.

This may not be *the* formal template for all fiction, but it is certainly *one* of them, along with the tragedy, the picaresque odyssey, the love story, the tale of the Trickster, the bedroom farce.

For the Hero with a Thousand Faces, unlike the hero of *The Emperor of Everything*, is Everyman on a mystical quest.

His guide is his shamanistic spiritual master. His journey is the tale of his spiritual awakening. The battles he fights are with the lower aspects of his own nature, either overtly or imagistically transmogrified into villains or monsters. The underworld or center to which he at last penetrates is the Void at the center of the Great Wheel, the level of the psyche where ego and consciousness emerge out of the collective stuff of creation.

And the final battle at the center is the struggle to achieve the mystical fusion of his spirit with the world, the successful climax of which is his attainment of spiritual transcendence, graced by which he returns to the world of men as Lightbringer and heroic inspiration.

Thus the ability of this tale both to attract an avid audience, no matter how often it is told, and to inspire yet another literary masterpiece, no matter how many great writers have retold it in the past.

The Hero with a Thousand Faces is, after all, the story of ourselves, or anyway the story of our lives that we all would write if *we* had our fingers on the Keyboard in the Sky, which is why our professional storytellers keep telling it to us again and again throughout the world and across the millennia, and why we're always willing to live it vicariously one more time.

And if it is truly told, like Vonnegut's foma, it can make us feel brave and strong and happy, and by so doing encourage us to feats of spiritual bravery in our lives.

Take for example, *The Stars My Destination* by Alfred Bester, recently reissued in hardcover by Franklin Watts after an inexcusable sojourn in the underworld of publishing limbo. This novel is generally recognized as one of the half-dozen best SF novels ever written and the prize blossom of the SF novel's 1950s flowering.

Gully Foyle, space freighter deck-ape, Everyman at a karmic nadir, opens the novel marooned on a wreck and about to expire. A spaceship approaches within rescue distance but passes him by, lighting up the depths of his dormant spirit with the fire of vengeance.

Hate drives him to mighty deeds. He survives, escapes, begins his quest to ferret out and destroy *Vorga*, the spaceship that left him to die, in the opening acts of which he discovers the corporate powers and machinations behind the deed, and ends up thrown in the literal underworld, the Gouffre Martel, a deep cave in which prisoners suffer total darkness and total isolation. There via the "whisperline," he meets the Princess-cum-spirit-guide, Jisbella McQueen.

They escape from the underworld, and Foyle transforms himself into Formyle of Ceres, a rich and powerful figure able to pursue and hunt down the powers behind *Vorga* at the highest political and social levels.

Foyle does not merely amass the fortune and assume the identity of Formyle of Ceres; we see him grow, through a process of worldly and spiritual education, into his true manhood, and we see his quest for vengeance transform itself into a quest for social justice.

At the climax of the novel, Bester, through a brilliant synergy of prose and something like illustration, puts Foyle and the reader through what can only be called a genuine psychedelic peak experience. Trapped and burning in another underworld, his senses crossed and mixed into synesthesia, Foyle teleports wildly through space and time while morally wrestling with the question of what to do with the secret substance PyrE.

PyrE is a thermonuclear explosive that can be detonated by thought alone. Anyone can do it. Foyle, through his evolution into The Hero with a Thousand Faces, has gained the power to "space-jaunte," to teleport anywhere in the galaxy. At this moment, he is the Emperor of Everything for fair. He has the power to literally open the universe to man. He has a secret that, if it gets out, will give whoever knows it the power to destroy civilization. The fire of the gods is in his hands for good and/or evil.

What is a true hero to do? Sit on the secret of PyrE and arrogate the ultimate power unto himself? Leave it in the hands of the "responsible" power structure for safety?

The ultimate moral greatness of *The Stars My Destination* is that Gully Foyle does neither.

As the avatar of the fully awakened Everyman, he turns the fire of the gods over to Everyone: he places PyrE in the hands of the people.

"We're all in this together, let's live together or die together," he tells the worlds of men. "All right, God damn you! I challenge you, me. Die or live and be great. Blow yourself to Christ and gone or come and find me, Gully Foyle, and I make you men. I make you great. I give you the stars."

Everyman, transformed into the Lightbringer, like the true Bodhisattva, eschews the pinnacle of egoistic transcendence and returns to the worlds of men not as an avatar of the godhead, but as Everyman reborn, as the *democratic* avatar of the godhead within us all. And *that*, not the magnificence of some anointed Darling of Destiny, is the true light of the world.

This is the true telling of the tale for the modern world, a version that in a sense would have literally been inconceivable prior to the advent of the democratic ethos, though there are echoes of it in Buddhism and the myth of Prometheus. Indeed, this spiritual message is one that the majority of people still don't seem ready to hear, or at least the avid readers of all those clones of *The Emperor of Everything*.

Just as republics tend to degenerate into empires, paths of enlightenment into hierarchical religions, and inspirational leaders into tyrants, so does the tale of The Hero with a Thousand Faces tend to degenerate into *The Emperor of Everything*, and for much the same reasons.

Gully Foyle is a true hero not because of his derring-do, though he does his share of derring, nor because of the godlike powers he attains, but because he achieves at the end the moral heroism and clarity of the Bodhisattva.

But few mighty heroes, fictional or otherwise, eschew the throne of transcendent power. Even noble Caesar, republican at heart, accepted the crown of empire the fourth time around.

Paul Atreides, the overtly transcendent hero of Frank Herbert's Dune sage (which is to say *Dune, Dune Messiah*, and *Children of Dune*, the novels in the series that chronicle his life), prescient superman that he is, wrestles with this final task of the true hero and ultimately fails, to his own sorrow.

Paul is the hunted, exiled, rightful heir to the dukedom of Arrakis. He undergoes a whole seies of initiation mysteries under many spiritual masters and mistresses as he raises up the Fremen into the People's Army, which will free the planet from the evil Harkonnens. Paul is destined by breeding to become the Kwizatz Haderach, a being of such godlike prescient power that he will be worshipped as a god in whose name jihad will sweep the worlds of men. At the triumphant end of *Dune*, he not only destroys the Harkonnens but stands fully revealed as the avatar of the godhead and quite literally crowns himself Emperor of Everything.

Superficially, *Dune* seems like the ultimate power fantasy for nerdish adolescents. One meets the identification figure as the special young boy that is one's own dreamself; follows him through battle, spiritual adventure, and derring-do; and finally one becomes the transcendent object of worship of all the worlds and crowns oneself Emperor of Everything. The perfect wank, or so it would seem.

But not to Paul Atreides.

The drug melange has made Paul prescient, so that quite early on he envisions the jihad that he is destined to bring. And he abhors it. Everything he does, at least on a certain level of self-deception, is designed to prevent it, but everything he does ends up leading him back along the timeline to the inevitable. At the end of *Dune*, he can only surrender to his unavoidable destiny, assume the godhead, crown himself emperor, and become the icon of the jihad.

Thus, the superficially triumphant denouement of *Dune* is really a tragedy. The Hero achieves everything up to and including the crown of god-king of the universe, but unlike Gully Foyle, he cannot transcend his transcendence, he cannot achieve the grace of the Bodhisattva, he cannot place the scepter of enlightenment and power in the hands of Everyone, he cannot stop his own jihad.

And his personal tragedy is that he knows it. Indeed, he has known it all along. He spends most of *Dune Messiah* as the enthroned messiah in question, a crabbed and cranky figure presiding over the bureaucratic institutionalization of his own cult of personality. He dies in *Dune Messiah*, is reborn in *Children of Dune* as a desert Jeremiah, and he dies again without destroying his own mythos.

This is what makes the first three books in the Dune series a literary achievement instead of a masturbatory power fantasy, even though the elements of the latter are all there to the max. Herbert has irony in these novels, and so does his archetypal Hero. In a sense, the novels are a mordant commentary on the story of the Hero with a Thousand Faces. Paul may become god-king of the universe, but he cannot escape the destiny that has raised him to this pinnacle, he cannot abdicate to the republic of the spirit, nor can he escape the dire consequences of his own godhood. He is a god who can do everything but attain his own final enlightenment, without which his life is a failure and this retelling of the tale a tragedy.

This is also why the rest of the Dune books, the ones that take place after Paul is finally gone for good, degenerate into a series of retellings of *The Emperor of Everything*, in which messianic figures and Jesuitical conspiracies battle for spiritually meaningless power in the long, long pseudo-medieval aftermath of his passage.

Taken as a whole, the Dune series is almost a perfect textbook example of how and why the tale of The Hero with a Thousand Faces so easily devolves into its unfortunate mirror-image, *The Emperor of Everything*. In superficial terms, one is as much a power fantasy as the other, but the true tale also has a moral and spiritual dimension. Shorn of its derring-do, The Hero with a Thousand Faces is a myth of enlightenment like *Siddharta* or *The Magic Mountain* or *The Dharma Bums*, in which the payoff for the reader is vicarious mystic transcendence and elevated moral consciousness.

But shorn of its inner spiritual heart, shorn of Gully Foyle's climactic mystical democracy or Paul Atreides' tormented ironic prescience, the tale can only become what Hitler made of Nietzsche.

For alas, the Führerprincip is the dark flip side of the tale of The Hero with a Thousand Faces. For without the moral vision of a Bester or the tragic irony of a Herbert, the inner light of the story is lost, and in place of a paradigm of spiritual maturation, we are left with only the pornography of power, with the egoistic Faustian masturbation fantasy of the fascist mystique, with the reader's hands in his tight black leather pants as he envisions himself as the all-powerful Übermensch in the ultimate catbird seat.

Few of us, after all, are Bodhisattvas; most of us would like to feel a good deal more powerful than we really are, and so all too many of us are attracted to the Führerprincip just as long as we can fantasize ourselves as Der Führer in question.

That's why, given reasonably skilled retelling, the latest clone of *The Emperor of Everything* will still move off the racks, especially if it is properly packaged with bulging thews, phallic weaponry, and suitable fetish items. Remove the inner light from the eyes of The Hero with a Thousand Faces and the face that leers back at you has a cowlick and a Charlie Chaplin moustache.

That's also why Adolf Hitler has become as powerful an archetype as the Hero, why Nazi imagery still has such a baleful appeal forty years later, and in a certain sense how Hitler mesmerized Germany. And also why the despiritualized version of the tale is so dangerous to the mental health of the reader and the body politic.

In my own novel, *The Iron Dream*, I attempted an exorcism of this demon in terms as overt as I could manage. Here is *The Emperor of Everything* to the putrid max. Feric Jaggar, our hero, destined in his genes for rule, fights his gory way from ignominious exile in the lands of the mutants and mongrels to absolute rule in the Fatherland of Truemen, after which he wages a successful holy war to purge the Earth of degenerate mutants and sends off clones of himself to conquer the stars.

But within *The Iron Dream* is an internal novel, a thing called *Lord of the Swastika* by one Adolf Hitler. Feric Jaggar is Hitler's dream of himself as the tall blond Aryan superman, and *Lord of the Swastika* is Hitler's fantasy of the triumph of the Third Reich in an alternate world after nuclear war has polluted the gene pool, written in yet another alternate world in which Nazi Germany never happened and Hitler himself was a lowly SF hack.

Lord of the Swastika begins with a science fantasy feel and small-scale mutant bashing, but Hitler's brain is rotting away from paresis as he writes it, he begins to gibber, the violence becomes surreally horrid and grand-scale, military technology advances by leaps and bounds, and by the time the novel is two-thirds over, the reader who has been getting off on this stuff finds himself confronted with the awful revelation that he has been getting off on the racism, Sturm and Drang, military fetishism, and inner psychic imagery of the Third Reich itself, replete with swastikas, Nuremberg rallies, SS Panzer divisions sweeping across Europe, carpet-bombing of population centers, genocide, concentration camps, and gas ovens.

Hitler ends his novel by cloning seven-foot-tall blonde SS supermen in toilet bowls and sending them off in great spurting phallic rockets to exterminate mutants and monsters and aliens throughout the galaxy, each division of Werewolf SS heroes led by a clone of Der Führer himself.

The idea, of course, was to suck the reader into the standard *The Emperor of Everything* power fantasy and then point out, none too gently, what this dynamic had actually led to in *our* alternate world by bringing the Nazi symbology right up front and laying on the violent loathsomeness with a trowel. The Emperor of Everything *really is* Der Führer, suckers, and you have been marching right along behind him.

To make damn sure that even the historically naive and entirely unselfaware reader got the point, I appended a phony critical analysis of *Lord of the Swastika*, in which the psychopathology of Hitler's saga was spelled out by a tendentious pedant in words of one syllable.

Almost everyone got the point. . . .

And yet one review appeared in a fanzine that really gave me pause. "This is a rousing adventure story and I really enjoyed it," the gist of it went. "Why did Spinrad have to spoil the fun with all this muck about Hitler?"

And the American Nazi Party put the book on its recommended reading list. They really liked the upbeat ending.

Apparently, the appeal of *The Emperor of Everything* to the longings for power within all of us save the true Bodhisattva is so powerful that some readers can get off on it, even when it means reveling in genocide and identifying with Adolf Hitler.

This is admittedly as extreme as an example of the phenomenon can possibly get, and the overwhelming majority of the readers of *The Iron Dream* did get the point.

More commonly though, the writer himself may not be entirely aware of what he is doing, for it is all too easy to lose the inner meaning of The Hero with a Thousand Faces, at which point entropy and commercial pressure almost always pull the tale down into *The Emperor of Everything*, as witness what happened to even such as Frank Herbert in the latter Dune novels, or Robert Silverberg's descent from the brilliant version of *Son of Man* to the skilled but passionless rendition in *Lord Valentine's Castle*, or Orson Scott Card's trajectory from *Songmaster* and *Hart's Hope* through *Ender's Game* and into *Speaker for the Dead*.

In *Hart's Hope* and *Songmaster*, Card amply demonstrated that he understood the inner meaning of the archetypal hero tale and could bring it home to the reader with power and clarity.

Hart's Hope is a fantasy novel set in a densely symbolic pseudo-medieval landscape largely of Card's own imaginative making. It is an overtly mystical retelling of the hero tale in which self-sacrifice is elevated over egoistic triumph, and it works admirably.

Songmaster plays *The Emperor of Everything* off against the artistic impulse, music in this case, and Card comes down squarely on the side of esthetics, on the side of the human spirit against worldly power.

So how did a writer like this end up producing *Ender's Game* and

Speaker for the Dead? And why have these latter-day works gained him the sales and awards and readership denied him for artistically and morally superior work like *Hart's Hope* and *Songmaster*?

The chronology of how the first two novels (in what appears to be the continuing saga of Andrew "Ender" Wiggin) came to be written may prove instructive. Card first published the novella version of *Ender's Game*. Then he apparently wrote the outline for *Speaker for the Dead* as a sequel to it but decided to turn *Ender's Game* into a novel first, perhaps because he realized in medias res that he had started himself a trilogy without knowing he had done so initially.

Structurally, it really shows. The final chapter of *Ender's Game* seems entirely dissociated from the rest of the novel and seems to exist entirely as a bridge to *Speaker for the Dead*, which in turn takes certain clumsy pains to establish the back-story of *Ender's Game*, which Card could have almost completely ignored if he had conceived of either book as a freestanding novel.

The weird effect is that of a phantom missing novel in the series between *Ender's Game* and *Speaker for the Dead*, a novel that *Speaker for the Dead* alludes to as if the reader could have read it, and for which the last chapter of *Ender's Game* reads like the marketing outline.

In fact the missing novel, to judge by the outline, would have been much more interesting than the books Card actually wrote, and indeed might be most of the real story.

Ender's Game takes the hero from boyhood through combat-game training to his destined apotheosis as commander via game machine of the human fleet that exterminates the misunderstood alien Buggers, an act of genocide he is tricked into committing, but for which he nevertheless feels a guilt he must expiate.

Speaker for the Dead, through time-dilation effect, gives us a period centuries later, in which Ender, now approaching middle age, has become a wandering "Speaker for the Dead," speaking the truth of dead lives upon invitation as he sees it, a saintly figure or so we are told, while the legend of Ender the Genocide lies darkly on the worlds as a warning against xenophobia.

Meanwhile another alien race, the Piggies, has been discovered on the planet Lusitania. The Piggies are technologically primitive and believe that certain trees are the wise and transcendent reincarnations of their dead ancestors.

Having been taught a lesson by Ender's extermination of the

Buggers, the human colonists fence themselves off on a reservation and leave the Piggies to their own devices, with only the anthropological team of Pipo, Libo, and Novinha studying them under a restrictive covenant of non-interference. Pipo is Libo's father. Novinha and Libo love each other and plan to be married.

They are appalled when their favorite Piggy, a respected figure in Piggy society who has seemingly just achieved an increase in status, is found dead, flayed by his compatriots with a sapling planted in his chest. Worse still, when Pipo, the senior anthropologist, is given the same treatment after appearing to have merely done the Piggies a good turn.

Ender is summoned to speak for the death of Pipo, necessitating a trip that will take objective decades but will not significantly age him, thanks to the time-dilation effect.

During this long storyline hiatus, Card is constrained to force poor Novinha to act like a complete idiot. She knows that the reason why the Piggies killed Pipo is buried in a data bank to which Libo would gain access by law if they married. Trained anthropologist that she is, does she delve into the data bank to learn the truth?

Uh-uh, because if she did, there would be no novel. She would easily learn the secret that Card has the puissant Ender winkle out hundreds of pages later as the climactic denouement, and that anyone who has read much science fiction has probably guessed already. (Hint: could it be possible that the primitive Piggies actually *do* understand their own life-cycle? Might a bear *really* know how to shit in the woods?)

So in order for the story to proceed, Card has Novinha refuse to marry Libo in order to save him from gaining knowledge that might somehow make him suffer Pipo's fate. Instead, she marries someone she doesn't love, and conducts a decades-long secret affair with Libo, whose children she bears, making the lives of all concerned miserable.

And all to no avail. By the time Ender arrives, the Piggies have done it to Libo anyway.

The rest of the novel, that is, the bulk of it, consists of Ender's uncovering the truth about Novinha's secret affair with Libo and the truth about the life-cycle of the Piggies, his unconvincing falling in love with the unpleasant Novinha, and what would appear to be a set-up for yet another Ender novel, in which Ender, having resurrected the Buggers and made peace between the humans and Piggies, will be constrained to defend Lusitania from a new set of baddies.

There just might have been enough real material here for a solid novelette, a xenobiological puzzle piece of the sort Philip José Farmer did so well in the collection *Strange Relations*. But then Novinha's long secret affair with Libo would have no motivation, and Ender Wiggin would be entirely superfluous to the tale.

But what about the phantom novel, the outline for which formed the final chapter of *Ender's Game*? Paradoxically enough, the last chapter of *Ender's Game* contains more novelistic material than *Speaker for the Dead*; indeed, in terms of The Hero with a Thousand Faces, the unwritten novel is the true ending of the tale of Ender Wiggin.

In a mere twenty-two pages, Ender journeys to the planet of the Buggers, makes psychic contact with the last remaining Bugger queen, learns the full truth of the mutual misunderstandings that led to the genocidal human-Bugger war, creates the mythos-cum-religion of Speaking for the Dead, rescues the bugger queen, stuffs her in a jar, and sets off on his long journey among the planets as the first Speaker for the Dead, looking for a suitable planet on which to resurrect the Buggers he has all but exterminated.

In general terms, the adolescent Hero descends to the underworld of his own guilt, achieves true knowledge through psychic communion with the alien spirit guide he finds there, and emerges as the fully mature Lightbringer to resurrect the higher consciousness he has unwittingly destroyed, and speak the wisdom he has gained in the process to the peoples of the worlds.

No wonder Card had to resort to an idiot plot to write Ender Wiggin into *Speaker for the Dead*! His true story was over before the book began.

But why didn't Card write the middle novel, which—if executed as well as *Ender's Game*, let alone *Hart's Hope* or *Songmaster*—would surely have been the best of the three? And why did he feel constrained to inject Ender Wiggin into the thematic material of *Speaker for the Dead* when the whole thing would have worked better if he had stuck to the story of Libo and Novinha?

From this vantage one can only guess. Perhaps Card felt he had already told the true tale of his hero's spiritual coming of age twice to his own satisfaction in *Hart's Hope* and *Songmaster*. Perhaps the relative indifference with which these fine, heartfelt novels were greeted persuaded him to take the same successful career strategy Robert Silverberg did with *Lord Valentine's Castle* and stick to the basics of the commercial series format.

Or just maybe his own craft was sufficient to run the reader-identification number on *himself* to the point where Ender Wiggin became the *writer's* alter ego as well as the reader's, a character he couldn't let go of and couldn't delve into too deeply because he had evolved into a mouthpiece for Card's own political and philosophical passions.

It wouldn't be the first time a writer lost the psychic separation between himself and his hero. Mickey Spillane ended up playing Mike Hammer in a movie. Hal Mayne degenerated into a mouthpiece for Gordon Dickson's sociopolitical theorizing in *The Final Encyclopedia*. Marion Zimmer Bradley has been known to administer the Amazon's Oath at Darkover conventions. Barry Maltzberg details this process definitively in the hilarious but harrowing *Herovits' World*.

To my knowledge Orson Scott Card has never been seen carrying a mysterious cocoon or speaking for the dead at conventions, but the dangers of *writing The Emperor of Everything* can be a lot subtler than that.

As I pointed out before, most of us would like to feel a good deal more powerful than we really are, no one more so than a writer whose worthy work as thusfar not gained him his just portion of fame and fortune, so why shouldn't *he* be attracted to the Führerprincip when *he* can easily enough write his own wish-fulfillment figure into the story as der Führer in question?

Card's first Ender, the one in the original novelette, lives out the nerdish adolescent power fantasy of *The Emperor of Everything*, conquering the baddies, only to have the triumphant payoff turn into a moral tragedy. Shorn of the hot air and incest subplot blown into the novel version, this is the Card of *Hart's Hope*, a nice little story with real mordant bite.

Card's second Ender, the Ender of *Speaker for the Dead*, has already degenerated into a stock figure, a "hero" like Conan or Perry Rhodan or Doc Savage, "heroic" only in the sense that he is the identification figure who wins the battles and gets the girl.

Actually, like most incarnations of the Emperor of Everything, he is something of a self-righteous prig and moral monster, a pur sang power fantasy without inner light, differing only in degree from Feric Jaggar.

He is the only man alive who has access to all the data banks in the galaxy through Jane, an Artifical Personality who has evolved therein beknownst only to Ender. Jane also gives him the magic power to manipulate electronic machinery. The hacker's ultimate power fantasy.

He is almost always right, and his (and by extension the author's) words of wisdom time and again have the power to enlighten hearts and cure deep-seated neuroses because Card tells us so.

He is a hero because he is smart, possessed of secret knowledge and powers, gets the girl, and is one hell of a stump speaker. But what of the inner light of the true hero?

Card has worked up a wonky ecology for Lusitania in which only four, count 'em, *four* species survive on the entire planet. This is due to a virus of which everyone on the planet is now a carrier. Scientific absurdity aside, the point is that anyone from Lusitania traveling off-world can devastate entire planetary ecosystems.

The higher authorities learn this, declare a quarantine, and dispatch a fleet to enforce it. Our compassionate hero, however, successfully machinates to send his crippled stepson (a child of Libo and Novinha), infectious though he is, off planet for personal reasons. As the novel ends, the humans, Piggies, and Buggers are about to unite under Ender to fight the wicked quarantine fleet, which, understandably enough, is ready to destroy Lusitania if necessary to preserve the ecospheres of the human worlds.

Lebensraum for the Piggies and the Buggers and the Lusitanian humans under the leadership of the great hero at the risk of exterminating all life on many other planets.

Ender Wiggin über Alles.

And that is what the true heroic myth is always on the edge of degenerating into under the pressure of commercial realities, which militate against dissipating the targeted audience's reveries with irony or moral ambiguities or terminating the identification figure's tale with a spiritually sophisticated closure.

In the process of pushing all the reader's power fantasy buttons, the writer of *The Emperor of Everything* all too often ends up pushing his own.

Worse still, in Skinnerian terms, this often receives positive reinforcement in the form of sales and awards, making it that much more difficult for a writer of worth to separate his hero's success from his own, to regain the clarity of the inner light necessary to attempt something like *Hart's Hope* or *Songmaster* or the phantom Ender Wiggin novel.

But at least Orson Scott Card *did* apparently know this well enough to outline the missing Ender Wiggin novel as the final chapter of *Ender's Game*, perhaps as some kind of spirit message to himself from the author of *Songmaster* and *Hart's Hope*.

And now we have *Seventh Son*, the first novel of who knows how many in the *Tales of Alvin Maker*, a fantasy set in an alternate America of the early nineteenth century in which the United States never came into being and magic of a kind works. Alvin is another of Card's young nascent heroes, and *Seventh Son* takes him no further than the encounter with his first spirit guide and the beginning of his life's journey, so it is far too soon to say whether he will evolve into another Emperor of Everything or a true Lightbringer.

So far the signs are fairly promising. The background is far richer and better realized than anything in *Ender's Game* or *Speaker for the Dead*, and the character relationships more ambiguous and complex; these are good signs that Card may be returning to the form of *Songmaster* and *Hart's Hope*.

On the other hand, it seems certain that Alvin Maker is destined for Great Things. Whether they will be the Great Things of The Hero with a Thousand Faces or the Great Things of the Emperor of Everything remains to be seen. Orson Scott Card has proven that he contains both potentials within him. And he is far from the only one.

If the danger in writing *The Emperor of Everything* is that the writer may lose sight of his own inner light in the process, the prize for the writer who successfully carries through with The Hero with a Thousand Faces is the recapture of same.

Writers, too, embark on this marvelous but perilous quest each time out, and let us not kid ourselves, brothers and sisters, each time out the outcome is in doubt.

Masters of the Form:
Careers in Profile

It is amazing, in a way, how little criticism of science fiction in either the SF specialty magazines or the general daily and monthly press seeks to provide overviews of the literary careers of the major writers. Those writing monthly reviews for the SF specialty magazines must perforce concentrate on a narrow timewise slice, to wit the latest books, and those squeezing reviews of science fiction into newspapers and general-interest literary journals even more so. Taplinger, Borgo Press, and Starmont do publish series of academic studies of individual authors as freestanding pamphlets, but even most of the papers in the ongoing academic journals, where critics exert most influence on other critics, and hence the shape of science fiction criticism itself, tend to concentrate on a thematic aspect of a writer's work, or a theme running through the work of several writers, and seldom on an oeuvre entire.

Mostly, I believe, it is the publishing exigencies that have skewed critics in the field away from this sort of thing—exigencies under which, happily enough, I do not labor at *Isaac Asimov's Science Fiction Magazine*. Yet I myself fell into it by accident, not design.

I wanted to review Sturgeon's *Godbody*, and I realized no sense could be made of that book without a consideration of Ted's whole career, and one couldn't consider Sturgeon without bringing up Kilgore Trout, which led into my writing "Sturgeon, Vonnegut, and Trout."

I was in England and France when I first read J.G. Ballard's *The Day of Creation* and was commissioned to do a very short review for the London *Sunday Mirror*. Attempting to say anything coherent about Ballard in such a short compass led me into the notion of considering his whole career.

The piece on Philip K. Dick, which was written especially for *Science Fiction in the Real World*, explains its own raison d'etre, as you will see shortly.

Peculiarly enough, without setting out to do so, I have, by picking the careers of Sturgeon, Vonnegut, Ballard, and Dick, ended up writing a kind of hologrammic and nonsequential outline of the evolution of science fiction from the 1950s into the 1980s, not from a linear historical perspective but from a consideration of the careers of four writers who, each in his own way, have been pivotal to that evolution.

I have done little rewriting of the column versions here, except to update the piece on Ballard a bit, for it was written before the release of the American edition of *The Day of Creation*.

Sturgeon, Vonnegut, and Trout

Theodore Sturgeon's death and the posthumous publication of *Godbody*, the only new Sturgeon novel to be published in a quarter of a century, brought well-deserved new attention to the work of a great writer, who, incredibly enough, never achieved as much fame in the world at large as Kilgore Trout, the strangely ambivalent Sturgeon-figure who haunts many of the latter-day works of Kurt Vonnegut.

So it goes.

When Vonnegut permitted the publication of a "Kilgore Trout novel" mentioned in his own work, *Venus on the Half Shell*, it wasn't even Sturgeon himself behind the pseudonym, it was Philip José Farmer who cashed Trout's checks. Ted, like Trout, stayed broke as usual.

So it goes.

Theodore Sturgeon is *still* probably the finest short story writer that the SF genre has produced, and arguably the finest American short story writer of the post–World War II era, period. Yet only one of his long golden string of stories of the '40s, '50s, and early '60s, "The Man Who Lost the Sea," ever made it into Martha Foley's mainstream year's-best series, and that was the high point of his recognition by the American literary establishment.

So it goes.

At least two of his very occasional novels, *More Than Human* and *Some of Your Blood*, are acknowledged masterpieces. Yet Ted Sturgeon was also constrained by finances not only to do the novelization of Irwin Allen's original *Voyage to the Bottom of the Sea* feature film but to put his own name on it.

So it goes.

And not until 1986 did we have the first publication of *Godbody*, Sturgeon's last novel, a novel whose first draft was written in the early 1970s, and which Donald I. Fine finally published, unrevised, after his death.

So it goes.

But *what* goes here?

At a Norwescon convention banquet, Spider Robinson essayed a memorial to Theodore Sturgeon in the form of his version of a Lord Buckley rap in which Sturgeon, as a jazzman known as The Fish, finally gets to blow the critics away with a triumphant master riff.

Spider Robinson's intentions were no doubt informed by nothing but the warmest sentiments, and indeed when his performance was over, the fans gave a good round of applause to the happy ending.

But Robinson's rap was what Vonnegut calls a "foma," a lie that makes the listener feel brave and strong and happy.

Alas, it never happened. Oh yes, The Fish could have blown the socks off any short story writer extant and did it quite regularly in the SF cellar clubs, but they never let him up there on the stage at Birdland to jam with the acknowledged immortals.

So *that* goes.

Certain critics, including Robert A. Heinlein in the loving foreword, have opined that *Godbody* is the capstone of Sturgeon's career, while others have deemed it a mess whose posthumous publication does a disservice to Sturgeon's reputation. In a weird way, both opinions may be right.

Godbody is formally audacious to the max. Except for a final section, which is told in author-omniscient third person, the entire novel is narrated in multiple first person. Eight characters narrate the story in sequence, and none of them reappears later as point of view, though they all figure in each other's narratives. I can't think of another novel that uses precisely this form (the closest literary parallels being Faulkner's *The Sound and the Fury* and Durrell's *Alexandria Quartet*), and certainly no science fiction novel.

And Sturgeon almost makes it work. Only at the end does he seem to find himself constrained to break form to tie things up in third-person author-omniscient.

On a prose level, *Godbody* is positively breathtaking. Almost no one but Sturgeon ever understood how to use style like this.

As Heinlein so rightly points out, you can open the book at random, and know which character is narrating after reading only a line or two.

But that is the least of it.

Much invidious advice has been offered the innocent on the subject of prose style, and just as much on the subject of point of view. Some savants advise aspiring writers to develop their own consistent prose styles, and others advise them to entirely eschew first-person narration.

Godbody demonstrates just what riches we may lose thereby in glorious words of many syllables.

By choosing the multiple-first-person narrative technique, Sturgeon allows himself the freedom to develop *eight* consistent prose styles in the course of one rather short novel.

Each character narrates his section in his own true voice, which, emerging into print, becomes the *character's* prose style, not the author's, with the character's idiosyncratic rhythms, vocabulary, philosophy, twitches, and conversational tropes.

Ted Sturgeon used first person frequently and never developed a consistent prose style. Even when he was writing in third person, the style was more often than not *the character's*, not Sturgeon-sprach.

Sturgeon's best work was character-centered. Oh yes, he knew how to tell stories and he had wondrous stories to tell, but the epiphanies and even the plot-climaxes always occurred within the human heart.

And Sturgeon's inner psychic landscapes were not just unicorn gardens, as he sometimes liked to pretend. Ted *was* genuinely a sweet and loving man, and he certainly had a lot more to say about the varieties of love than about the varieties of hate, but even within the confines of a song of love like *Godbody*, he shows he can invent quite credible loathsomeness too.

But always with compassion.

The main first-person narrator in *Some of Your Blood* is a vile vampire who commits unspeakable acts. Sturgeon puts him under psychoanalysis, lets him speak for himself, and the monster comes out the other end as someone we care for.

Sturgeon at the top of his form brings his readers deep, deep inside his characters, as, of course, he can do only by being willing to go there himself. Thus Sturgeon's moral courage, the courage to love his characters and thereby make the reader love them, no matter who and what they are.

This was the greatness of Sturgeon's vision, but the core of his greatness as a writer was that he could convey this vision through the medium of prose.

Yes, yes, I know, I have merely described what every writer of fiction should strive for.

But Theodore Sturgeon *knew how to do it*, and on the deepest possible level.

He knew that, in the real world, what people say and how they say it is the closest mirror we can have into what they are saying to themselves inside their own heads. He knew that in the world of fiction, the only real instrument we have for conveying the style of a character's consciousness is the style of the prose in which we tell his story.

You don't necessarily have to do it in first person, as Sturgeon does in *Godbody*, and Sturgeon himself used third person as often as not. True too that some writers with one consistent prose style do manage to get as deeply inside the spirits of their characters as Sturgeon does, and even with as much caring, as witness Philip K. Dick.

But no one who does not allow his style to mutate with his characters the way Sturgeon does can hope to have his range and depth at the same time.

Parts of *Godbody* are told by, variously, a cop, a rapist, a sincere minister, his sexually frustrated wife, a village Machiavelli, a plain girl with inner complexities, a slimy gossip columnist, and a middle-aged flower child. All of them have the same level of believability. All of them, including the rapist, are people we come to truly understand. All of them are quite real.

Sturgeon achieves this by letting them all speak for themselves in their own voices. By using multiple first person instead of third, he is able to combine eight separate prose styles embodying eight different varieties of human spirit in the same novel without disorienting the reader.

In these terms, Robert Heinlein is right on: in terms of form and depth of characterization and prose style and their unification, *Godbody is* a masterpiece and the capstone of Sturgeon's career. Even though this is essentially a raw first draft, he hardly ever hits a stylistic sour note or lets one character's style leak over into another's.

But alas, those who believe that perhaps a first draft like this should not be published have a point too, especially since Sturgeon agreed with them.

For, as published, *Godbody* has a huge and rather obvious flaw, and that flaw is quite literally a flaw at the center of the novel, namely Godbody himself, the title character, the void about which the eight-fold wheel rotates, what the Vonnegut of *Cat's Cradle* might call the "wampeter of the karass."

Who is Godbody?

This is a question that reappears every once in a while, and it is also the last line of the novel. The problem is that Sturgeon never answers it in his own terms.

Godbody is a beautiful naked man who appears out of nowhere to the point-of-view characters and catalyzes deep changes in most of their lives, principally by awakening their positive libidinal energies and making them love one another in every possible sense. At the end he is tragically murdered by the unconverted and rises on the third day.

So what we have quite explicitly here is a sexualized Jesus figure, and indeed Dan Currier, Sturgeon's minister, attempts to use Scripture to suggest that the true Christianity, the Christianity of Jesus himself, was in part a sexual mystery religion like tantric yoga—that in the true Christian spirit, sexual love is at least as valid a spiritual transcendence as Mass or Communion.

This is not entirely a new concept for Sturgeon. We hear echoes of it in *Venus Plus X*, "The Lovebirds," "Affair with a Green Monkey," even *Some of Your Blood*. But here it is stated most fully and candidly in a manner sure to raise the blood pressure of the Bible Belt.

Nor is this conceptual core the problem with *Godbody*. There is a brilliant if obscure novel, *Jesus Christs* by A.J. Langguth, which consists entirely of numerous retellings of the passion of Christ in different alternate world incarnations. Sturgeon's concept *could* have worked just as well.

But it doesn't.

The problem with *Godbody* the novel is Godbody the character, and the problem with Godbody the character is that Sturgeon didn't seem to be able to figure out whether he should be played as a man on the same reality level as the viewpoint characters or played as a pure symbol, a forthright abstraction, a piece of magic realism.

He doesn't use Godbody's first-person viewpoint, he doesn't get inside him at all, but that's not the problem either, that's conceptually appropriate to this sort of story in this sort of form. Philip K. Dick does it all the time; you can find it in a whole genre of political novels like *A*

Face in the Crowd and *All the King's Men*; I used it in *Passing through the Flame*; and even Milton didn't attempt to portray the psyche of God.

If the central character is simply too vast for empathy, make him the void at the center about which the others rotate. aka the unmoved mover, the wampeter of the karass.

But if you are going to give the godhead speaking lines at all, they had better be good! Sturgeon, alas, does give Godbody a few lines of his own dialog, and their studied ordinariness jarringly breaks the limpid realism of the rest of the novel.

You can see what he was *trying* to do.

The recurring question in the novel is, who is Godbody?

And of course the only proper Zen Jesuit answer is—Everybody.

Sturgeon was trying to portray the ordinariness of true saintliness, and—what can I say?—he blew it. To see how it actually *can* be done, read Philip K. Dick's *The Transmigration of Timothy Archer*, in which Dick demonstrates the saintliness of a slightly retarded mechanic through his discussion of the characteristic flaws and virtues of various makes of cars.

Sturgeon also blew the ending of the novel when he was forced to break form and describe the denouement in author-omniscient third person, because, apparently, he couldn't frame a first-person viewpoint that would be in all the right places to tie the threads of the story together.

So what we have as published is neither the capstone of Sturgeon's career nor a misconceived failure. What we have here, quite simply, is the *first draft* of a potential masterpiece, that, alas, never got the necessary revisions.

A successful rewrite might not have been so difficult. One could, for example, reserve the first-person viewpoint of the gossip columnist to narrate the resolution. Indeed, one could let her be transformed too, and let it happen then. And if you can't make Godbody speak magic prose in the rewrite, you can always leave him mute and make him more remote.

Theodore Sturgeon was a conscious and conscientious craftsman. He sat on this first draft for twenty years of bad road. It wasn't that he couldn't sell it, and it certainly wasn't that he didn't need the money. Indeed the book *was* sold to at least three different publishers during this period. But Sturgeon quite properly refused to have it published until he gave it the rewrite he knew damned well it needed.

But alas, he never rewrote it, not even with the wolf at the door already inside his premises and biting him on the ass.

Why he never rewrote it may have to remain a literary mystery, for Ted isn't around to tell us, may very well not have known himself, and the only witness remaining is, in a manner of speaking, Kilgore Trout.

The choice of name clearly proclaims that Vonnegut's failed science fiction writer is based on Theodore Sturgeon. But Vonnegut's Trout is not quite the Sturgeon that his friends and readers knew.

Not that there wasn't any Trout in Sturgeon. Like Vonnegut's version, the real Kilgore Trout was also chronically broke, enmeshed in marital and extramarital complexities, and had a million little self-destructive mechanisms for keeping it that way. Like Trout, Sturgeon still managed to keep his sweetness and his optimism through it all.

But while Theodore Sturgeon might have lived the *life* of Kilgore Trout, Sturgeon, *the writer*, was the mirror-image of Trout.

Trout was a prolific hack who cranked out hundreds of potboilers. Trout's novels were superficially written, botch jobs of brilliantly bizarre conceptual notions.

Ted Sturgeon was a slow, careful craftsman whose modest production of wordage was the hard won product of an almost career-long battle with writer's block. Sturgeon was a deeply empathetic writer who lived and died with his characters, and his works were based solidly in their inner lives. Sturgeon was a master prose stylist, with hundreds of orchestral voices at his command, a far more accomplished stylist in terms of range, than, say, Vonnegut himself.

But while Kilgore Trout may have more to say about Kurt Vonnegut as a writer than about Theodore Sturgeon's work, Vonnegut certainly *has* given us a bitterly affectionate send-up of the business end of Ted's career.

And while the first draft of *Godbody* is Sturgeon the literary genius caught in the act of creation with his pants not quite pulled up, how it came to be written is truer Trout than anything Vonnegut ever wrote, and true Theodore Sturgeon too.

Ted hadn't written a novel in at least a decade, and as usual was in need of money when Brian Kirby offered him something like $1,500 to write a novel for his Essex House line. Now in those days $1,500 was a pretty standard advance for an SF novel, but the likes of Sturgeon could have gotten perhaps as much as $5,000. So why did Ted agree to take a $1,500 deal?

Well, for one thing, he *had* gotten contracts for several SF novels, received the signature half of the advances, all long gone by now, and now, from a certain warped perspective, couldn't afford to write them. A good Marxist explanation of writer's block. Having failed to deliver on a number of contracts with SF publishers, new contracts with money up front became somewhat difficult for Ted to obtain. A good capitalist explanation of writer's block, you better believe it, Karl!

Then too, Brian was a friend of Ted's and knew him well. All too well. "I know you Ted," he told him. "The only way I'm going to get a novel out of you is if I pay you chapter by chapter. A hundred bucks up front, a hundred fifty every time you turn in a chapter."

Ted, who on a certain level of sanity, the same level that made him the writer that he was, knew *himself* all too well too, and agreed.

And that is the Kilgore Trout of how *Godbody* came to be written.

But, ah, the Theodore Sturgeon of it!

A porn publisher had commissioned Brian Kirby to do a line of "high-quality stiffeners." What Kirby's company knew about literature could be contained on the front page of the *National Enquirer* and often was. Kirby could publish anything he wanted to as an Essex House book, as long as it had a good measure of explicit sex in it.

Kirby's thesis was that "there's no reason why good literature can't give you a hard-on." So he signed up poets like David Meltzer and Michael Perkins, rescued a Beat novel from years of nonpublication, became an early publisher of Charles Bukowski, and went to science fiction writers like Charles Platt, Hank Stine, Philip José Farmer, and Theodore Sturgeon.

"Get it all out," Kirby told his writers. "Get crazy. There are no taboos or limits here. Anything you want as long as it's got fuck scenes in it."

Unlike other porn publishers, Kirby would not let respected authors hide behind pseudonymns. "I don't want to publish something you're ashamed to put your name on," he told his writers.

Under these conditions, Philip José Farmer produced wild and sometimes terrifying sex-and-adventure romps like *Image of the Beast*, *Blown*, and *A Feast Unknown*. Hank Stine write a stylistically brilliant psychosexual novel, *Season of the Witch*. Bukowski wrote the usual gross sardonic humor. Meltzer wrote a long series of dark and violent science fiction novels reminiscent of William Burroughs. Perkins wrote, among other similar things, *Evil Companions*, my choice for the most brilliantly vile and fascinatingly repellent novel ever written, beside which *120 Days of Sodom* rates a soft "R."

And Ted wrote *Godbody*.

And *that* is the Theodore Sturgeon of it!

Released from all taboos and restrictions and told only that he had to write about sex, while most of the Essex House writers did gross-out comedy or cast spotlights on the creatures mating in the deepest, darkest cellars of the savage id, Theodore Sturgeon produced this paean to the spiritually uplifting power of sexual love.

Well, needless to say, while there's no reason why good literature can't give you a hard-on, it's not going to sell like hotcakes in stroke-book stores, where the patrons are sufficiently challenged by the task of holding the book and turning the pages with the same hand.

So Essex House folded before Kirby could extract the rewrite from Sturgeon, and Ted sat on the first draft unto death two decades later, neither rewriting it nor allowing it to be published as it stood.

Why?

Easy enough to understand why Ted refused to publish it in the form we have now. It needed revision, and he knew it, and he was Theodore Sturgeon to the end, and wouldn't publish something he knew didn't work.

But why couldn't he figure out how to make it work?

The answer is no foma, it is not going to make anyone feel brave and strong and happy, and perhaps it is gauche of me to even mention it in print, but it's the only answer there is.

Ted was blocked for the last twenty years of his life. He wrote a few fine stories, but only a few, and revising an entire novel conceptually may have been beyond his creative energies at the time.

For too many years had this dedicated sensitive literary artist been forced to live the life of Kilgore Trout. *Godbody* could have been The Fish's master riff, but alas, Spider, he never got up there to blow it. They never let him in the door. And they didn't even let him die with his horn in his hand.

Kilgore Trout's creator, Kurt Vonnegut, also found himself, at an early stage in his career, in danger of being trapped on the outside looking in.

Like Sturgeon, Vonnegut was a literary artist whose thematic concerns, rather than genre ambitions, led him to write his own idio-

syncratic kind of science fiction, hardly calculated to win him a man-
tlepiece lined with Hugos. Unlike Sturgeon, Vonnegut also wrote an
idiosyncratic sort of mainstream fiction, too, and was able to place much
of his short fiction in the big-league slicks.

These days, of course, Vonnegut shrilly proclaims he was never a
science fiction writer, but had he been making his move in the '80s
instead of the '60s, he might now be just as righteously proclaiming he
was never a mainstream writer, and with equal literary justification.

Because the borderline between Vonnegut's full-bore SF and his
so-called mainstream fiction was always nonexistent. He no more
wrote mimetic contemporary novels than he did action-adventure space
opera.

He was always a kind of American magic realist, a combination of
Twain and Heller, Pynchon and Dick. In this part of the fictional
universe, the contemporary present behaves like science fiction, and
science fiction behaves like silly putty, so who is to say where the phase
change takes place? Or whether there is any at all.

Only the packagers, dummy!

Player Piano, Vonnegut's first novel, was a fairly gritty SF dystopia
in which the American middle class is automated out; it was obviously
decades ahead of its time, but all too plausible today. It was quite a good
novel, but it was published in a small hardcover edition and won no SF
awards.

Sirens of Titan, his second novel, curiously enough, reads as if it
could have been written by Trout, if only Trout could write with
Vonnegut's mordant panache. Human history is revealed as an incredibly
convoluted scam concocted by stranded aliens on Titan to send an idiot
message back home to Tralfamador. There are more SF gimmicks, time
loops, and reality tricks than a barrel of space monkeys. The message is
really as grim as a message can get, but the book is a pleasure to read, a
classic of its kind. This was published as straightforward SF and got
some genre attention, but no one was calling Vonnegut the man of the
hour.

Mother Night, his third novel, concerned the identity crisis of one,
ah, Howard W. Campbell, Jr. (get it? Vonnegut never did sell to
Astounding), an American sleeper agent in Nazi Germany whose cover
is his work as a Nazi propagandist and who ends up not quite knowing
who he is or which side he's really on.

Now while a certain case for *Mother Night* as SF could be made by fanzine mandarins, in the real world it should have been eminently publishable as a major mainstream novel.

But it didn't happen. *Mother Night* was published as a paperback original in a package that leaned toward hinting that maybe it *was* science fiction in order to guarantee a certain base market. You could hear the truckdrivers say, as they filled the rack pockets, "Hey, this guy Vonnegut, he goes with the sci-fi, right?"

Well unlike Sturgeon, Vonnegut (or at least his agent) had publishing street smarts or the right connections, probably both. He read the handwriting on the order forms, got his act together, and took it on the road, just in time to get *Cat's Cradle* published more or less in the manner it deserved.

If a novel that pivots on a speculative piece of very hard science, contains a made-up religion that in a curious way really works, and climaxes with the end of life on Earth may be said to contain at least marginal SF elements, then *Cat's Cradle* may be said to be science fiction, but fer chrissakes not on the cover!

While *Slaughterhouse Five* was the book that made Vonnegut a literary superstar, *Cat's Cradle* and then *God Bless You, Mr. Rosewater* were the solid base that made the rapid ascent possible.

Cat's Cradle is still my favorite Vonnegut novel, and it was the first novel that brought Vonnegut to my attention; and while the former may be a minority opinion, the latter was a common experience, for it was the first Vonnegut novel to be published in a first-class manner.

And it richly deserved to be. It is savage, mordant, funny as usual, but there is something more, a kind of sad but jaunty affirmation largely missing from Vonnegut's other novels. Bokononism, the Rasta-like religion of foma, of lies we can tell each other to feel better, seems a genuine affirmation of the best thing that Vonnegut can find to believe in, fictional creation itself. And when Bokonon lies down and freezes himself in a final posture of ultimate cosmic comic defiance, giving the finger to You Know Who, we feel the real Vonnegut displaying a rare moment of kinship with poor fucked-over humanity as he flips the malignantly indifferent universe the final juicy bird.

Cat's Cradle didn't become a big best-seller, but it sold a lot of trade paperbacks over time, and justly made Vonnegut's reputation in the wider literary world as an important American novelist to watch.

God Bless You, Mr. Rosewater completed Vonnegut's disengagement from any lingering SF image. It is the story of the misadventures of a millionaire trying to give away his money to do good, a rather gentler version of Terry Southern's *The Magic Christian*. It has no SF elements at all and cemented Vonnegut's standing reputation as a major mainstream novelist.

But curiously enough, Eliot Rosewater's favorite writer is none other than Kilgore Trout. Just as Vonnegut had finished wiping the SF mud off his bootheels, Kilgore Trout began to haunt his work.

Then, of course, came *Slaughterhouse Five*, generally recognized as Vonnegut's masterpiece, and certainly the cornerstone of his reputation, and the rest is literary history.

Literary history with a rather Vonnegutian ironic kicker.

At the height of his success, literarily and financially, something elusive seemed to seep out of Vonnegut's work. The mordancy turned a bit over-bitter, storytelling tended to become perfunctory for want of any burning story to tell, characters became mouthpieces for the author, and most ominously, the work started becoming indulgently self-reflective.

And Kilgore Trout, who indeed had been Billy Pilgrim's favorite writer in *Slaughterhouse Five*, kept popping up to haunt him. He appears in *God Bless You, Mr. Rosewater; Slaughterhouse Five; Breakfast of Champions; Slapstick*; and is the wampeter of *Galapagos*, even as a kind of ghost.

If Kurt Vonnegut had lived the life of Kilgore Trout, we would probably say that he'd reached SF burn-out, the point at which imagination flags and you start setting everything in the same fictional universe, books start referring to other books, characters make guest appearances in each other's novels, and, in the terminal phase, the author ends up holding long fictional conversations with himself in his best-selling rubber room.

Which is not to say that Vonnegut has quite reached condition terminal. *Jailbird* and *Dead Eye Dick* were more solid novels, and while *Galapagos*, his return to straight-on science fiction in everything but the cover copy, may seem genuinely depressed and fatigued, at least Vonnegut seems to be wrestling with the strange public warning he gave himself after the publication of *Slaughterhouse Five*.

He was quoted as saying, "Now that I've said everything I have to say, I'll shut up." In *Breakfast of Champions* he even attempted to lay off the cast of characters he had created.

Indeed, *Galapagos* seems like the ultimate attempt to shut down the works. Human assholery finally destroys the species. The only humans left a million years later are the descendants of Galapagos survivors, who have developed into a clade of mindless aquatic mammals, and good riddance to the bad rubbish of their "overdeveloped brains."

And who, you may ask, is around as a viewpoint to narrate this grim tale from a million-year retrospective?

None other than the son of Kilgore Trout, who on the Day of Judgment was summoned to the other side of the Blue Vortex by the shade of his dead father and, turning back, was constrained to endure the next million years of boredom for his sins until the Vortex and Kilgore Trout came for him again.

Well obviously, if Kilgore Trout began as Vonnegut's mordant send-up of the karma of science fiction writers like Theodore Sturgeon, he has by this time long since become a character of *Vonnegut's* literary psychodrama.

Trout's life is exactly what Vonnegut rescued himself from living with his worldy wisdom, what he might have become if, like Theodore Sturgeon, he hadn't been able to make the right moves to rescue himself from undeserved obscurity.

Buy why should such a literary ghost have the power to haunt Kurt Vonnegut? There is no danger of Vonnegut's relapsing to such a state. The numbers say anything he writes will be a best seller. Surely no part of him can mourn for *Kilgore Trout's* way not taken!

Maybe. . . .

But if Theodore Sturgeon was the template for Trout's karmic dilemma, it was Vonnegut who wrote Kilgore Trout's novels in both the literal and literary senses.

Obviously all Trout's bizarre sci-fi premises are really the product of Vonnegut's imagination, but less obviously, Trout's work as described sounds much more like Vonnegut's earlier oeuvre than anything of Sturgeon's.

Sturgeon was no cosmic stand-up comic, and his worlds were almost always carefully and even conservatively well worked out and plausible. If he had one weakness as a writer, it was that he was no surrealist; he played the reality game by the universe's rules.

Sturgeon's fiction is always realistic, in the sense that his worlds are rendered with verismilitude, and his stories take place on a deep empathic stage of character. They don't zen dance across the surface like Vonnegut's successful novels, and they're anything but wise-guy cosmic gimmick stories like Trout's.

Vonnegut's Trout seems more like the voice of the science fiction writer Vonnegut escaped becoming, spouting out the ream of sci-fi potboilers that Vonnegut mercifully never had to write. Half sigh of relief, half a shudder at what might have been, but for some fancy footwork and the right connections.

But *Sturgeon* was never in danger of devolving into a hack like Kilgore Trout. True Ted, like Trout, was not a fancy publishing dancer and, like Trout, never had the right connections to get himself on the best-seller list, or—half the time—to pay the rent.

But unlike Trout, Sturgeon was incapable of churning out fast wordage for money. At his rate of production, he had no choice but to rely on quality and an understanding bank manager. Could it be that Vonnegut knows in his heart of hearts that *he* could have and probably would have ended up writing Trout's five-foot shelf if his back had been pressed to Sturgeon's wall?

Of course, Kilgore Trout can't really be *Vonnegut's* own doppelganger, can he? After all, unlike either Trout or Sturgeon, Vonnegut prevailed—he followed his own star and it took him to the big time.

Yet now it seems, in retrospect, Vonnegut has gifted the fictional Kilgore Trout with one modest saving virtue that both he and Sturgeon might both wistfully admire as brothers under the skin.

Trout is a hack. He has the literary genius of neither Sturgeon nor Vonnegut. But, chronically depressive though he may be, he doesn't dry up, he doesn't stay blocked, and he doesn't become cynical either. He keeps on cranking it out, he keeps on truckin' with all these crazy dreams in his head.

If Trout had had Sturgeon's talent, he might have been the champ. But if Sturgeon had Trout's sheer persistence at the typewriter, *Godbody* would have been rewritten into a masterpiece on a hot weekend in the early '70s, and The Fish might have gone on to knock 'em dead in the big time for the next decade.

And if Kurt Vonnegut had listened to what the voice of Kilgore Trout was starting to whisper to him as early as *God Bless You, Mr. Rosewater*?

If he had trusted more in his crazy dreams after *Slaughterhouse Five* and not been quite so cagy, if he had spent his literary riches to good cause like Eliot Rosewater, if he had given a little freer reign to the Trout in him, might not the world look a little brighter now?

Would we and he have been spared the listless self-indulgence of

Breakfast of Champions and *Slapstick* and the de-energized terminal pessimism of *Galapagos* and had instead another *Cat's Cradle* and *Slaughterhouse Five*? Even a string of good solid SF novels like *The Sirens of Titan* might have been preferable to what was actually produced.

What is Kilgore Trout trying to tell Kurt Vonnegut? That a hungry writer is a creative writer, that fame and fortune are harmful to the soul, that it is better to starve in a garret than to luxuriate in literary salons?

Give him a break, folks!

Sturgeon's career went that route, and look where it got him. Curiously enough, in a kind of psychic sense, much the same place Vonnegut seems to be now. Sometimes You Know Who likes to give us all the finger back.

Bokonon lay down on the ice and died with his finger in the air, Sturgeon died with an unfinished masterpiece in first draft that gathered dust for two decades, but maybe in the end Kilgore Trout had the right idea. He just made the best of the bad hand of cards fate dealt him and just kept cranking out his crazy ideas till the Blue Vortex came and got him.

The Blue Vortex has already gotten Trout when *Galapagos* begins, but even in the terminal bleakness of the extinction of earthly consciousness, Vonnegut lets us glimpse him shining through on the other side.

Maybe this is a good sign in a weary novel.

Maybe this is Vonnegut's foma to himself.

And if he finally believes it, it will make him strong and brave, and make his future readers happy.

Theodore Sturgeon could explain it better than I could. No one could explain it better. *Godbody*, for all its first-draft flaws, still shines through with his warm knowing smile from the other side. But he's not here to enlighten our hearts anew any more.

The Blue Vortex came and got Ted too.

The Strange Case of J.G. Ballard

He has been publishing his own idiosyncratic brand of science fiction for thirty years now. He was a central figure — arguably *the* central figure — of the New Wave of the 1960s. He is acknowledged as a seminal influence by the Cyberpunks of the 1980s. He was short-listed for the Booker Prize. He had a number one best-seller in Britain. He is a major literary figure in France. He has been talked about for the Nobel. He was major motion picture.

He has never won a Hugo. He has never won a Nebula. His books have never really sold well in the United States, and truth be told, at times he has had difficulty placing them with American publishers at all. His collection, *The Atrocity Exhibition*, was bought, scheduled, and announced, and then its publication was cancelled by two American publishers before it finally appeared as *Love and Napalm: Export USA*. *Empire of the Sun*, the aforementioned Booker Prize nominee and number one British best-seller, flopped as a hardcover in the United States and didn't even have a real mass-market edition before the Spielberg film.

J.G. Ballard began publishing in 1956, and his early stories appeared in conventional SF publications. Over the next few years, stories like "Prima Belladonna," "Billennium," and "The Voices of Time" earned him a reputation as a unique and powerful voice in science fiction on both sides of the Atlantic.

1962 saw the publication of his first novel, *The Wind from Nowhere*, the first of a series of disaster novels, the others being *The Drowned World, The Burning World*, and *The Crystal World*, in which civilization is destroyed by wind, flood, drought, and crystallization, respectively.

These books established him as a major science fiction novelist in America as well as Britain.

In the middle to late 1960s, during the crest of the New Wave, Ballard wrote a series of so-called condensed novels—"The Assassination of JFK Considered as a Downhill Motor-Race," "Why I Want to Fuck Ronald Reagan," "You and Me and the Continuum, "The Atrocity Exhibition," etc.—many of which were first published in Michael Moorcock's *New Worlds*, and most of which were collected in *The Atrocity Exhibition*. Ballard also wrote occasional criticism of fiction, nonfiction, art, and culture for *New Worlds*. He was not only a central literary figure of the New Wave, he was deeply involved in the development of its esthetic theories, and it was Ballard who coined the catchphrase "inner space."

In the 1970s, while continuing his prolific production of short fiction, Ballard published *Crash*, a bizarre novel centered on car-crashes, and two urban-disaster novels, *Concrete Island* and *High-Rise*, in which the disasters, rather than being climatological, are entirely man-made. By this time, Ballard had established himself as an important figure in international literary circles. Contrariwise, his commercial viability as a science fiction writer in the United States was on the wane.

In 1984, Ballard published *Empire of the Sun*, an autobiographical novel of his days as a boy in Japanese-occupied China during World War II. *Empire of the Sun* was an enormous literary and commercial success in Britain but pretty much bit the Big One on its own in the United States.

It has nevertheless been turned into a major motion picture by no less than Steven Spielberg.

The Day of Creation, his latest as I write this, did well in Britain, though not as well as *Empire of the Sun*, and was well published in the United States thanks to the film, but has met with only indifferent commercial success.

This capsule publishing history epitomizes, at least to an extent, the corresponding three decades of dialectic between British and American science fiction.

In the 1950s and into the early 1960s, science fiction as a whole was dominated by works written in English (as it still is), and Anglophone science fiction was both strongly transatlantic and economically dominated by American publication.

British writers like John Brunner, John Christopher, Brian Aldiss, and John Wyndham were able to compete in the American market (where the wordage rates, advances, and royalties were more lucrative) with the native science fiction writers. What they were actually writing was not very much different from the broad mainstream of American SF, and they were hardly perceived as identifiably British on this side of the Atlantic.

The same could more or less be said of J.G. Ballard at this phase in his career. The early stories did not have too much trouble seeing print in the United States; they were even published here in collections; and if they were regarded as somewhat more "literary" than the usual run of stuff and more than a little weird, they were no more so than, say, Sturgeon, Cordwainer Smith, Dick, or Bester.

The first three disaster novels were published in the United States as science fiction in a regular Ballard program and were perceived as such, disaster novels in the tradition of John Wyndham, John Christopher, Balmer and Wylie, et al.

The Wind from Nowhere, The Drowned World, and *The Burning World* were more or less straightforward ecological disaster novels, or so it seemed, at least, until the publication of the final book in the series, *The Crystal World*, in 1966. *The Crystal World* was something else again, and cast the three previous novels in a new perspective.

Wind, water, and heat were the straightforward McGuffins in the first three novels, readily acceptable and comprehensible in realistic science fictional terms, even rather scientifically rigorous in their extrapolation. But the disaster McGuffin in *The Crystal World* was mumbo-jumbo in hard science terms and made sense only on a metaphysical and metaphorical level.

Organic forms begin to crystallize into inorganic versions of themselves, the effect radiating from a center deep in the jungle. While the protagonist penetrates deep and deeper towards the center of crystallization, the effect spreads outward with an inevitability that makes it clear that the whole planet will eventually be transformed into the Crystal World of the title. The protagonist becomes infected by the "crystal disease," and the deeper in towards the center he goes, the more he himself becomes crystallized, physically and psychologically.

And as the novel progresses, the disaster, the spreading crystallization within and without, is transformed from a sinister plague into a thing of physical and metaphysical beauty, so that by the time the novel ends and the final crystallization is completed, it is seen not as a devolution of the organic and human sphere into something dead and inorganic but as a kind of mystical apotheosis. The transformed protagonist and the transformed landscape are united in an eternal moment of crystalline clarity.

You will notice that I refer to the viewpoint character of *The Crystal World* as the "protagonist," not the "hero." From the retrospective advantage of *The Crystal World* it is easy enough to see that the previous three Ballardian disaster novels have no "heroes" either.

In contrast to the traditional SF disaster novels, in which heroic characters struggle against—and more often than not triumph over—the altered physical realm, Ballard's characters devolve into and as often as not merge psychically with the transformed landscape. In the first three disaster novels, this process can be and was seen as the simple psychological devolution of people under the pressure of physical disaster, but *The Crystal World* makes it clear that all the Ballardian disaster novels have the merger of character into landscape, inner space into external environment, and vice versa, at their thematic core, and that Ballard's concern is more esthetic and coldly metaphysical than moral or even conventionally characterological.

In a sense then, the four disaster novels are indeed a kind of tetralogy. The first three dissolve devolving characters into a devolved landscape, and then *The Crystal World* throws the whole thing into a deeper and more subtle perspective by portraying much the same melting of character into landscape, inner space into environmental surround, as a kind of *evolution*, a metaphysical transcendence.

The Crystal World marked Ballard's emergence from genre SF as a significant general literary figure in Britain and as a minor literary light in the United States, where the book was brought out as a "literary" novel. It also marked his emergence as a novelist of subtlety and power.

And the beginning of his eclipse as a science fiction writer within the SF community and as a commercially viable writer in the United States.

By the time *The Crystal World* was published, in 1966, the New Wave controversy was already in full flower, the SF community was already becoming polarized, and Michael Moorcock and J.G. Ballard were at the center of the storm.

Moorcock was the editor of *New Worlds* (where most of the New Wave short fiction was being published and some of the novels in serial form as well), he was the major critical theorist (the Bruce Sterling of his day), and the writer he most frequently held up as an exemplar was Ballard.

With all the Sturm und Drang over establishment versus counter-culture, hero versus antihero, outer space versus inner space, literary freedom versus censorship, upbeat versus downbeat, dope versus pro-peller beanies, the technical literary thesis that was at the heart of at least the British New Wave tends to become obscured.

Moorcock believed that traditional mimetic contemporary fiction had exhausted its material and fossilized its technique. He believed that science fiction offered theoretically boundless new vistas but was frozen into stylized action-adventure forms, slavish mimesis of reality, stereotypical image-systems, and conventionalized traditional prose.

What he sought to foster was hybrid vigor—the material of science fiction, the psychological depth and thematic ambition of traditional "high literature," written in new forms and new prose styles in the process of being invented. And he had a notion of the direction those forms and styles might take.

Moorcock proposed a fiction whose skein of events, instead of following the linear logic of a conventional plotline from problem through complication into successful climactic resolution, were organized nonlinearly, as montage, in the manner of a film, so that the final closure would be an accumulation of images, an ultimate union of metaphor with event, signifier with significand, inner with outer, in a resolution satisfying on both a content level and an imagistic level, like a successful poem.

To achieve this, a prose line was required that avoided obvious statement, that eschewed the constraints of mimetic reportage of events in favor of imagistic transformation, that skipped selectively over the surface of reality, that transmuted the mundane into the extraordinary, that grounded the extraordinary in the dreamlike but somehow familiar psychological landscape of the characters' and the readers' inner space.

Examples of such writing were to be found in the work of William Burroughs, Jerzy Kosinski, Mervyn Peake, the Moorcock of the Jerry Cornelius stories, and most preeminently in the work of J.G. Ballard.

Earlier short stories like "The Voices of Time" and "Billennium," particularly the stories set in the decaying resort of Vermillion Sands, followed much of Moorcock's schema before the fact. And the disaster novels, with their morally neutral imagistic observance of the transformation of the inner landscape to match the altered environment, with their reliance on physical description rather than conventional storytelling to convey inner meaning, were already moving in that direction before culminating in *The Crystal World*, in which the metaphorical system *is* the surface of the novel's reality, in which the protagonist's inner space becomes one with the metaphorically transmuted outer landscape, in which the resolution, horrific in conventional plot and character terms, becomes satisfying on an entirely imagistic level, a closure that succeeds on metaphorical esthetics alone.

This, needless to say, is a far cry from what makes Hugo- or Nebula-award-winning SF succeed, and has very little to do as well with what makes commercial fiction, SF or otherwise, move off the racks.

With the publication of *The Crystal World*, Ballard was already beginning to come under attack from traditional SF circles, particularly in the United States, and the criticism was applied in a somewhat revisionary manner to his previous work, too.

Ballard's characters were antiheroes. They did not respond to the challenges of disaster by fighting back with pluck and courage and technological puissance like good SF heroes should. They despaired, they devolved, they gave up, they allowed themselves to be gobbled up by the hostile universe, they accepted it, they even came to welcome it. Science and rationality did not inevitably triumph in Ballard's scheme of things, far from it. The man was a nihilist. Anti-rational. Downbeat. A real bummer.

And he was in the forefront of this damn New Wave thing over in London.

And indeed he was.

About the time *The Crystal World* was published, Ballard's condensed novels began to appear, mostly in *New Worlds*. And if *The Crystal World* and the earlier short fiction were New Wave only in retrospect, helping to formulate the theoretical underpinnings, the condensed novels were written under the early influence of the movement and in turn served as exemplars of what the new SF could become.

These short stories — and most of them are quite short — really *are* condensed novels in a formal sense. Scenes are rendered as sequences of rapid-fire images, each of which is redolent with multiple and ambiguous meaning. The scenes in turn succeed each other in rapidly cut montage, the structure arises out of their successive and sometimes repetitive juxtapositions, the psyches of the characters are seen to mutate in a series of isolated cuts rather than linearly, and the resolutions, such as they are, are imagistic, rather than climactic.

It is as if Ballard took whole novels and edited out all the transitions, all the build-ups to situations, all the personal interactions, most of the dialogue, all extraneous description, and condensed them to a series of freeze-frames, extracted moments of epiphany, a kind of flip-book version in which the essence of a whole novel is conveyed in a perfectly selected series of still-shots.

Though the condensed novels were a brilliant technical achievement whose influence on short science fiction in particular has been enormous, they were hardly the sort of thing likely to be short-listed for the Hugo or even the Nebula, nor likely to appeal to any but a quite literate audience, defying as they did all conventional mimetic and story expectations. And the bizarre and obsessive imagery that permeates them did not exactly make them more accessible to science fiction enthusiasts or the general mass audience.

Unlike those of the disaster novels, Ballard's settings in the condensed novels are relentlessly technological—decaying cityscapes, the malfunctioning technosphere, the randomly mutating media landscape. And the condensed novels are largely set in an America that Ballard knew only as contemporary myth. And the same images appear over and over again.

Motorways. Marilyn Monroe. Car crashes. JFK. Ronald Reagan. Abandoned airfields. Jacqueline Kennedy. Eniwetok Atoll. Ralph Nader. The Enola Gay. Sexualized car parts and crashes. Hospitals. The Dallas Schoolbook Depository. The atomic bomb. Lee Harvey Oswald.

Ballard seemed to be ransacking contemporary media coverage for images. And the imagistic montages he put together out of these bits and pieces of contemporary mythology were deeply disturbing, not to say outraging, to conventional and even to unconventional sensibilities.

Surely the two most notorious of these condensed novels were "The Assassination of JFK Considered as a Downhill Motor-Race" and "Why I Want to Fuck Ronald Reagan."

"The Assassination of JFK Considered as a Downhill Motor-Race" narrates the events of the Kennedy assassination as if the whole thing were indeed a motor race. Ballard sets up this metaphorical assumption and proceeds to describe the dire events in Dallas in terms of racing imagery, as if they were being described by some kind of Martian sportscaster.

"Why I Want to Fuck Ronald Reagan" would seem to have been too much even for Moorcock. It first appeared in something called *Ronald Reagan, the Magazine of Poetry*, published in London by Thomas M. Disch and John Sladek, two Americans who, like me, had migrated to Britain to be at the heart of the New Wave ferment. When it appeared in the first American incarnation of *The Atrocity Exhibition*, at Doubleday, it caused the entire print run to be trashed.

Nelson Doubleday, so the story goes, was taking some VIPS on a tour through the printing plant as the book was coming off the presses, picked it up at random, saw the story, freaked, and ordered the entire print run, save six author's copies, fed directly into the pulper. Ballard, so the legend goes, then sent one copy to the then-governor of California with an anonymous note saying, "Just thought you should see what filth Doubleday is printing about you."

"Why I Want to Fuck Ronald Reagan" is just that—the undescribed narrator's explication of the charismatic sexual appeal of the man who was to become president a decade and a half later, and it draws an imagistic equation between the sexual appeal of Reagan and that of a car crashing into Ralph Nader's pudendum. Really. And makes it work.

For those open to such outré literary experimentalism, that is; which is to say, let's face it, an elite minority. In retrospect, it cannot be denied that the British New Wave was an elitist movement. In technical terms, it was centered on a complex literary theory epitomized in Ballard's condensed novels, Moorcock's Jerry Cornelius stories, Aldiss' *Barefoot in the Head*, and the short fiction of James Sallis, Langdon Jones, and M. John Harrison. In commercial terms, Moorcock was quite willing to see the circulation of *New Worlds* shrink to the natural audience for the sort of fiction he wished to publish. In audience terms, the writers began with the assumption that their hypothetical ideal reader was at least as intelligent, sophisticated, and literate as themselves.

This is how dedicated wirters expand the bounds of the literary possible, but it is not the ideal way to separate Joe from his beer money.

As a kind of literary laboratory, the New Wave succeeded admirably. For while Moorcock's theoretical new fiction never took hold in its pur sang form, and even Ballard abandoned the condensed novel for the most part after he had thoroughly mastered it, the literary lessons of the New Wave diffused into the general literary culture of science fiction, and their liberating influence can be seen today in the work of American writers as varied as Lucius Shepard, William Gibson, Gregory Benford, Bruce Sterling, Greg Bear, Gene Wolfe, and Lisa Goldstein.

The primary audience for fiction as uncompromisingly experimental as Ballard's condensed novels is other writers, writers who absorb technique from it, which they may then apply to the production of fiction with appeal to a more general audience. The obsessive imagery in the condensed novels, like that of William Burroughs, was too personal and recondite to render them accessible to a mass audience or even devotees of conventional "high literature."

But even Ballard himself was able to apply what he discovered in the lab to the writing of superficially more conventional and much more generally accessible fiction.

In the middle 1970s, as the New Wave was being absorbed into the generality of science fiction, he published three novels, *Crash, Concrete Island*, and *High-Rise*, which did much to transform his European reputation from that of an interesting experimentalist to that of a significant British literary figure read by "serious readers," if not by a mass audience.

Crash is a condensed novel writ large, almost impossible to describe or paraphrase, that works Ballard's obsessive car-crash imagery to the max, transmogrifying the car crash into an immense, murky, convoluted, and powerful image for the intersection of sex, power, death, and the technosphere. It is in many ways the culmination of the condensed novels.

And perhaps the exorcism of the obsessional material of this period, the content that made the condensed novels even more inaccessible than did the formal experimentalism, obscuring to some extent the technical achievement. For a new clarity of vision, a new narrative power, a new sheer storytelling ability, appears in *Concrete Island* and *High-Rise*, a melding of the disaster novels with both the concerns and the absorbed techniques of the condensed-novel period.

Both *Concrete Island* and *High-Rise* are disaster novels, but unlike the previous disaster novels, they are *urban* disaster novels, taking place not in an altered natural realm but in the Ballardian technosphere of the condensed novels. *Concrete Island* takes place entirely on a traffic island in the middle of a motorway interchange. *High-Rise* takes place entirely inside an enormous self-contained apartment building.

These are huge and powerful images for the modern western world, made all the more powerful because they are no mere metaphors. The high-rise and the motorway are not only dominant images of the contemporary urban consciousness, they dominate the landscape of modern reality itself. Here Ballard has found node-points where the inner landscape and the outer landscape merge perfectly in a manner that needs no surreal dreamtime connection. The image *is* the reality, the reality *is* the image, and these two novels are therefore easily accessible on a mimetic level.

Concrete Island opens with crashing of the protagonist's car onto the traffic island, and the entire novel takes place on this bizarre yet entirely credible pocket universe beneath the motorway ramps, as the driver first seeks to escape from the traffic island, then begins to undercut his own efforts, and finally surrenders to the landscape in the prototypical Ballardian manner.

There is no surrealism here. The elements of the traffic island do not undergo imagistic transformation. They don't have to, for the car bodies, garbage dump, and bulldozed village of the traffic island, and the motorway ramps soaring above it, are *already* a perfect image system in the real world for what Ballard is trying to convey about modern reality. The story he tells is a series of failed escape attempts, reminiscent structurally of the fate of poor Wiley Coyote in a Roadrunner cartoon; straight-line, taut with narrative tension, illuminating of character, and yet because of the concretized metaphorical setting, rife with imagistic opportunities that Ballard fully exploits for irony and epiphany.

High-Rise is the perfect metaphorical yet realistic urban horror story. It takes place in a building that is designed to be a completely contained model of modern urban culture, with supermarkets, liquor stores, parking lots, boutiques, schools, pool, everything it takes to encapsulate urban man. The internal society *is* a pocket universe, and as it devolves, it mirrors general urban society in extremis.

The building was designed with a class structure built in—the apartments are more expensive the higher you go, and the more expensive your apartment, the closer to the building you get to park—and so, Ballard implies, with the potential for class warfare also built in.

As things devolve, as conflicts, battles, tribal warfare, and finally permanent ongoing chaotic savagery break out, the evolution of modern urban man runs backward as the inhabitants come to welcome this stepwise shucking of civilized constraints as a liberation from the superego of modern society and a return to the feral innocence of the psychic jungle. As their pocket universe devolves toward the civilized vanishing point, they devolve toward creatures of pure egoistic lusts, characters merging into a ruined urban landscape that their own devolving interior landscapes are creating, both landscapes becoming perfect images for each other, and both of them literally concretized by the real-life metaphor of the high-rise apartment block.

By the late 1970s, then, Ballard was established as a significant literary figure in Britain and on the Continent, even while his career as a science fiction writer was in eclipse in the United States. From the vantage of today, we can see that the present schism between British and American science fiction began in the 1970s, and the strange case of J.G. Ballard nicely epitomizes what happened.

In the United States, science fiction was transformed from a minor publishing genre with consistent low sales from book to book, no matter who wrote them, into a major sphere of commercial publishing. In Britain, this never quite happened. In Britain, science fiction writers like Ballard and Aldiss were able to achieve general literary acceptance, Ballard via the congruence between New Wave SF and experimental literature, Aldiss via the publication of a series of literate mainstream best-sellers. In America, *this*, generally speaking, did not happen.

So while American science fiction writers had the possibility of bestsellerdom dangled before them, British SF writers, thanks to the New Wave, had the possibility of acceptance into the general literary culture. As one American editor has observed, "The New Wave lost in the US and won in Britain."

And while this is certainly an oversimplification—since many of the literary techniques of the New Wave were absorbed by American writers who used them for the most part in the service of more generally accessible SF than their British brethren were producing—it certainly is true that *Ballard*, the archetypal New Wave figure on both sides of the Atlantic, lost in the United States and won in Britain.

Ballard never wrote for a mass audience. Back before American SF publishing went major-league, neither did any other science fiction writers, so the low sales figures for his admittedly difficult work didn't matter and he was able to enjoy at least regular American publication on a par with his American colleagues. But once American science fiction started appearing regularly on the best-seller lists, once true commercial success was a real possibility, so was commercial failure, and once the publishers started paying rapt attention to the sales figures, writers like Ballard came to be deemed commercially nonviable.

He was certainly not best-seller material. Nor was he a fave rave among SF fans. And he was too much the experimentalist and still too much the SF writer to be a mainstream literary lion. What he was was an experimentalist most appreciated by the avant garde and other writers, and what that means in terms of American publishing is small printings of obscure trade editions and nonviability in mass market. And that's how J.G. Ballard had been published in the United States for years.

In Britain, though, with reduced economic expectations, with a long literary history of non-genre science fiction in the tradition of Wells, Huxley, Orwell, and Burgess, with the penetration of a sector of the literary establishment by the energy of the New Wave, it is possible for a writer like Ballard to be adequately reviewed enough, to achieve stature enough, to find his natural audience—not SF fans or the average general reader, but those interested in literarily adventurous fiction plugged in to the contemporary zeitgeist.

This would seem to be what many of the better British SF writers are after—an educated audience large enough to support them, economically and psychically, at the full stretch of their powers, rather than the maximum number of readers for their lowest common denominator. This has always been an elusive goal for science fiction writers in the United States, where Ballard, like most of his British colleagues and many American SF writers as well, has failed to achieve it.

And then in 1984, *Empire of the Sun* was published, and J.G. Ballard became a superstar in Britain. Not only did the novel zoom up the best-seller lists, it received wide critical acclaim, which also brought favorable retrospective attention to Ballard's previous work and unquestionably established him as one of the most important living British writers.

Empire of the Sun was a quantum leap for Ballard, not only in terms of sales and public stature but in absolute literary terms, and what is more, in it Ballard casts a psychohistorical perspective on his own inner landscape in a manner few if any other writers have attempted or achieved. Still further, it was the first Ballard novel to be readily engaging to a mass audience.

And no wonder.

Empire of the Sun is an autobiographical novel of Ballard's own boyhood experiences in and around Shanghai during the Japanese invasion and occupation during World War II. The novel opens with the invasion of Shanghai, follows young Jim through the occupation, and ends with the atomic bombing of Hiroshima and Nagasaki and the liberation. Jim is separated from his parents, survives on his own in their empty house, ends up in an internment camp, escapes, wanders solitary through the chaos and horrors of the Japanese occupation, and survives to become, all these years later, the James G. Ballard who has finally come to tell the tale.

On one level, the level that no doubt made *Empire of the Sun* a best-seller in Britain, this is an exciting action-adventure story with a plucky young hero, set in an exotic wartime locale. Ballard's eye for detail is formidable, he writes action sequences very well indeed, the novel is utterly realistic, and the viewpoint stays superficially within the consciousness of young Jim.

This is probably the level upon which Steven Spielberg was attracted to the story in the first place, and certainly the level upon which his film primarily operates—the tale of the young boy's lone survival of the horrors of war and occupation.

But on another level, the level that no doubt got the novel short-listed for the Booker Prize, *Empire of the Sun* is the archetypal Ballardian disaster novel, rendered with the hard-edged realism of *Concrete Island* and *High-Rise*, but also with the imagistic intensity of the short fiction.

Ballard is totally in control of all the diverse aspects of his writing here and, for the first time, has managed to bring all of it together to grab the mass readership with real emotional appeal while surrendering none of his subtlety, depth, intensity, or imagistic obsessions.

This is Jim's story, and the author's third-person narration never wanders from the viewpoint of the boy, but this is J.G. Ballard the mature consciousness explicting his own boyhood tale, giving it historical perspective, psychological analysis, and prescient overtones of the coming postwar world, and doing so by transmuting the realistically rendered settings into the archetypal Ballardian imagistic landscape.

Actually, that's got it a bit backwards. For what Ballard reveals here is that his real-life experiences as the Jim of *Empire of the Sun* were the template of many of the imagistic obsessions of the short fiction, the devolving characters of the disaster novels, the distance of his characters from each other, the urban disaster areas of *Concrete Island* and *High-Rise*.

Empty buildings. Abandoned airfields. Wandering refugees from disaster. Barbed wire. Bombers. Wounded and/or ill protagonists. Eniwetok. Hiroshima. The Atom Bomb. Cracked concrete. The Disaster Area.

It's all here, in its original prime-reality version as Ballard lived it during World War II. Here is much of the source material of all the fiction that has gone before: the imagery, the Ballardian protagonist alienated from the landscape but finally merging into it, the impending ruins of the twentieth century and the existential plight of modern man within them.

Empire of the Sun is not science fiction, but it is informed by a characteristic Ballardian science fictional perspective, for, in light of his total oeuvre, what Ballard finally manages to achieve here is the illumination of not only the roots of his own career but the genesis of the postwar world of its thematic obsessions. He does it by demonstrating just how those imagistic obsessions and modern icons arose out of the real landscape of a real Disaster Area, the Second World War.

And he does one more thing in *Empire of the Sun* that he has never done before: he creates, in Jim, a sympathetic hero who survives by his wits, with whom the reader can emotionally identify, a character who may warp into the landscape of disaster, but who matures rather than devolves.

Why then was the novel not a commercial success in the United States when Spielberg was so quick to sniff out the story's appeal to a mass audience? Because the buyers for the bookstore chains could not credit such appeal in a Ballard novel? Because the hero is British? Because the book was not properly promoted in trade?

The indifferently successful film made the paperback tie-in reissue a near best-seller, but, packaged as it was with Ballard's name writ small to promote the film rather than the writer-protagonist, it did not exactly introduce Ballard's other work to a mass American audience or convince distributors that he had become a superstar on the racks.

On the other hand, it did get most of his backlist reissued in small editions, and it does seem to have finally secured Ballard decent American publication for his future work, even if he has not yet emerged as a major literary figure in America.

But who is to say it can never happen?

The Day of Creation, Ballard's next and latest novel, clearly demonstrates that the creative breakthrough of *Empire of the Sun* was no fluke generated by the autobiographical nature of the material; that, perhaps through the cathartic effect of writing it, Ballard has achieved and consolidated a new level of literary clarity and emotional balance at this mature stage in his career.

The Day of Creation is a Ballardian disaster novel in reverse. Dr. Mallory, a typical alienated and ill Ballardian protagonist who narrates the novel in first person, accidentally triggers the birth of a new river, the Mallory, in drought-stricken Central Africa. The river grows, generating a lush new Eden in the desert along its banks, and Mallory, pursued by the local police captain, the local guerilla forces, a degenerating documentary film maker, his Indian assistant, and an obsessed widow, flees by boat up toward its mysterious source, accompanied by Noon, a young African girl who may or may not be a figment of his fevered imagination.

For the first time, Ballard gives us a natural landscape in the process of glorious exfoliation rather than degeneration. And he describes it with a precision previously applied only to the technosphere and a passionate naturalist's eye that he has never really displayed before.

And here the protagonist does not devolve into a hostile altered landscape. Instead, a hostile landscape is gloriously transformed into a new Eden that emerges out of his inner space in a magical act of creation. Mallory openly identifies the river with his own body and blood and, in keeping with his ambivalent attitude towards himself, cherishes the river even as he seeks to destroy it at its source, pursued by the demons of the western technosphere, petty third-world empire-building, and his own self-alienation.

Mallory has an awareness of his own ambivalence towards himself and his river throughout, a Ballardian character possessed for the first time with a degree of Ballardian insight, rendered thereby emotionally closer to the reader than such obsessives have been before, sympathetic in his self-defeating behavior, if not exactly lovable.

That the Eden of the Mallory is eventually polluted and destroyed by these forces and Mallory's own obsessions is therefore a true tragedy, in the context of which Ballard succeeds in closing the novel on a note of pathos rather than despair.

In its condensed imagistic prose, *The Day of Creation* does skirt perilously close to self-parody of middle-period Ballard. But it never quite goes over the top. For it is balanced by the emotional intimacy and straightforward narrative drive that emerged in *Empire of the Sun* in a manner that indicates that Ballard, like Mallory, has penetrated to the headwaters of his own flow of creation but, unlike Mallory, has emerged from the experience a wiser and more truly mature creator.

Although Ballard has been writing for three decades now, amazingly enough, he is still maturing and still evolving. Whatever he does next is bound to be no less than interesting. What happens to his career next should be interesting one way or another, too, for it will tell us much about the realities of American publishing, the publicity value of a major film to a writer's total oeuvre, the differences between American and British reading publics, and perhaps, who knows, the health of Anglo-American letters itself.

The Transmogrification of Philip K. Dick

I really didn't want to write this essay, for Philip K. Dick was a close friend, his untimely death affected me deeply, and aside from a brief obituary I was cozened into writing at the time and an introduction to one volume of his collected short stories, I have been unwilling and perhaps unable to write about Phil since.

But this book is intended as a critical overview of the modern literature, and Phil Dick is arguably the greatest science fiction writer who ever lived and certainly a central figure in the literary history of the field, so *Science Fiction in the Real World* would not only have a gaping void at its heart if a consideration of Dick's work were omitted, it would do a disservice to his literary legacy.

However, I will not be so disingenuous as to pretend to objectivity; indeed, it is obvious from the two opening paragraphs that I cannot even decide upon a comfortable way of referring to my late friend and literary comrade. I cannot help but commit innumerable sins against conventional critical objectivity in this essay, which perforce must be as much a personal memoir as a piece of literary criticism.

Furthermore, I freely admit that what finally moved me to break my grieved silence on the subject of Philip K. Dick was the growing amount of cultish rubbish written about Phil since his death, which, I believe, has done a disservice to the serious critical perception of the true greatness of his oeuvre by obscuring its center, which has little to do with relatively minor works like *Valis* and *The Divine Invasion*, let alone the so-called "Exegesis."

Gregg Rickman has entitled one book of interpreted interviews with Phil *The Final Testament*; it concentrates mainly on *Valis, The*

Divine Invasion, Phil's experience with the "pink light" and the dybbuk of a fourteenth-century rabbi who supposedly dictated to him the material of the "Exegesis" upon which these novels were based. All too much of post-mortem examination of Dick's life and work has focused on this admittedly bizarre material, which R. Crumb has even turned into a comic strip.

Given all this, given that Phil eventually died as the result of a stroke, given that *Valis* and *The Divine Invasion* have a certain air of babblement to the nonbeliever, it was perhaps not unreasonable for Eric Rabkin to opine that the "pink light" was a symptom of an earlier and smaller stroke that unbalanced Phil's brain on a biological level and led to the delusionary state in which he unfortunately produced his last works.

But both Rabkin and Rickman ignore one fact—Rickman perhaps because it does not fit his mystical obsession, Rabkin because it obviates his otherwise cogent explanation of what he calls Phil's final insanity and what Rickman and others consider Phil's transcendental revelation.

And that fact is that neither *Valis* nor *The Divine Invasion* nor the "Exegesis" nor Gregg Rickman's book of interviews is the final testament of Philip K. Dick.

The final testament of Philip K. Dick is *The Transmigration of Timothy Archer*, the last novel Phil wrote, a work that is luminously lucid, eminently sane, a literary breakthrough for Phil at the end of his career and in a certain sense a wise and gentle piss-take on the Philip K. Dick of *Valis, The Divine Invasion*, and the "Exegesis"—a negation of all the complex and confused kabbalistic mystification of the previous period, and a return to the melding of the quotidian lives of very real people with the clear and genuine metaphysical insight and loving warmth that made him the great writer than he was, redoubled here by the palpable return to true mystical clarity in and rising out of the real world that, I would contend, made him a metaphysical writer like no other.

And here is where literary criticism must segue into personal memoir, for I had a hand in the genesis of this novel, or at least in the form that it took.

I had returned to New York from Los Angeles before the "pink light" period and had seen Phil only a few times on visits back to the Coast. I am a lousy letter writer when I am working, and I felt that, in a certain sense, I had abandoned Phil during this difficult period. Had he really flipped out? Had I let him down?

But on my next trip back, I visited Phil in Santa Ana, and things seemed much the same. Phil was not barbled. He was having the usual troubles with his car. He had spoken to me occasionally about the "pink light," his possession by the dybbuk of the fourteenth-century rabbi, the automatic writing of the Exegesis, but even at the time, he had discussed all this on the same level as his transmission problems or his troubles keeping his weight down, and now he had put all that behind him and was in the process of trying to put some totally different material together into a new novel.

It seemed that a female relative of one of his wives had had an ongoing secret affair with James Pike, the maverick Episcopal bishop of California, who had eventually been relieved of his post by the hierarchy and had died in the Negev in Israel, apparently having ventured into the desert in a bad car in search of Essene sites or artifacts, provisioned only with two warm bottles of Coke.

Phil had come to know Pike through this connection and wanted to write a novel about Pike's spiritual odyssey. Somehow, perhaps because he felt he was irrevocably typed as an SF writer, Phil had gotten it into his head that the only way he could get such a novel published was to tart it up with a lot of thriller-cum-SF paraphernalia involving CIA plots, alien invasions, and the usual razzmatazz.

"Jeez, Phil," I told him, "you've got a great story here, you don't need all that crap. Why don't you just tell it straight?"

"You think I could get it published?"

I told him I thought he could, and he decided to discuss the matter with Russell Galen, his agent and friend, whom he really trusted. Galen concurred, encouraged Phil to go ahead, and the result was *The Transmigration of Timothy Archer*, which I believe is one of Phil's three or four best novels, and a return to the level of *The Man in the High Castle*, *The Three Stigmata of Palmer Eldritch*, and *Ubik*, after too many years of floundering around with lesser work. Certainly it is far superior to *Valis* or *The Divine Invasion*, utterly coherent, totally controlled, spiritually lucid, and filled with loving clarity.

Dick, furthermore, narrated the novel in first person—something he had never done before—and he made the first-person viewpoint character a woman, Angel Archer, who, in her detached distance from the Bishop Timothy Archer of the title, is a peculiar but effective transmogrification of Phil's own peripheral position in the story of James Pike.

Timothy Archer is recognizably Pike but, in his spiritual maunderings, his loss of faith, and its eventual transmogrified recovery after death, bears a certain resemblance to Dick himself, in his own wanderings through the quagmire of the Exegesis, *Valis*, and *Divine Invasion* period into the clear white light that enabled him to write this very book. And Angel herself, Dick's sexually transmogrified alter ego, emotionally distanced and spiritually cynical throughout most of the telling of *The Transmigration of Timothy Archer*, finds a kind of spiritual center herself at the conclusion of the novel.

That *The Transmigration of Timothy Archer* was Philip K. Dick's last novel is a tragedy and a triumph.

It is a tragedy because it broke bold new literary ground, in terms of form, viewpoint, clarity, and control, for a writer who already had many great works behind him and was only in his fifties when he died. Where would Philip K. Dick have gone from here?

It is a triumph because it is a fitting final testament for Philip K. Dick the writer and Phil the man—a return to the height of his literary powers at the untimely end of his career, a return to the true metaphysical vision and human insight of *Ubik* and *The Man in the High Castle* and *The Three Stigmata of Palmer Eldritch* and *The Martian Time-Slip* after a long period of secondary work.

And it is also somehow the purest statement of the spiritual center of Phil Dick's work as a writer and his being as a man, as if Phil, like one of his own characters, knew somehow that the end was near, and left us this piece of clarity to give the lie to the obfuscatory cult he somehow knew was to come.

The story, though directly metaphysical and even straightforwardly religious, is, quite unlike *Valis* or *The Divine Invasion*, simple, clear, and direct. Angel, the narrator, is the wife of Bishop Archer's son, Jeff. She introduces Tim Archer to Kirsten Lundborg, and Kirsten and the bishop become lovers. Archer becomes obsessed with the scrolls that have been found in Israel and identified with the Zadokites, a sect that predated the birth of Christ by some two hundred years. As the translations proceed, it becomes apparent that the writings of the Zadokites were the template for the parables of Jesus, and the bishops's faith in the divinity of Christ begins to erode.

Jeffery Archer commits suicide. Bishop Archer learns that the Christian sacrament of the Eucharist derives from the Zadokite practice of consuming hallucinogenic mushrooms, that is, that the mystical communion between Christians and Jesus engendered by the eating of the wafer and the drinking of the wine is nothing more than a ritual derived from a preexisting mystical mushroom cult where an actual psychedelic experience of the godhead was delivered, and this destroys his faith.

Kirsten dies. Bishop Archer goes off into the Negev desert in a rented car in search of the mystical mushroom and his own lost faith, guided only by a gas station roadmap. The map is faulty, the car fails, and he dies in the wilderness.

Later his spirit returns, its faith reborn, via the person of Kirsten's schizophrenic son, Bill, thereby restoring Angel Archer's spiritual center, after a fashion.

Needless to say, such a plot summary does not convey the full depth and power of the book. Dick throws almost as much metaphysical speculation and biblical, kabbalistic, and even Hindu scholarship into *The Transmigration of Timothy Archer* as he does into *Valis* or *The Divine Invasion*, and a lot of arcane material about Wallenstein and the Thirty Years War to boot, as well as other esoterica—nowhere else has he displayed the full range of his sheer intellectual breadth and depth as he does here.

But there is nothing pretentious or boring or didactic about it, for it is all conveyed in the realistic dialogue of characters, particularly the narrator, Angel, who are products of a Berkeley milieu in which all this is quite natural, a milieu in which Phil himself lived and worked for many years, and that he never portrayed with this detail, depth, and humor until this final work.

Then too, all of this metaphysical speculation, all of this high-falutin' table talk, is perfectly balanced by an equal attention to the details of daily life and popular culture. Angel, Jeff, Kirsten, even the bishop, segue from heavy intellectual rapping into questions of popular music, down-and-dirty politics, and their problems with their cars (which seem, like Phil's, to have been endless), within the same sentence.

And this is not mere balancing technique. There is something behind it that is at the mystical core of the novel.

Bill Lundborg, Kirsten's schizoid son, is a character critical to the denouement of the novel; in order for Timothy Archer's spirit to speak credibly through him at the end, in order for the reader to believe in this as a spiritual reality and a peak moment, the reader must first have been convinced that this simple man, this victim of shock therapy and the psychiatric establishment, this mere auto mechanic, has been a kind of innocent saint all along.

How does Dick bring this off?

By a bravura piece of writing that is at once thematically central to the novel and quite impossible to paraphrase or explain, that one must quite literally read to believe.

He does it through a long conversation between Archer and others in which the bishop discusses Christian theology while Bill discusses the merits and flaws of various makes of cars. And makes it work. If there is such a thing as literary magic, this surely is it.

This is worth more than the whole Exegesis and all the gobbledygook surrounding it. This is Phil's true spirit shining through at the very end, and it not only works on a literary level, it is real. Even in death, Phil had the power to raise up the human spirit in this strangely humble manner.

I last spoke on the phone to Phil from New York while I was waiting on a movie deal that was to make me more money than I had ever seen in one piece in my life and he was about to travel to Europe with his new girlfriend. He was buoyant, in high spirits. He had seen a rough-cut of *Blade Runner* and liked it. I was chewing my fingers to the bone waiting for Universal to pay me the buyout money on *Bug Jack Barron*. As he had so many times in the past, Phil helped me see it through.

A few days later, I got a summons to jury duty the next week. A few days after that, I got my long-awaited $75,000 phone call. I had about two hours to enjoy it. Then I got another phone call, telling me that Phil had had a massive stroke and had lapsed into a terminal coma.

I had just made more money than I had ever made in my life. And Phil lay dying. And next Monday I had jury duty. It was like being suddenly dropped into one of Phil's own novels.

What was I to do? Cop out of jury duty (on a certainly justified excuse) and party to celebrate my good fortune? Or fly to California, where ex-wives, children, and girlfriends were already swarming around Phil's deathbed in a feeding frenzy, to exactly the death scene Phil would have written for himself?

Well, I decided, if Phil was writing this, then the only thing to do was do what Phil would have done.

And what Phil would have done was his jury duty, not out of respect for the majesty of the law or fear of the consequences, but because copping out of it even in these circumstances, somehow *especially* in these circumstances, might have deprived someone he didn't even know of the only good thing that could come of this confusion and pain.

"Hey, if you were the guy they were about to send to the joint," Phil's voice seemed to say in my head, "wouldn't *you* want you on the jury with what you're feeling right now?"

I pulled a petty burglary trial. The defendant was obviously guilty of something, but the way the charges were framed, I had a shadow of a doubt. I was one of the two holdouts against conviction. The jury was sequestered overnight. The next morning, another juror, knowing only that I was a science fiction writer, showed me the obit section of the newspaper. "You know this guy?" she asked.

Indeed I did. While I was wrestling with my conscience over sending a petty burglar to jail in New York, Phil had died in California.

Somehow Phil had written this part for me too.

I was now the last holdout against conviction. I was shattered emotionally, but I wouldn't let it go. I had testimony read over and over until I finally found a section in which the defendant convinced me of his guilt beyond all doubt, for I knew beyond all doubt that that would have been what Phil would have wanted me to do. He would never have wanted me to shrug my shoulders and send a man to prison just so I could escape that jury room to grieve.

That is the end of the story of my friendship with Phil, and that was the kind of man Phil was when he died, the kind of man who could write *The Transmigration of Timothy Archer*, and—in literary terms, at least—it was a strange sort of happy ending for me, for I had never known the Philip K. Dick who wrote *The Man in the High Castle* and *The Three Stigmata of Palmer Eldritch* and *Ubik* and *Do Androids Dream of Electric Sheep?* and *The Martian Time-Slip*, which is to say the Philip K. Dick of the 1960s, the era when he was writing the core of his oeuvre at the top of his form, a form I would contend he returned to only at the very end.

That Philip K. Dick I knew only as a writer, and, weirdly enough, as one of the clients I handled briefly as an anonymous wage-slave at the Scott Meredith Literary Agency.

As a neophyte literary agent, I was appalled at the cheap hackwork Dick was doing to survive. *The Unteleported Man*, for example, was written as a novella around a cover painting for *Amazing* and later blown up into a novel for about $1,500. *The Zap Gun*, I kid you not, was written because Tom Dardis of Berkley Books had this *title* he thought would sell a science fiction novel, and asked Scott to find someone to write the book.

As I was to learn much later, a good many of Phil's minor works of this period—*The Unteleported Man, The Zap Gun, Counter-Clock World*, etc.—were churned out as unrewritten first draft on speed because Phil needed quick cash.

As a reader, though, I devoured the major Dick novels of this period, and as an aspiring young writer myself, I was inspired by them, studied them, considered them just about the best science fiction extant, and made my future friend one of my main literary idols and gurus.

These novels, at least, I can view with some semblance of objectivity, for I had never met Philip K. Dick when I first read them.

The Man in the High Castle, published in 1962, was the novel that made Dick's reputation, and with the possible exception of *Do Androids Dream of Electric Sheep?* (courtesy of the film *Blade Runner*), is still probably his best-known book, and, with its alternate present of a Nazi- and Japanese-occupied America, certainly his most imitated.

In a certain sense, that is. For while there have been many novels and stories in which the Nazis have won World War II, there has been nothing like Dick's vision.

In most of Dick's previous short stories and novels, he made comparatively little attempt at genuine extrapolative verisimilitude. *Solar Lottery* posits a political system based on chance, *Eye in the Sky* takes its characters through a bizarre series of ersatz realities, *Dr. Futurity* is a time-paradox novel, and so forth; while many of these earlier works are metaphysically interesting indeed and contain well-rounded characters, they all make full self-conscious use of the tropes, imagery, gimmicks, jargon, and schtick of SF; in Alexei Panshin's phrase, they are "science fiction that knows it's science fiction."

The Man in the High Castle is something quite different. Here Dick posits a single assumption—that Nazi Germany and Imperial Japan won World War II and split America down the middle—and proceeds to write a realistic, characterologically based novel in the quite believable world he has created.

The novel jettisons all the familiar SF paraphernalia, centers on the lives of relatively ordinary people, concentrates on their human stories more than the macropolitics (in the manner of mainstream fiction), and yet remains science fiction, albeit a science fiction that *anyone* could pick up and read without familiarity with the genre. It was something that Dick had not done previously, and would not really do again until the very end with *The Transmigration of Timothy Archer*.

And yet most of the themes and virtues of the work to come, the work that was to make Dick one of the premier science fiction writers of the twentieth century and one of the premier metaphysical novelists of all time, are present in *The Man in the High Castle* and in rather fully developed form.

The dichotomy between the spiritless ersatz and the humanly real, as epitomized in the macrocosm by the anomie of the Nazis versus the more spiritually centered Japanese conquerors, and in the microcosm by Frank Frink's drive to create authentically new American jewelry instead of phony antiques.

Ordinary people like Frink and Mr. Tagomi as genuine heroes. Larger figures seen in the distance or in glimpses, like Abensend, the author of *The Grasshopper Lies Heavy*, the alternate-world novel within the alternate-world novel in which the Nazis and the Japanese *lost* the war. Characters, who, for the most part have real workaday jobs, and ordinary work as something that can have spiritual and personal meaning.

A blending of passionately political themes (in this case an utterly convincing portrait of two Americas as molded by two very different occupying powers) with the metaphysical and mystical (here the I Ching and the Sino-Japanese concept of wu) in a manner that demonstrates the one arising out of the other. A sense of the author's genuine love for his characters. The multiplex subjectivity of reality—in this alternate America, a writer has written a book about another alternate America, and Mr. Tagomi's small moment of heroism is triggered by a fugue state in which he finds himself briefly in *our* America.

This is not to suggest that *The Man in the High Castle* laid out all of Dick's future obsessions and concerns and that all else was repetition or even that it is necessarily his best novel. But it certainly was a great writer finding his true voice, creating his first truly mature work, presenting us with the broad outline of the scope of his vision and the style and spirit of what was to come, and in that, much older, medieval sense, *The Man in the High Castle* can literally be said to be his "masterpiece."

What followed in the next decade was an enormous burst of creativity, in which Dick explored, exfoliated, and deepened the thematic concerns he had opened up in about half a dozen major novels and even more minor ones, though no two critics are likely to agree on complete lists of which was which.

Indeed Phil himself made it quite clear, publicly and privately, that some of these novels were hacked out at top speed for quick money, that some of them he took more seriously, that others were like Graham Greene's "entertainments," and a few didn't even make sense to *him* in retrospect, though he could be cagy and contradictory about which he thought were which.

While we can all argue the relative importance of novels like *Clans of the Alphane Moon, Dr. Bloodmoney, A Maze of Death, Galactic Pot-Healer, The Simulacra,* and *Now Wait for Last Year,* and few would contend that *The Zap Gun* or *The Unteleported Man* or *Our Friends from Frolix-8* or *Counter-Clock World* or *The Crack in Space* are major works, few critics or readers of Dick will deny that *Martian Time-Slip, The Three Stigmata of Palmer Eldritch, Do Androids Dream of Electric Sheep?* and *Ubik* are unquestionably at the core of Dick's oeuvre, whichever of his many, many, other works they may choose to rank with them.

While these are four very different novels with four quite different settings, they have many things in common with each other and with many of the other Dick novels of this enormously creative period.

All of them have viewpoint characters, which is to say the viewpoint character through whose consciousness we experience the largest portion of the novel, who are not really movers and shapers but find themselves placed in a central role that requires from them heroism of one kind or another. And they are all real people with real jobs that mean something to them and with real and troubled personal lives and relationships of one kind or another.

All of these novels but *Martian Time-Slip* have a larger-than-life, reality-altering, charismatic figure at the center of what is happening in the macrocosm but not really quite central to the actual events in the story, though their relative importance to the plot and the set-up vary from book to book. Mercer, the TV messiah expiating the guilts of the ruined world, is fairly incidental to *Do Androids Dream of Electric Sheep?*, Runciter is quite central to *Ubik,* and Palmer Eldritch at the end is virtually the deity of *The Three Stigmata.* Even *Martian Time-Slip* contains such a figure in a peculiar way, functionally split between the worldly powerful union leader Arnie Kott and his reality-altering autistic son Manfred.

We see such figures in other Dick novels—in *Dr. Bloodmoney, Now Wait for Last Year, Galactic Pot-Healer*, and in some of the earlier novels as well—and while all of them are highly individuated and finely drawn, they do have more in common than their functional ability to create, in one way or another, alternate realities.

Even though they are not central to the plotline in tems of their time on stage in the novel, they are rendered as viewpoint characters with real and understandable inner lives more often than not, rather than as cardboard figures, stock villains, or unmoved movers. Arnie Kott may be rough and tough and ruthless, but he is not really a bad sort. Glen Runciter, even in the semi-death of half-life, is trying to do good by his people. Even Palmer Eldritch is to some degree the victim of his own screwed-up good intentions.

Finally, the thread that runs strongly through these books, and indeed through most of Dick's work in one form or another, is his central theme with its many well-explored corollaries, which put one way is the distinction between the authentic and the ersatz—humans versus androids in *Do Androids Dream of Electric Sheep?*, realities themselves in *Ubik, Palmer Eldritch* and to an extent *Martian Time-Slip*—and put another way is the Dickian concept of the *multiplexity* of reality, and, in that sense at least, of the lack of hard and clear-cut distinction between "reality" and "illusion," "authentic" and "ersatz."

This is the great theme of Dick's oeuvre, of the core novels of his most productive period and the minor works too, of what leads up to the burst of creativity that began with *The Man in the High Castle*, as well as his later works; it is an enormously vast theme, bottomlessly deep, endlessly complicated. Small wonder then that Dick often seems to contradict himself on these matters from novel to novel, indeed often within the same book, for what he is wrestling with is the nature(s) of reality(ies) it(them)self, and the overall wisdom that one takes away from a reading of his work as a whole is that *reality itself* is multiplex, non-objective, and indeed internally self-contradictory.

Martian Time-Slip seems to take place in the single reality of a future colonized Mars, and Manfred's autism seems to be merely a mental disease. But by the time the novel is over we are left with the perception that the autistic boy is living in a kind of precog vision of a future decaying into "gubbish," into a dead simulacrum from which all animating spirit has been leached (a key Dickian concept), as real or more so in some sense than the consensus reality of the other characters.

The realities of *Ubik* take place inside a subjective universe created by Runciter, who is himself trapped in the subjective reality of half-life, but what Joe Chip, the main protagonist does inside them affects the "real" world and vice versa.

The Three Stigmata of Palmer Eldritch is perhaps Dick's fullest and grandest and most humane statement of his enormous central theme. Via the drug Chew-Z, brought back from Centauris by Eldritch, the characters' subjective realities fold into each other like nested boxes along a Möebus strip, Eldritch himself the god of many of them, but Eldritch himself occupying a reality in which he is far from an unmoved mover.

What allows Dick to explore such material without lapsing into mere babblement? Indeed, such is the nature of his thematic core that sometimes, when he attempts to knock out a quick minor work along these lines, such as *The Zap Gun* or *Counter-Clock World* or *Our Friends from Frolix-8*, he *does* go over the edge.

But when he's got it right, as he certainly has in *Martian Time-Slip, The Three Stigmata of Palmer Eldritch, Do Androids Dream of Electric Sheep?, Ubik,* and elsewhere, he is able to give us, out of this very multiplex and self-contradictory metaphysical confusion, a true vision, a genuine clarity that illumines our lives on the deepest spiritual level.

He does this in two ways.

The first is technical. Dick is the master of the multiple-viewpoint narrative. He may not have invented the technique, but he did more to introduce it to science fiction than anyone else, he uses it in almost all of his novels, he never breaks form, and the form he has chosen is ideally suited to his material.

There is no auctorial overview in novels like *Martian-Slip, Palmer Eldritch, Androids,* etc., no Philip K. Dick telling the reader what is real and what is not. These novels are mosaics of realities, the realities of the viewpoint characters, not of the author; in this sense, there is no overall base reality to any of these novels, only the interfacing of a multiplexity of subjective realities.

And that is what "reality" is *really* like, Dick is not so much saying as demonstrating—consensus reality, to the extent that there is such a thing, is the interfacing of our subjective realities with those of other consciousnesses, not an overall matrix in which we all live. What is, is real.

Much has been made of Phil Dick's involvement with drugs and the prevalence of consciousness-altering drugs as central elements in his work, at least in the 1960s, and to lapse into memoir, it is certainly true that no one I ever met, including Timothy Leary, knew as much about psychopharmacology as Phil or had pondered more deeply the metaphysics of consciousness-altering drugs and the relationship of that metaphysics to the metaphysics of mental illness, particularly various forms of schizophrenia.

For Phil Dick, consciousness-altering drugs like Chew-Z in *Palmer Eldritch*, mental states like Manfred's autism in *Martian Time Slip*, and ersatz subjective realities as in *Ubik* or *A Maze of Death* or *Eye in the Sky* serve the same function, literarily and metaphysically. Namely, to demonstrate that altered mental states, *however they may be created*, create altered realities that are as "real" as what we individually think of as "base reality," since each of our individual "base realities," far from being the absolute we like to pretend it is, is *itself* a unique subjective reality, arising as it does in our own unique biophysical matrix.

In this perception lies either the solipsistic madness of total psychic relativity or transcendent wisdom, and the greatness of Dick as a writer, what makes him by far the greatest metaphysical novelist of all time, is that, having opened the door to this ultimate spiritual, perceptual, and metaphysical chaos, he leads us through it to true wisdom along a *moral* vector.

What ultimately makes the androids in *Do Androids Dream of Electric Sheep?* less than human is not their synthetic origin, but, like the Nazis in *The Man in the High Castle*, their lack of caritas, their inability to empathize with the existential plight of other life caught in the same multiverse. What raises the android Roy Batty to human status in *Blade Runner* (the film version of *Androids*) is that, on the brink of his own death, he is able to empathize with Decard.

What makes Joe Chip, Rick Decard, Mr. Tagomi, Joe Bohlen, Barney Mayerson, and Leo Bulero true heroes is that ultimately, on one level or another, whatever reality mazes they may be caught in, they realize that the true base reality is not absolute or perceptual or metaphysical, but moral and empathetic, and they act accordingly when push comes to shove.

What is really real is what is felt on both sides when two subjective realities intersect; what is really real is the spiritual connection between isolated subjectivities, the caritas, the empathy, the love, without which we are all lost, like the Nazis and the androids and poor Palmer Eldritch, in our own solipsistic subjective universes.

Or as Phil Dick has Leo Bulero put it in the opening epigram of *The Three Stigmata of Palmer Eldritch*; "I mean, after all; you have to consider we're only made out of dust. That's admittedly not much to go on and we shouldn't forget that. But even considering, I mean it's sort of a bad beginning, we're not doing too bad. So I personally have faith that even in this lousy situation we're faced with we can make it. You get me?"

And that is about where any pretense this essay may have to objectivity must end, for that is the point at which my friendship with Phil began, after I had read, and had been moved and deeply influenced by, all these great works, after I had learned the possibilities of the multiple-viewpoint technique from Philip K. Dick and applied it to *The Men in the Jungle* and *Agent of Chaos* and *Bug Jack Barron*.

I had been in the same room with Philip K. Dick only once, at the Berkeley Worldcon in 1968, and I couldn't say that I had actually met him; I had been too much in awe even to try to begin a conversation.

Then, late one night in 1972, at my house in Los Angeles, I got a phone call from Vancouver and found myself in a strangely familiar somewhere where fiction intersected reality.

It was Phil Dick. "Listen," he said, "my girlfriend just left me, and I think I'm going to kill myself, but I read your story *Carcinoma Angels* in *Dangerous Visions*, and I thought I should talk to you first."

And that was how our friendship began, in midstream, as if it were a preexisting condition, or as if Phil had had a precog flash of the subsequent years, and was acting now on the basis of it, or. . . .

Whatever it was, it suddenly seemed totally natural, and I found myself on the phone for an hour, deep in intimate conversation with this old friend who had been a literary inspiration but a total personal stranger before my phone rang.

"On the other hand," Phil said, "I've got this offer from Willis McNelly at Cal State Fullerton to come down there to Orange County to live. What's your honest opinion, would I be better off moving to Orange County, or killing myself?"

"Well, Phil, personally, I can't stand Orange County," I found myself saying, "but you might as well give it a try. If you don't like it, you can always kill yourself later."

"Yeah, that makes sense," Phil said reasonably, and moved to Southern California.

So I came to know Phil personally in the 1970s, the period in which he wrote *Flow My Tears, the Policeman Said* and *A Scanner Darkly*, which to some critics were a repudiation of the point of view of the work of the 1960s, and *Valis, the Divine Invasion*, and *The Transmigration of Timothy Archer*, which some critics have mistakenly taken as a thematic trilogy, as well as the "Exegesis," which some have taken as divine inspiration and others have taken as proof of Phil's insanity.

Had too many drugs barbled his brain? Was his mind affected by an undetected minor stroke? Certainly the man who wrote *The Transmigration of Timothy Archer* was clear and lucid on the evidence of the text alone. But what about the Phil Dick I knew in the previous decade, the Dick of the so-called CIA break-in, the pink light, the dybbuk, the suicide attempt, the Exegesis? Was Phil insane during that period, recovering his balance only at the end?

First, one must define sanity, and that, one learns from a reading of Dick, is a pretty pointless exercise in the multiverse.

Item: the German edition of *The Man in the High Castle*, finally published a decade and more after the initial American publication. Phil, who read German, told me he had insisted on proofing the galleys himself, he just didn't trust the Germans. I told him he was really being paranoid.

When the galleys came through, great swatches of material about the Nazis had been removed.

Item: suicide attempt, as described to me by Phil. "I was really depressed, and I decided to do myself by taking a bunch of downers. After I dropped all the pills, I realized that since I would soon be dead, I didn't have to worry about my weight anymore. So there was no reason not to eat the chocolate cake I had in the fridge. So I gobbled up this whole huge chocolate cake and ended up puking my guts out, downers and all. Didn't die, but I must've gained five pounds!"

Is that crazy or is that eminently sane?

Item: the so-called CIA break-in. When Phil started telling me the story of how government agents broke into his house to steal his papers (before Paul Williams' article on Phil appeared in *Rolling Stone*), I thought he was being completely paranoid. I mean, why on Earth would the FBI or the CIA or military intelligence or whoever come after some science fiction writer? It made no sense, it sounded vey much like paranoid delusions of reference, until. . . .

". . . and then there was this guy who called me up from some Stanford University radio station for an interview," Phil went on. "And I said sure, why not, and he says he'll fly right down. Shows up with this guy he introduces as his pilot, asks a lot of really strange questions about dope and the sex lives of SF writers. And when I check it out later with Stanford, it turns out the radio station doesn't even exist."

I got a cold, cold flash.

The same two guys had run the same cover story and the same interview on me, too. The question I remember best, because it was certainly the weirdest, was "Is it true that Samuel R. Delany is really the illegitimate son of Philip K. Dick?"

In retrospect, it can clearly be seen that it was *the times* and the Nixon administration that had gone insane, for this was the era of White House plumbers and enemies lists, of utter paranoia in the highest places. And a few years earlier, the Department of Health, Education, and Welfare had paid Robert Silverberg a considerable sum of money to prepare a bibliography of science fiction novels and stories dealing with mind-altering drugs. And that, mind you, was the *cover story*!

Ultimately we are dealing here with a complex and charged area where questions of politics, sanity, metaphysics, drugs, and literature intersect, and no sense can be made of the work of Philip K. Dick and the last decade of Phil's life without confronting it; this is why, I believe, there has been so much critical confusion.

Phil was never apolitical, always left of the American center. Political analysis appeared central to his work in the eyes of many European critics, so the French were aghast when he appeared at Metz and made a metaphysical speech instead of the expected political one. Consciousness-altering drugs were a central McGuffin of many of Phil's novels, and during certain periods Phil himself did a lot of speed. Certain critics, to whom consciousness-altering drugs are personal anathema, welcomed *Flow My Tears, The Policeman Said* and *A Scanner Darkly* as repudiations of Phil's previous position on the subject; other people condemned these books as apostasy to the psychedelic creed. Certain critics have taken the "Exegesis" and the novels that it supposedly spawned as evidence of Phil's insanity or his drug burnout, even as other people have constructed a cult around the Divine Revelation of the Pink Light.

Alas, in the 1980s, the whole subject of drugs has become so shrilly politicized that a measured discussion of their relationship to creativity, literature, altered states of consciousness, and the development of science fiction has become difficult and dangerous indeed.

A few hard and currently highly unpopular truths:

At certain periods in his career, indeed during much of his most prodigiously productive period, Philip K. Dick wrote on speed. What this ended up doing to his health in the middle 1970s may indeed be tragic, but what it did for his creativity in the 1960s is self-evident.

Phil Dick may have done too much speed for his own personal good, but the literature he produced, partially under its influence, in the 1960s was some of the best science fiction ever written. Like it or not, this work is proof that consciousness-altering drugs can indeed enhance productive creativity.

Philip K. Dick was not preaching against drug use in *A Scanner Darkly* any more than he was advocating it in *Palmer Eldritch*. His great theme was the multiplexity of reality, and consciousness-altering drugs were one literary vehicle for exploring it, ersatz universes and schizoid states being others.

Phil used mind-altering substances as creative tools in the 1960s and they worked. But the price he paid in terms of his health was heavy, and in the 1970s he realized it and gave them up. And managed to make the exceedingly difficult transition to working without them, which is at least a partial explanation of the nearly four-year hiatus between *Our Friends from Frolix-8* and *Flow My Tears, the Policeman Said*.

It took a man of great courage, wisdom, and spiritual strength to make such a transition, and so it is hardly surprising that he may not have re-attained the literary level of the previous decade until *Timothy Archer*, nor is it really surprising that he should write a novel about narcs and dealers (*Flow My Tears*) and then one about the spiritually murderous potential of bad drugs (*A Scanner Darkly*) in the process.

For Phil the man, and for Philip K. Dick the writer, it was never a question of consciousness-altering drugs being "good" or "evil," any more than it was ever a question of "altered realities" being good or evil per se, for he knew that in a very real sense *all* realities are altered realities, one from another. And where the moral quality in a drug, or a mental state, or even a pocket universe lies is not in the chemistry or biology or physics of how one gets there, but in what kind of person you become when you arrive.

Drugs that create solipsistic states and psychopathic behavior are evil. Drugs that enhance empathy are not. Mental states that deaden the spirit are diseases. Mental states that enhance caritas are not.

How could anyone who had *this* as straight as Philip K. Dick did, in all his work and in his life as he lived it, be said to be insane? For this is the truest definition of sanity that I know of, and it is Phil Dick's own — eschew realities that harm your spirit or worse, cause you to harm others; seek to raise up the spirits of other consciousnesses in whatever reality and under whatever conditions you happen to find yourself.

What then, finally, of the pink light, the dybbuk of the fourteenth-century Rabbi, the Exegesis, and Dick's late turn into complex Christian and kabbalistic metaphysics in *Valis* and *The Divine Invasion*?

Since Phil's own definition of moral sanity, as demonstrated by the sum total of everything he had written, is also at the core of true essential Christianity, and since Phil himself was a believing Christian who wrestled with these questions all of his creative life, it should surprise no one who truly understands his work that a forthrightly Christian element could finally emerge in *Valis* and *The Divine Invasion*.

For on a moral and spiritual level it was there all along, and Phil attended church frequently during certain periods in his life and contributed to Quaker charities. That these two books move away from his more politically oriented science fiction is merely a matter of a shift of balance, for even his most political fiction, such as *The Man in the High Castle, Dr. Bloodmoney*, and the novella *Faith of Our Fathers*, have a metaphysical, and yes, a mystical dimension. Phil was always a Christian in the best and most original sense.

As for the pink light, and the possession, and the Exegesis, I don't really know. Phil spoke to me of these matters to some extent at the time, but he did not seem barbled at all. He told me that he had had this strange experience. He had done all this automatic writing. He claimed to have written coherent Hebrew, a language of which he had no knowledge.

Phil's attitude toward it all, at least as expressed to me, was that he didn't know what had happened to him either. But he had plenty of theories. Possession by a dybbuk. Contact with an alien intelligence. Divine inspiration. Secret rays from Saturn.

It seems to me now, as it seemed to me then, that, given the subjective reality in which Phil had found himself, his reaction to the experience was as sane as could be: to hypothesize various theories to explain it without necessarily believing that any of them were true.

It may very well be that *Valis* and *The Divine Invasion* were simply Phil's efforts to do this in the way natural to him, by taking the experience, premising some explanations, and turning it into science fiction. *Phil* didn't seem unbalanced about this material; the people who were unbalanced about it were the people who took it as other than science fiction.

Phil himself told me a little story about this. Upon reading Horse-lover Fat's conversations with Philip K. Dick in *The Divine Invasion*, Ursula Le Guin publicly voiced the opinion that Phil had flipped out.

"Hey, Ursula," Phil wrote back to her good-naturedly, "you forget that Horselover Fat is just a character in a novel."

As to what projected Philip K. Dick into the reality in which the events occurred that led to his writing the Exegesis and *Valis* and *The Divine Invasion*, we will probably never know, as Phil never did. A small stroke? A drug flashback? Or just maybe a real dybbuk or a real alien contact?

It isn't really important. What is important is how Phil dealt with the reality he experienced, which was with his usual extrapolative curiosity and moral lucidity.

In *The Transmigration of Timothy Archer*, the Bishop loses his faith when he learns the apparently awful truth that the cult that evolved into Christianity, the spiritual experience of Christian consciousness itself, was based on the ingestion of a psychedelic mushroom.

But Archer's true transmigration and that of the reader occur when it is realized that this does not at all negate Christianity's true core, which is neither the dogma of any church nor the divinity of any historical Jesus, but the spiritual essence of the message for the hearts of men that Jesus embodies, whether he was a historical figure, the Son of God, or the reality-altering effect of ingesting a mushroom.

And *that* is the moral clarity and insight that shines through the oeuvre of Philip K. Dick, *that* is how he reconciled all his grand themes at the very end of his career—the multiplexity of reality, the moral primacy of caritas, the dignity of work, the heroism of small moral clarities, and yes, the positive potentials of mind-altering drugs, too—reconciled them not only with each other but with the true Christian grace that he had always sought and that in this final work he so clearly attained.

That is why I, who am no Christian at all, can still say that *The Transmigration of Timothy Archer* is Philip K. Dick's true final testament. Few men, few Christians, few writers, have ever crafted better.

Science Fiction in the Real World

Finally, perhaps, I really should try to say something about what it feels like to be a writer of science fiction in the real world, as the title or this book more or less promises.

This may sound easy, considering that I have been writing science fiction myself for over twenty-five years now, have written criticism of it for over a decade, written extensively about the SF publishing industry, and have even been president of the Science Fiction Writers of America, but I still can't quite figure out how I got here and I'm still not sure quite where I am.

That is probably as good a thumbnail description as any of what it feels like to be a science fiction writer in the real world.

From the point of view of a writer of science fiction, the real world itself has uncertainty built into it on the particle level, where, quantum mechanics tell us, being conjures itself from nothingness as the universe bootstraps itself into existence. This is not mere metaphor, this is as hard as the scientific facts get, and this is the universe in which we really live, and the science fiction writer knows it.

In the real world of astrophysics and quantum mechanics, we ourselves are ultimately creatures conjured out of quantum uncertainties on the microlevel and into a universe that dwarfs us utterly on a macrolevel and operates on a time scale that makes our lifespans seem trivial in the cosmic scheme of things.

This is something that most people are unaware of or at least never think about, but the science fiction writer is aware of it all of the time, for part of the esthetic underpinning of science fiction is that it *must* attempt to factor in these cosmic ultimates and deal with them as emotional realities. So the science fiction writer does indeed spend a certain amount of time pondering the paradoxes and gazing off into the billion-year vistas.

Yet the same seer sooner or later finds himself autographing in the huckster room of some tacky science fiction convention, surrounded by tables full of old comics, *Star Trek* fetish items, medieval weaponry, and, if he is lucky, actual new copies of his current book to sign rather than huge stacks of moldy oldies, wondering how he got there too.

To a science fiction writer, quantum reality and sleazoid covers, island universes and Worldcon huckster rooms, literary obscurity and the power to summon spirits from the vastly deep, high visions and low farce, all are equally real, all are part of what he must deal with in the real world in which he finds himself.

To a science fiction writer, there often seems to be a literary Heisenberg Uncertainty Principle at work in his life too.

Generally speaking, the science fiction writer is not a solid citizen of the national literary culture, at least not in the United States, yet his access to and intellectual influence upon national *scientific culture* can be significant. The science fiction writer longs for the salons of the literary high life in place of the convention circuit but, on the other hand, sells more books than most of the denizens thereof, and when he does visit with the creators of the accepted literary canon, he does not always find them the intellectual equals of his comrades in the trenches.

Who, paradoxically enough, are often churning out schlock.

So it goes, as a writer of science fiction has frequently written.

That's the where, and the how you get there can only be pondered in terms of another central esthetic principle of science fiction, namely, that character and destiny, history and personality itself, are all the product of feedback between the environmental surround and the consciousness moving through it.

Which in this case means whatever constellation of genes and experience made you the sort of consciousness with the impulse to write this stuff, confronting both the long literary history of critical tradition and the current exigencies of the publishing industry.

There is no free will in the sense of some detached observer's choice to act as some unmoved mover; Einsteinian relativity ensures us of that much. But there is no determinism in this universe either, since uncertainty is built into it on the finest possible level, where the nature of events is actually altered by how the observer chooses to observe them.

Meaning that all sincere literary art is the product of human beings doing the best they can with the hand of cards they've been dealt, and the price of liberty is taking care of business.

How did you get here?

How else?

How does anyone get anywhere?

As the end-product of their relationship with the total environment up until the moment of arrival.

Think of it, as two other science fiction writers have written, as evolution in action.

So the science fiction writer isn't as interested in a deterministic detailing of how the past created the present—quantum mechanics assures him this is impossible anyway—as he is in examining the current situation with a view towards pondering what may evolve next, which is not so impossible, since quantum mechanics also assures us that the course of future events is indeed affected by the observer's chosen frame of reference.

And when a science fiction writer turns to pondering the evolution of science fiction itself, he is going to apply the same orientation to criticism.

Science Fiction in the Real World has not been a linear history of the literary evolution of science fiction nor of the evolution of SF as a literary genre in the real world of publishing pragmatics, but in some sense a novelistic attempt to render the ambiguities of the interface between publishing realities and esthetic imperatives, Muse and Mammon, psyche and society, art and commerce, which, you had better believe it, is the real world of real writers all of the time.

And this, I would contend, is the proper subject of literary criticism. Not because it is the only legitimate subject of critical discourse, but because all other subjects of critical discourse may be contained within its overview.

This is not Marxist criticism, but it certainly is concerned with the economic determinants of what actually gets written. This is not Freudian criticism, but it does not eschew pondering the state of mind of the creative artist or the psychological effect of the product on the reader and society. This is not historical criticism, but it certainly can't afford to ignore the history of culture and literature.

This is a novelistic approach to criticism, the peculiar approach of the science fiction writer to any culture, world, or reality: to create an illusion of totality by presenting it from as many camera angles as possible, freely borrowing from everywhere and anywhere in order to do so.

And since the science fiction writer has little class self-interest in accepting the canons of literary tradition and his place outside it as the pure product of Platonic idealism, it is hardly surprising that he will attempt to explain even *literary culture* as if it were another world he was evoking as the product of a history and evolution, too.

From where the science fiction writer stands in the real world, it's either that or the fannish notion that science fiction is something somehow unconnected to the mainstream of "mundane" literature, whose inner wonders can only be accessible to We Chosen Few, or worse, accepting the wisdom of the "pulp tradition" and its schlock-meisters that writing to sell is the ultimate raison d'etre.

So, like anyone presented with negative self-images by the culture, the science fiction writer will, like Blacks in the 1960s and women in the 1970s, seek to become self-defining. But unlike just anyone, the science fiction writer is peculiarly equipped, through the nature of the work itself, to take on the task.

So, in a sense, *Science Fiction in the Real World* is an attempt to redefine science fiction critically from the point of view of the microbes on the slide, to place it in a context that, while not exempting it from traditional literary standards, does not confine analysis of it to traditional critical conceptualizations, either.

Because from the point of view of the science fiction writer, science fiction as a genre and a literature, as a living art form evolving under evolutionary pressure in the real world, is sorely in need of less criticism that examines its minutiae or condescends to it as pop literature, and more criticism that will both place it in its proper cultural context and provide it with the internal literary standards that the genre presently so obviously lacks.

What science fiction needs is more *useful* criticism; criticism that explicates it coherently to the general culture, helps writers to improve what is being written, enhances readers' enjoyment of it by deepening their perceptions of the meaning of the work, or in the best of all possible worlds, all of the above at once.

Such work exists, and more of it continues to be published, but for the most part neither in forms nor publications that bring it to the attention of the practitioners of the art or the general literary readership, which is to say it has not yet noticeably improved the literary quality of what is written or brought science fiction into the accepted canon of modern literary art.

I hasten to add that these are not the only valid functions of criticism—criticism, like fiction, is a literary art form that may be written and read for pure pleasure as its own ding an sich—but I would contend that these are functions that, on the evidence of the results, criticism on the whole has not performed very successfully for science fiction as yet, which may be why some of the form's major figures publicly proclaim that criticism has no functional use to science fiction at all.

Obviously I don't feel that way myself, or I would never have written this book; still, if I were entirely satisfied with the critical status of science fiction or the state of science fiction criticism, I wouldn't have written this book either.

I have written *Science Fiction in the Real World* because I *do* believe criticism is important and that science fiction as a literature needs critical overviews that will both revise its perception in the real world of letters and resolve the internal identity crisis at its heart.

Science fiction, I hope this book has demonstrated, is an evolutionarily inevitable literary mode with its roots in the rise of the Age of Reason and its raison d'etre in the replacement of the lost fantasy landscapes beyond the sea with the scientifically plausible wonderlands beyond the bounds of the quotidian present.

As such, it is a literature peculiarly relevant to the transformation crisis our species is presently attempting to negotiate, to wit, the question of whether or not we will be able to handle the cosmic powers we have seized in our hot little hands long enough to evolve into a spacegoing culture with long-term survivability. Or whether we will destroy ourselves and our planet before we grow up.

All unknowing, perhaps, we have made ourselves the gods of the Earth, with the power of life and death over the planetary biosphere, whether we like it or not.

We have had the nuclear power to render the planet uninhabitable for decades now, so perhaps it's a good sign that we're all here to talk about it nearly half a century after Hiroshima.

Now, however, it begins to appear that our agro-industrial civilization has already unwittingly altered the climate and the atmosphere itself by the metabolic waste-products of its mere existence, for it is clear that the planet really *has* been warming up since we became the dominant lifeform.

What *else* we have done to the biosphere as the result of actions taken before their future consequences could be understood remains to be seen.

On the other hand, we now have the power to extend our civilization beyond the Earth's biosphere, and indeed to create new biospheres tailored to our specifications, or even redesign our genes to tailor our protoplasm to suit our needs and whims.

Oh yes, don't kid yourself, like it or not, for better or worse, we lunatics have already taken charge of the asylum, we've put ourselves in charge of evolution itself, and that's one genie that can never be tricked back into the bottle.

So what science fiction *should* be is one of our culture's main means for pondering not only the future consequences of what we are doing now but the effects of these inevitable, unpredictable changes on the human spirit. And since these enormities are absolutely central to the very survival of our species, our culture requires such a literature, requires such a science fiction, at its intellectual core.

But science fiction in the real world is nothing of the kind, and in the state of science fiction, and even more the state of the real world, can all too closely be read the results of this failure of form to follow function.

In the real world, as I would imagine this book has made all too clear, SF is a commercial publishing genre, and science fiction that even tries to tackle issues of central social concerns, while it certainly exists, is only a small portion of the total product, and, buried as it is amidst the rocket-and-ray-gun packaging and fannish fads, seldom comes to the serious attention of the intellectual mainstream of cultural life.

And this is the identity crisis at the heart of science fiction.

What is this stuff? Why are we writing it? Out of commitment to literature? To pay the bills? Out of messianic impulse? Out of genuine concern for the destiny of the species? Are these motivations really mutually exclusive?

Is science fiction commercial schlock or is it literary art? Is it visionary literature or militaristic alien-bashing masturbation fantasies for the next generation of gunfodder? Should we take ourselves seriously or are we just in it for Joe's beer money?

These are the real issues science fiction writers have to deal with, so these must be the central areas of concern to any criticism of science fiction that seeks after the truth of how it is actually called into being in the real world.

Are we the inheritors of H.G. Wells or of Jules Verne? Are we writing socially committed speculation or are we just walking tourists through the hardware? Are we illuminating the dark corners or pandering to the demons lurking therein? Are we being the best we are able to be or are we following the path of least resistance along the sacred bottom line?

These are not issues for critics to resolve but Zen paradoxes for them to ponder and meditate aloud upon, for of course science fiction and science fiction writers, taken as a class, are all of the above at once and much more.

For the truth of it is that by being thrust together under the same logo whether they like it or not, writers with very little in common literarily, writers just in it for Joe's beer money, high artistes and everything in between, have developed a sense of solidarity, of fraternity as "science fiction writers," at least when it comes to confronting our places as such in the real world.

Yet, to make fully rounded criticism of science fiction that much more difficult, science fiction is an industry, too, with a community of writers and publishers and editors, all of whom know each other personally, and the whole existing as the aristocracy of a tribe that has accreted around the literature, a tribe called Science Fiction Fandom, a tribe under whose aegis editorial interactions take place, a tribe out of whose ranks have emerged major editors and publishers and writers themselves, and a tribe whose effects can therefore hardly be ignored by any critic seeking the full story of the evolution of the literature.

That such an area of central cultural concern should chance to be ghettoized into a commercial publishing genre and a tribal subculture and removed thereby as a subject of serious intellectual discourse is a severe cultural failure. The effects on science fiction may be read in the book slots at the newsstand. The effects on the species we are reading in the newspaper racks.

And this cultural failure must be laid pretty squarely on the malfunction of the critical mechanism of at least American literary culture.

As we stagger toward the dawn of the twenty-first century, our emerging planetary culture needs an emergence of science fiction into the mainstream of cultural concern, even as science fiction needs to share common literary standards with all seriously intended literature if it is ever to escape from the sci-fi genre into the cultural mainstream.

This, I believe, is the broad critical agenda for anyone who wants to consider the place of science fiction in the real world, a savory smorgasbord of food for critical thought that, strangely enough, has gone largely untouched except by some of the better academic critics who have made the field their specialty.

Why?

Why has mainstream American literary criticism avoided the subject of science fiction by dismissing it as commercial cultural artifact rather than self-aware literature and shucking it off on the Popular Culture department?

Perhaps the conventional critical mechanism just isn't equipped to contain a phenomenon like science fiction, which can be serious literature, pop culture, and a transliterary phenomenon, and sometimes all three in the same book.

Perhaps traditional literary criticism simply doesn't have the critical equipment to deal with a literature that arose from the proletarian pulps rather than along any aristocratic trajectory, that has spawned a world-wide subculture and inspired the exploration of space, Scientology, the Manson family, and Mathias Rust, who, it turns out, flew his plane into Red Square in emulation of the derring-do of his idol, Perry Rhodan.

How could any retrospectively oriented critical tradition hope to understand such a phenomenon and integrate it into literary culture? It is different in *kind* as a literary phenomenon from anything in the annals.

Make no mistake about it, criticism that would seek to encompass this phenomenon must not only reexamine its own content, it must readjust its technique and angle of attack to suit the subject.

Too much literary criticism tends to regard the writing of fiction as taking place in a sociopolitical and particularly economic vacuum, as if writers were really Platonic idealists operating beyond the reach of cultural and economic forces.

But science fiction can be understood only by a criticism that examines the Room 101 where most criticism most fears to go—the interface between art and commerce itself, the interface between the total external environment and the psyche of the writer, where literary criticism transmutes into something not entirely unlike science fiction itself. The Marxists at least approach this from one direction and the Freudians from the other, but what is needed is a lot more criticism than we presently have that attempts to convey the whole story—*novelistic* criticism, if you will.

In precisely the manner of science fiction itself, such a criticism should attempt to explicate the literature to the culture at large by relating it to both the constellation of economic and cultural forces that have made the genre what it is and the vision of its exemplary work, but without condescension and with the kid gloves off.

Meaning that criticism that is attempting to redefine science fiction's position in the real world, in order to be credible, must be just as revisionary and maybe even a little more cold-eyed about applying general literary standards to what is produced within the genre, horrifying though that prospect may be in terms of facing the truth.

More such literarily hard-nosed criticism might be welcomed by more science fiction writers than critics might think. Such a bigger dose of intellectually uncompromising criticism might do more good than science fiction writers might think.

Enough of such criticism might, in the end, not merely redefine science fiction's standing in the literary canon, but who knows, by also improving what was actually written, might even in the end redefine science fiction's place in the real world itself.

Index

Norman Spinrad has been publishing science fiction for over twenty-five years and has been writing literary and film criticism for over twenty.

He is the author of fifteen novels, including *Bug Jack Barron, The Iron Dream, A World Between, Songs from the Stars, The Void Captain's Tale, Child of Fortune,* and *Little Heroes,* as well as four collections of short fiction. He has also written *Staying Alive,* a guide to publishing for writers, and is the editor of *Modern Science Fiction,* a textbook for science fiction classes.

He is a past president of the Science Fiction Writers of America and is currently president of World SF.

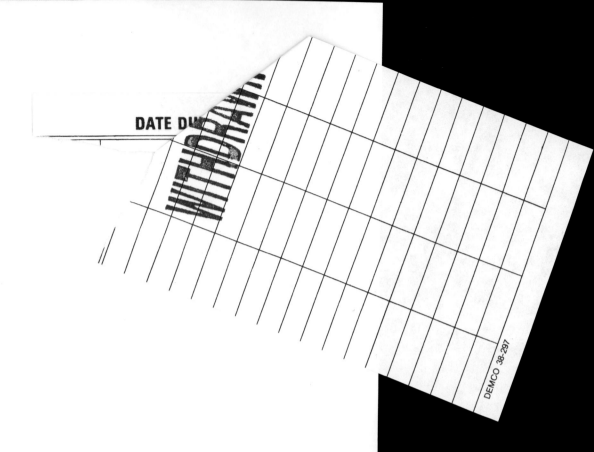